POWERING UP

POWERING UP

Unleashing the clean energy supply chain

Alan Finkel

Black Inc.

Published by Black Inc.,
an imprint of Schwartz Books Pty Ltd
Wurundjeri Country
22–24 Northumberland Street
Collingwood, VIC 3066, Australia
enquiries@blackincbooks.com
www.blackincbooks.com

9781760644598 (paperback)
9781743823071 (ebook)

 A catalogue record for this
book is available from the
National Library of Australia

Cover design by Tristan Main
Typesetting by Typography Studio
Cover image by Bobyramone / Shutterstock
Internal images by Alan Laver
Author photograph by Andre Goosen

Printed by McPhersons Printing Group.

To Elizabeth, who always challenges me

CONTENTS

Introduction

'It won't be easy getting to zero, Kathleen.'

We were at a dinner party soon after the May 2022 Australian election, which saw the Labor Party, led by Anthony Albanese, form government, with an unprecedented number of seats won by the Greens and by climate-focused independents. Rolling her eyes, Kathleen pressed on in a triumphal tone. 'With the new political will locked in, surely we'll get there quickly.'

Quickly? Kathleen was not in a position to see what lay ahead. Our energy system is a behemoth nourished on fossil fuels. Replacing that rich diet with lean wind and solar energy is a task of barely imaginable proportions. Think forests of wind farms carpeting hills and cliffs from sea to sky. Think endless arrays of solar panels disappearing like a mirage into the desert. What we have now has to be scaled up by a factor of twenty.

It will take mining on a massive scale to extract the minerals needed for batteries and solar panels. It will take giant factories to build the parts for towering wind turbines. It will take untold miles of high-voltage transmission lines to carry the electricity to power the mines and factories and the 24-hour buzz of civilisation. It will take engagement with and support for affected communities; financing at unprecedented scale; strategic government policies that convert targets into actions.

The sheer scale of the task, I pointed out to Kathleen, is why we'd barely made a dent in reducing global emissions despite three decades of effort and concern. Between 1990 and 2021, the behemoth known as global civilisation only reduced its fossil-fuel diet from 87% to 83%. Let me spell that out. We shaved off 4% in the last thirty years. In the next thirty we need to shave off 83%.

Kathleen's expression shifted from triumph to despair. In that moment, I realised I needed to write this book.

I am an engineer. I've been trained to solve problems. And I've spent over a decade thinking about the climate problem. As Australia's Chief Scientist I presided over the review of Australia's electricity market, the development of the national hydrogen strategy and the national low-emissions technology roadmap. Five years before that, I worked at Better Place, a start-up ahead of the times, conceiving the recharging infrastructure for electric cars.

The intention of this book is to help individuals like Kathleen, policy makers in government and strategists in companies appreciate the scope of what must be achieved so that we can power up our response. The task ahead is immense, but there is reason to be optimistic.

We know what to do. We need to replace fossil fuels with zero-emissions electricity. Our ambition must be to usher in the Electric Age to replace the Industrial Age.

The journey has begun. Although solar and wind supplied only 5% of total global energy consumption in 2021, they got there off a zero base in 1990 and are now increasing by a factor of four every decade. If that rate of increase can be maintained for the next two decades, we will be approaching full decarbonisation of the energy system.

To keep the engine of change operating at that pace, we will need an efficient global supply chain. The basic elements are there, built up over decades. But they are vulnerable – think Covid, think the Ukraine war.

With American leadership, after the Second World War protectionist tariffs and quotas around the world were dropped, resulting in a thriving international economy. But there have been quirks, including excessive concentration of supply. The dependence of Europe on Russian gas was made clear when Russia cut supplies in 2022. That alerted all countries to the risk excessive supply-chain concentration could pose to the clean energy transition. Nearly all the world's battery materials are refined in China, and the vast majority of solar panels are produced there. Most of the world's cobalt for electric vehicle batteries comes from the Congo.

We must massively expand mining for energy transition materials: lithium, cobalt, manganese, nickel and graphite for batteries; silver and silicon for solar panels; rare earth elements for magnets in electric vehicle motors and wind turbine generators; aluminium for lightweight vehicles and copper for their internal wiring; platinum and iridium for hydrogen production.

As mining expands, there is an opportunity to diversify supply across a broader mix of countries. Simultaneously, mining companies must shoulder their responsibilities to preserve biodiversity and rehabilitate the local environment. Their labour policies must without exception avoid child exploitation and forced labour. Welfare and education for workers, their families and affected communities must be provided.

Coal-fired plants have no future, but shutting them down before the firmed solar and wind generation plants are built would risk extended electricity blackouts. That would not just be a disaster for modern life; it risks rescinding the social licence for moving as fast as we can to net zero.

As coal mines and oil and gas wells shut down, and coal-fired electricity generators become obsolete, workforces will need to be trained and re-trained to support all aspects of the clean energy supply chain, from operating new mining vehicles through to extensive manufacturing opportunities in batteries, electrolysers and solar panels. Local and national governments will have to coordinate and collaborate with communities and companies to ease the pain, maximise the opportunities and minimise the dislocations.

Getting things right also means being alert to unintended consequences. The road to hell is often paved with good intentions. One example of this is the recent trend by companies under pressure from shareholders to improve their green credentials by divesting their fossil-fuel assets. However, for every seller, there is a buyer. If, as is often the case, the buyer is a private-equity company or a state-owned corporation, they are not accountable to the scrutiny of pesky shareholders and operate their new acquisition with poorer practices. Net result? The planet is worse off.

Another example of perverse outcomes is when rich countries improve their emissions scorecard by offshoring heavy industries to developing nations. Again, the planet is worse off because the developing countries tend to run their factories on higher emissions energy sources.

Instead of divesting or offshoring, industry and governments should invest in renewable technologies to make them ever more competitive and render fossil fuels obsolete. The mantra should be *investment, not divestment.* By investing in renewables such as hydro, solar and wind electricity, more countries than before will enjoy the geopolitical security of a domestic energy supply. Equally important, they will benefit from the cheapest form of energy, completely decoupled from global price spikes.

Given the goal of getting to net zero, communities will have to accept technologies that many would prefer to forever banish. Nuclear power is one, since not every country is blessed with the land and climate to build solar, wind and hydro power at scale. Another is carbon capture and storage (CCS), which according to the United Nations and the International Energy Agency is the only way we can get to net zero, as there will always be residual emissions such as methane from agriculture and decaying waste, and carbon dioxide from the chemical reactions in cement production and other industrial processes.

Where there is an alternative to fossil fuels, it must be pursued. The supply chain for steel making is poised to be flipped on its head. Instead of using coal to melt and chemically transform iron ore into pure iron in blast furnaces, new facilities are being built that will use solar, wind and hydropower electricity for heat and to make hydrogen. The hydrogen will be used to chemically transform the iron ore into pure iron. The amount of coal used in future iron production will fall to precisely zero.

The transition to clean energy systems cannot be left to chance. There are two ways that governments are nudging industry and investors.

The first is through carbon pricing, either as a carbon tax or an emissions trading scheme. While this is the favoured approach of economists and sensibly operates by putting a price on emissions to encourage a shift to low-emissions alternatives, where it has been instituted it has been limited in breadth of coverage and undercut by exemptions that are necessary to protect trade-exposed industries. Further, instead of investing in low-emissions alternatives, companies can and do take the short-term option of purchasing credits that often have very little long-term benefit. These practical limitations mean that the rate of decarbonisation is too slow.

The second option for governments is to offer incentives to make investing in clean technologies more attractive. This worked well to stimulate the solar markets in Germany, China and Australia, and the wind markets in Denmark and the UK. Driven by these and other government incentives around the world, solar deployment has rapidly increased and solar electricity prices have dramatically fallen. Onshore wind is not far behind, and the price of offshore wind is now highly competitive. California led the world with incentives for buyers of electric cars. Direct incentives have also been strongly adopted in the United States through its *Inflation Reduction Act*.

China, of course, continues to invest despite the trade war started by President Donald Trump and maintained by the Biden administration. China's dominance in solar panels is now being replicated in electric vehicles, with nearly 60% of electric vehicles sold in 2022 worldwide made by Chinese companies. This success was stimulated by strong industrial policies backed by government mandates and incentives. These approaches are so effective that the US *Inflation Reduction Act* has been described as the United States trying to out-China China.

These direct incentive packages will speed up the clean energy transition by focusing investment on low-emissions technologies. The concern is that because some of these climate incentive packages double up as domestic industrial policy, they could undermine the benefits of globalisation.

The task ahead is daunting, but I am a great believer in human ingenuity to overcome such challenges. NASA's James Webb Space Telescope defied decades of setbacks and pessimism and is now revealing the beginning of our universe in all its glory. At the other end of the scale, microprocessors continue to defy predictions that we will reach the limit of what can be packed onto a computer chip. The technological improvements and cost reductions in solar panels, wind turbines and lithium-ion batteries are equivalently astonishing.

In Australia's case, with our abundant minerals and renewable energy, we have the opportunity to become an *electrostate* of the future, supplying the world with the energy transition materials it needs and with decarbonised products.

Technology can deliver the clean alternatives that will enable us to continue to enjoy the benefits of our existing and evolving modern civilisation. This book is not about the technologies, but about how we can nurture the supply chain of materials, markets, government policies and finance to put them into practice at scale, and fast. It is an acknowledgement of the essential role of energy in modern civilisation. It is about the importance of deploying zero-emissions electricity to push fossil fuels out of the market rather than shutting down fossil fuels and hoping that zero-emissions electricity will fill the void. It is about getting the parameters right for responsibly mining the massive quantities of energy transition materials required to usher in the Electric Age. It is about the importance of governments stimulating private sector investments without undermining the benefits of globalisation.

The task is not easy. However, if we optimise the supply chain, ensure integrity in financing, invest in constant technological improvement and keep open minds, we will get there. The famous American architect Buckminster Fuller said, 'You never change things by fighting the existing reality. To change something, build a new model that makes the existing model obsolete.'

Let's do what we can to build and scale up our new model – clean technologies.

By doing so, we will make the old model – fossil fuels – obsolete.

1.
Setting the Scene

In the first week of March 2020, coronavirus panic gripped Melbourne. Driven by the nightmare scenario of being in the bathroom without a square of toilet paper in sight, vast numbers of my fellow Melburnians flocked to the local supermarket and cleared the shelves. Purchasing quotas were imposed, enterprising social media entrepreneurs offered toilet paper rolls for hundreds of dollars online and there were even reports of rolls being stolen from public toilets. After decades of smoothly operating retail markets, the Covid-19 pandemic was the first introduction to the issue of supply-chain bottlenecks for most Australians.

For me, professionally, the issue of supply-chain efficiency was sheeted home when I became involved in helping to secure intensive care unit (ICU) ventilators for Australia. In the middle of March, I received two calls from senior medical colleagues, who independently asked me, 'What are you doing about ventilators, Alan?' Given that I was Australia's Chief Scientist at the time, they had good reason to expect an answer. The next day, I checked with officials from the Australian Department of Health and the Department of Industry. They were already geared up to secure supplies of personal protective equipment and diagnostic kits, but ventilators weren't yet on their radar.

'Can you help?' was their response, and that simple question was the start of an extremely busy period of my life. Within 48 hours, I had spoken in depth to more than a dozen ICU physicians, respiratory specialists and hospital procurement executives. I came to a tentative conclusion as to what type and how many ICU ventilators we could clinically utilise in Australia and I submitted a report to the federal minister for health, Greg Hunt. Three days later the Australian Government COVID-19 Ventilator Taskforce was established, with me as the advisor.

Our strategy to ensure that Australia would have enough ventilators included purchasing from international vendors and creating a domestic manufacturing capability. Our timeline was short; the pressure was on for those ventilators to arrive in just a few months. Both approaches were difficult, but to my surprise, purchasing from international vendors was the harder of the two.

There was fierce competition from other countries desperate to purchase. It was the toilet-roll-hoarding phenomenon played out between countries, each seeking to procure its supply of life-saving ventilators no matter the cost and mostly irrespective of their immediate needs. The established manufacturers could not meet the demand. In just a few weeks, shady vendors were offering novel products that didn't exist, and dubious wholesalers were offering established products from warehouse stocks that didn't exist. In both cases, the suppliers wanted payment upfront. They were like internet scammers targeting national governments.

Prior to these events I hadn't personally experienced serious problems with the supply chain. I ran a manufacturing company headquartered in Silicon Valley for 23 years until the early 2000s. We used lots of electronic and mechanical components, sourced from American and international suppliers. Of course, not everything was available off the shelf, but if we were quoted an eight-week delivery time, in most cases that's how long it took for the parts to arrive.

Broken supply chains were things I read about in history books, in a military context. A resonant lesson was the nearly complete loss of French Emperor Napoleon Bonaparte's army of more than 600,000 soldiers in his disastrous 1812 invasion of Russia. The surprise realisation is that the French army did not lose a single battle against the Russian army until they began their retreat. Instead, they were defeated because Napoleon underestimated the difficulty of supplying his men and horses with food and water. His lack of preparation was compounded by the decision by the Russian command to feint and withdraw, pulling the French army ever further into Russia until their supply chain collapsed and the French soldiers literally starved to death or died of dysentery at the end of the advance and during the retreat.

Would Napoleon have won the war if he had paid as much attention to his supply-chain logistics as he did to his battle tactics? That would be idle speculation, because a good supply chain is necessary but not sufficient for success.

Fast forward to the present. During 2020, 2021 and 2022, workforce shortages occurred repeatedly, because of lockdowns to stop the spread of disease and because large numbers of workers were unable to attend their workplaces because they were in personal isolation. Inevitably, shipping and factory outputs were disrupted, resulting in shortages and rising prices. The term 'supply chain' became a regular phrase in the popular lexicon, invoked, for example, to explain the shortages of toys and luxury goods in the lead-up to Christmas.

And now, in the modern era, Russia's involvement in supply-chain disruption looms large again, this time at a global level. The horrific and unprovoked Russian invasion of Ukraine in February 2022 and Russia's manipulation of gas supplies to Europe created shortages and price rises that resulted in a global energy crisis.

The war in Ukraine has acted like a catalyst to speed up the investment in energy supply chains, but the response has been complicated, with affected countries doubling down on their commitment to clean energy sources while at the same time augmenting their non-Russian supplies of coal, oil and gas. The consequences of overreliance on Russia for fossil fuels sounded a warning for the world's clean energy transition – customers should value supply-chain diversity and avoid overdependence on single countries such as China for any essential commodities and products.

Awkwardly, these global supply-chain problems are occurring at a time when most countries have committed to reinventing their economies to achieve net zero while continuing to drive economic growth. We must get it right. At the Sydney Energy Forum in 2022, Gauri Singh, deputy director-general of the International Renewable Energy Agency (IRENA), observed, 'Supply chains are essential if we are going to keep up with the pace and scale needed for renewables.'

The story so far

Greenhouse gas emissions – mostly composed of carbon dioxide and methane – cause global warming, which in turn causes climate change.

The dominant source of these emissions is our use of fossil fuels, accounting for more than 70% of total annual greenhouse gas emissions. The process of replacing the use of fossil fuels is known as the clean energy transition.

Greenhouse gas emissions are what we can directly control. However, despite international agreements at Kyoto in 1997 and Paris in 2015 – despite targets, declarations of intent and all our efforts to date – as shown in Figure 1, the atmospheric carbon dioxide concentration continues to rise.

Because of the rising atmospheric concentration of carbon dioxide, methane and other greenhouse gases, global temperatures are relentlessly increasing and extreme weather events driven by climate change are punishing communities across the planet.

In 2021 we saw the temperature reach an Australian record of 50.7°C in the Pilbara region of Western Australia, and experts began warning us to prepare for 50°C in metropolitan areas such as Western Sydney.[1] In the European summer of 2021, with one country after another reporting record temperatures, wildfires raged across the continent, incinerating crops and destroying homes. In the United States, the Great Salt Lake in Utah dried out and explosive

Figure 1: Atmospheric carbon dioxide concentration is continuing to rise, at an accelerating rate. There has been no slowdown since the first international treaty calling for a reduction in greenhouse gas emissions was agreed in Kyoto 1997, nor since the Paris Agreement in 2015. (Source: capegrim.csiro.au)

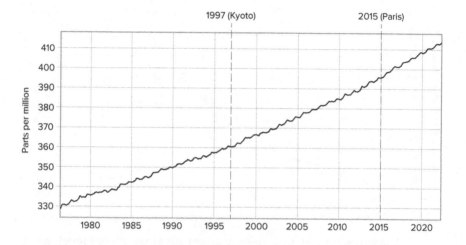

wildfires burned out of control in California. During the northern summer of 2022, extreme drought in China dried the mighty Yangtse River to its lowest level ever, halting shipping, cutting irrigation for farmers and reducing hydropower for the electricity grid. At the same time, unprecedented floods devastated Pakistan.

In most countries, the intellectual battle has been fought and it was a win for science. The reward is the widespread adoption by governments and companies of targets for emissions reduction and an associated boom in new investments. At the highest level, targets were agreed at the United Nations Climate Change Conference in Paris in 2015 and beefed up six years later at the Glasgow conference.

However, to state the obvious, it is important not to take comfort in targets. We should focus on outcomes. And there, at a global level, we are far behind. Look at the global greenhouse gas emissions shown in Figure 2 and you can see that annual emissions continue to rise.

Figure 2: Worldwide greenhouse gas emissions, mainly carbon dioxide, plus other greenhouse gases such as methane converted into carbon dioxide equivalents. (Source: World Bank, 'Total Greenhouse Gas Emissions', worldbank.org)

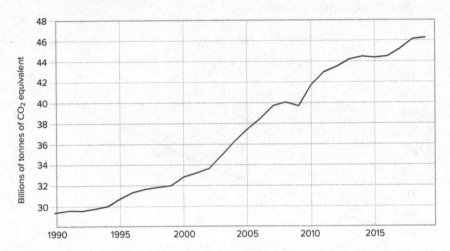

Notwithstanding this gloomy situation at the global level, we should take heart that in some countries there is substantial progress. OECD countries that have cut their emissions by 20% or more between 2005 and 2019 include Australia, Belgium, Denmark, Germany, Italy, Spain and the UK.[2] Emissions in the United States, the second-highest-emitting country in the world, are down by about 12%.

However, while much of the progress in these countries is the result of the clean energy transition, a substantial fraction results from deindustrialisation and the replacement of domestically manufactured products by imported products. This reduction of emissions-intensive manufacturing in importing countries merely pushes the emissions into the national greenhouse inventory of the countries where the products are made, particularly the industrial powerhouses of Asia. Partly for this reason, the emissions in China and India, the first and third largest emitting countries, have risen compared with their 2005 baseline.

Given the globally dominant emissions from fossil fuels, the clean energy transition to replace them is the most important step we can take in our pursuit of net zero.

Figure 3: Growth in global energy supplied from non-fossil energy sources such as solar, wind, hydropower, nuclear power and modern biofuels has been against a background of relentless growth in the use of coal, oil and gas. In this graph, primary energy is calculated based on the 'substitution method', which takes into account the inefficiencies in fossil-fuel production. (Source: ourworldindata.org/energy-mix)

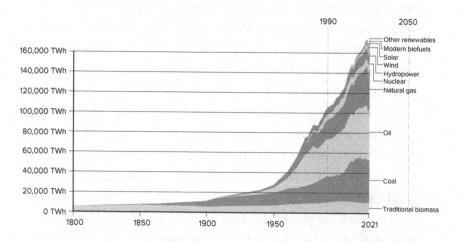

We've known this for a long time. I presented a speech in 2013 titled 'Electric Planet' about my vision for a future in which zero-emissions electricity would replace coal, oil and gas. The reality is that although the title of my speech was novel, the core concepts had been touted for decades. Nevertheless, despite awareness and considerable successes, there is still a long way to go.

The global effort to achieve the Electric Planet must be accelerated. In support of this ambition, the main focus of this book is consideration of what can be done to optimise the supply chain so that clean energy solutions can be deployed much faster, at much greater scale, across all nations and at an ever-decreasing cost.

To date, at a global level, progress in the clean energy transition has been sluggish. The numbers tell the story. The first number to consider is that back in 1990, 87% of all energy consumed came from oil, coal and gas. The balance came from traditional biomass, nuclear power and hydropower.[3] Fast forward thirty-one years to

2021, and the share of global energy provided by fossil fuels had fallen slightly, to 83%.[4]

This is a surprisingly small reduction given that during that period, solar and wind electricity deployment began and continued at an ever-increasing rate. However, the introduction of solar and wind electricity occurred in the context of total global energy consumption simultaneously rising by 72%. Despite the investment in renewables, most of this overall growth was provided by fossil fuels. The increase in fossil-fuel energy during this period and the emergence of solar and wind power can be seen in Figure 3.

The stark reality is that despite only achieving a four-percentage-point reduction in 31 years from 1990 to 2021, we have to eliminate the remaining 83 percentage points before 2050.

For thousands of years, and still to this day in many parts of the world, humans used traditional biomass – wood, agricultural waste, dried manure – to provide heat for cooking, warmth and hot water. Around 1850, coal started to be used in earnest. It was valued as a high-density fuel, much more cost-effective and easy to transport than biomass. It powered the Industrial Revolution and enabled the rapid growth of modern civilisation. Coal use consistently increased in the last 170 years, and while demand has plateaued recently, it continues to be used in huge quantities.

Around 1900, abundant free-flowing oil was discovered. It had many advantages over coal, such as being suitable for internal combustion engines. It powered the transport revolution on the ground, in the oceans and in the air, enabling the realisation of a connected planet where people can travel with ease virtually anywhere in the world. But it didn't replace coal; it added to the mix.

Around 1930, natural gas was discovered in commercial quantities. It had many advantages over oil, such as being easier to distribute to houses, factories and commercial buildings. It powered industrial, building and water heating, cooking and fast-response electricity generation. But it didn't replace oil or coal; it added to the mix.

Consumers adopted these fossil fuels because they were cheap, reliable and empowering. Despite occasional price spikes due to wars, embargos or failures in the supply chain, they have remained so. Now, for the first time in human history, we must push these major energy sources out of our lives. We must replace coal. We must replace oil. We must replace natural gas.

This will not happen on its own, driven by cost and convenience. It will happen because people and the governments who represent them are rightly convinced that we must do this to mitigate climate change. Some of the global replacement will be nuclear power and hydropower, but there is a limit to how much these sources are likely to be permitted. Thus, most of the replacement energy will come from solar and wind electricity.

We have no alternative to replacement. We cannot cease using energy. Take away modern medicine and we would be back to the conditions at the start of the Industrial Revolution, when your risk of dying was greater if you went to a doctor than if you didn't. Take away modern education and we would be back to the Middle Ages. Take away energy and we would be back to the Stone Age.

Planetwide behavioural changes such as dramatically reducing the global population, slashing domestic and international travel, convincing most of the population to become vegan and forgoing economic growth have been proposed for decades but have had no global impact. We have no choice but to implement zero-emissions solutions that will continue to deliver the benefits of modern civilisation and meet the aspirations of people in the developing world.

Solar and wind electricity generation would never have achieved their current success if left to the same market drivers that led to the adoption of fossil fuels. If it wasn't for massive direct government incentives and investment in research and development, solar and wind electricity would not have come down the cost curve to the point where they are now cheaper than their fossil-fuel alternatives.

That, however, is not the end of the story, because when it comes to their connection to national electricity grids, solar and wind electricity are difficult because they don't have the load-following capabilities of coal, oil and gas-fired electricity generation. But what they lack, solar and wind make up for in other ways: they are zero-emissions sources of unlimited electricity; their operating costs are not subject to international fuel prices; they require very little maintenance; they provide energy security through energy independence.

Power and energy

Before we proceed, let's discuss what we mean by power and energy.

Take two athletes. The first is a sumo wrestler who does little but drink beer, eat sushi and sleep. The second is a skinny marathon runner who practises 40 kilometres every day. Who is more powerful? The wrestler could flick the runner across the room, so he is clearly the more powerful. But which one would you describe as more energetic? I am sure you would join me in choosing the runner.

In the case of the sumo wrestler and the runner, few people would use the words power and energy inappropriately. However, when discussing electricity, the terms power and energy are often used inaccurately or ambiguously.

When a new utility-scale battery is described as having 100 megawatts output, does this refer to electrical *power* or to electrical *energy*? And does it matter? It does.

Energy is a fundamental measure of the ability of a system to do things, while power is a measure of how quickly energy is used. For example, a 100-watt light globe operates at four times the power of a 25-watt globe, and therefore is four times as bright. If they both run for one hour, the 100-watt globe will use four times the amount of electrical energy.

The metric unit for measuring energy is the 'joule', named after the English physicist James Prescott Joule. A single joule is a fairly small amount of energy, roughly equivalent to the energy required to lift an apple from the floor to a tabletop.

The metric unit for measuring power is the 'watt', equal to one joule per second, named after James Watt, the Scottish inventor whose steam engine heralded the Industrial Revolution. A thousand watts is a kilowatt (kW); a thousand kilowatts is a megawatt (MW); a thousand megawatts is a gigawatt (GW); a thousand gigawatts is a terawatt (TW).

Although the joule is routinely used in various industries, and almost always used by scientists, it is almost never used in the electricity industry. Instead, electrical energy is measured in 'kilowatt-hours'. Take a look at your electricity bill. You will find that you have been charged for the number of kilowatt-hours (kWh) you used in the billing period. The kilowatt-hour measures the amount of energy consumed over the course of an hour when the power is one kilowatt. One kilowatt-hour is equal to 3.6 mega-joules.

Whenever you feel confused distinguishing power from energy, remember that while power tells you how fast electricity will be consumed, you pay for energy. From a monetary perspective, energy is more important than power. The wholesale price of electricity is based on megawatt-hours (MWh). As an example, 25 cents per kilowatt-hour is equivalent to $250 per megawatt-hour.

The last thing to clarify before we proceed is the use of the terms electricity and energy. Electricity is the flow of electrons along a conducting wire. That flow of electrons can do work, thus it is a form of energy. But electricity is only one of many forms of energy. When gas burns, it produces heat energy. When the wind blows, the air carries kinetic energy. If we are particularly focused on electricity as energy, we sometimes use the term 'electrical energy'.

Where the difference between the terms electricity and energy becomes important is when thinking about total energy consumption. A nation's total energy consumption consists of the sum of electrical energy consumption plus the direct combustion of fossil fuels in automobiles, factories and buildings plus the combustion of biomass.

To be pedantic, 'renewable energy' is the energy in the sun, wind, reservoirs, geothermal heat, waves, tides and biomass. 'Renewable electricity' is what we get when we convert some of that renewable energy into electricity.

Now consider renewable electricity sources such as solar. We tend to think of a 100-megawatt solar electricity generator as a direct replacement for a 100-megawatt coal-fired electricity generator – but this is far from being the case. If the solar generator is rated at 100 megawatts, this refers to the *peak power* that the solar panels can generate in bright sunshine. If that output power is maintained for one hour, we say that the amount of energy generated is 100 megawatt-hours.

Coal-fired power stations can operate at peak power most of the time, but in practice, because they respond to the demand and the demand is not constant, they average about 60% over the course of a year.

A solar generator operates at peak power only when exposed to sunlight. In the early morning, late afternoon and on cloudy days its output is diminished, and at night it switches off. In a good location, a well-designed solar farm might generate an average annual output of about 25% of its peak. This is referred to as the capacity factor. Over the course of a year, this solar farm produces less than half of the electrical energy of our coal-fired generator. In this example, a 240-megawatt solar farm would be needed to replace the annual energy generation of the 100-megawatt coal-fired generator.

Wind electricity generation does better, with an onshore wind farm perhaps generating an average annual output of 35% of its peak. That is, over the course of a year, the wind farm in this example produces somewhat more than half of the electrical energy output of the coal-fired generator of the same peak capacity. Therefore, a 170-megawatt wind farm would be needed to replace the annual energy generation of the 100-megawatt coal-fired generator.

For solar in particular, the capacity factor is highly dependent on location. In parts of Australia, northern Chile and other sun-drenched countries, solar farms with single-axis tracking enjoy a capacity factor of better than 30%. In most of the United Kingdom and Japan, the capacity factor is less than 12%.

Shaping the Electric Age

Back in the real world, the fact that solar and wind electricity generation is dependent on sunshine and wind does not rule them out of contention. This variability is something we must overcome, because in Australia and most other jurisdictions we need solar and wind generation to deliver zero-emissions electricity. For this overwhelmingly important reason, we must find ways to make solar and wind electricity so attractive they will replace all instances of fossil-fuel use.

As is becoming increasingly clear, the solution is to support solar and wind generators with storage, power electronics, overbuilding, demand-side management, control software, transmission lines and implementation diversity, such as using both onshore and off-shore wind. It is a massive task but already well proven and within our ability to scale up.

We will shift from digging and drilling fossil fuels out of the ground to mining energy transition materials out of the ground. The former practice helped us to achieve our modern civilisation, but at high cost to the environment. The latter will enable us to continue with our modern civilisation, sustainably and responsibly. Fortunately, the enthusiasm for making this happen is growing rapidly.

My 2021 essay *Getting to Zero* was about the science of global warming and the technology that can get us to net zero emissions.[5] In it, I acknowledged that technology does not exist in a vacuum. In this book, my goal is to discuss the broader political, economic and social-licence settings that will enable zero-emissions technologies to be deployed faster and at huge scale. Key among these are the operations of markets and global supply chains to support this enormous endeavour.

The process is conceptually simple: electrify everything. That is, convert the existing electricity supply to a zero-emissions supply, expand it greatly and use clean electricity to replace oil, coal and natural gas. Where the electricity is not directly suitable, use it to make hydrogen and synthetic fuels.

Many people think to themselves, 'Look, I've just installed solar panels on my roof and a battery in the backyard. It worked for me. Why can't the government just get on with it?' Oh, that it were so simple.

Across the planet, governments, businesses and communities need to pull out all the stops. We have most of the technology we need to tackle the problem, but the world is not responding at the necessary pace and scale. Keep in mind that there are only 28 years remaining till the end of 2050. This is a very short amount of time. Note, for example, that the liquefied natural gas (LNG) industry in Australia took 50 years to establish itself to the present level. It took much longer for global coal, oil and natural gas consumption to grow to today's levels.

Hard as the task is, a reason to be confident is the exponential growth of solar and wind electricity generation.

We have reached a tipping point. A good one. Deployment of solar and wind has reached warp speed, as can be seen in Figure 4. In 2021, solar and wind combined generated more than 10% of the word's electricity, up from 2.3% just ten years earlier.[6] That's more than a four-fold increase in a decade.

One could say that 2021 was an *annus mirabilis*, because we reached a second tipping point. Of 66.7 million new car sales worldwide, 6.6 million were electric vehicles.[7] That's another 10% milestone. Where they can afford it, consumers are voting with their wallets. Electric cars are better for the environment, and a superior driving experience.

In 2022, the miracle continued. Worldwide, electric vehicle sales reached 10.3 million. This represented about 15% of all new

Figure 4: Hydropower is by far the largest renewable electricity source, but its rate of growth is roughly linear and possibly slowing down. Solar and wind, on the other hand, are growing exponentially. (Source: our-worldindata.org/renewable-energy)

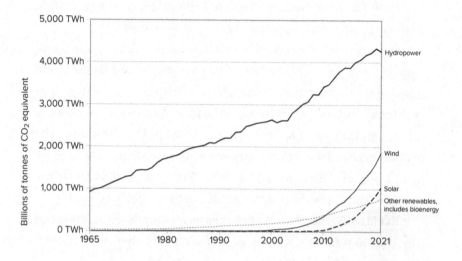

car sales. The figures in China were stunning: electric vehicle sales nearly doubled from the previous year to 6 million, being a quarter of China's new vehicle sales.[8] And in Norway, nearly 80% of new cars sales were electric.[9]

Another good sign is that according to analysis done by *The Economist* in November 2022, 33 countries have severed the link between economic growth and ever-increasing emissions of greenhouse gases. Those countries have managed to reverse the pattern of hundreds of years and increased their gross domestic product (GDP) in recent decades while reducing their emissions.[10]

Let's return to the electricity half of the *annus mirabilis*. Today, electricity from all sources combined provides about a fifth of the world's energy consumption. If we were to use electricity to replace all the non-zero-emission energy sources, you would think we would need five times as much electricity as today. But we will not need that much, because electricity is more efficient than other energy sources. A good example is automobiles. While the efficiency of both a battery electric car and a petrol engine car depends on the drive cycle, the United States Department of Energy concludes that in typical driving circumstances, a battery electric vehicle converts 77% or thereabouts of the electrical energy from the grid to power at the wheels, whereas a conventional petrol car converts as little as 12% to at most 30% of the energy stored in the petrol to power at the wheels.[11]

Considering the superior efficiency of electricity across all applications, replacing the fossil-fuel energy used worldwide would require about three times as much electricity as is generated globally today, instead of five times. If the fourfold increase per decade can be maintained for the next two decades, that would see the global solar and wind electricity share increase from 10% to 160% of today's global electricity generation. That is more than half of the threefold multiple that we will need! That's reason to celebrate.

Eventually, the percentage increase per decade will decline and the shift to renewables will follow an *S* curve rather than an *exponential* curve, but that turning point is not yet in sight.

Trillions

Do you remember the first time you heard the word 'trillion'? I first heard it years ago, to describe the number of cells in our bodies. That's human cells, such as red blood cells, skin cells, brain cells and fat cells, but not counting bacteria. The latest careful estimate is that we each contain about 38 trillion human cells.[12]

In the last few years, the word trillion has been bandied about in relation to the clean energy transition as if it were an ordinary word. The word billion is inadequate to gauge the level of interest; trillion is the new black.

The clean energy transition will not come cheap. In its report *Net Zero by 2050: A Roadmap for the Global Energy Sector*, the International Energy Agency estimates the cost of deploying clean energy solutions will ramp up to about US$4 trillion per year by 2030, for a total of about US$100 trillion by 2050.[13]

These are large numbers indeed. However, this expenditure is an investment in capital assets that will generate long-term returns. In addition, much of that expenditure will drive a dramatic reduction in the US$3.7 trillion spent annually today on fossil-fuel extraction and refining. For further comparison, global GDP in 2021 was about US$96 trillion.

The Sydney Energy Forum

Much of what will be presented herein was crystalised for me through the Sydney Energy Forum, held in July 2022, in the shadow of the Russian invasion of Ukraine.

The topic was the need for an optimised supply chain in the Indo-Pacific region to increase the pace and scale of the clean energy transition. To the best of my knowledge, this conference was the first of its kind.

The Forum was an initiative of the Australian government, first raised at a 2021 meeting of the Quadrilateral Security Dialogue (the 'Quad') attended by then prime minister of Australia Scott Morrison, US president Joe Biden, prime minister of India Narendra Modi and then prime minister of Japan Yoshihide Suga. Nevertheless, it was not a formal Quad project and the geopolitical region of interest for the Forum expanded to encompass the Indo-Pacific.

I was asked by Morrison to chair the steering committee, and as such I was deeply involved in the planning and delivery over a six-month period, which included a change of government in May 2022. The incoming prime minister, Anthony Albanese, and the minister for climate change and energy, Chris Bowen, agreed the Forum was important and they actively participated.

Shortly after the Forum was proposed, the Australian government issued an invitation to the International Energy Agency (IEA) for them to co-host the event. Their executive director, Fatih Birol, immediately agreed and made the decision to release a series of new studies contemporaneously with the Forum. The Business

Council of Australia provided support as the Forum Partner. The Forum brought together ministers, international organisations, industrialists, innovators, financiers, researchers and market operators to share their experiences and identify ways to diversify and strengthen the clean energy supply chain.

The starting position of the Forum was that it is essential to rapidly reduce global greenhouse gas emissions to mitigate climate change, and that the most effective way to achieve this is to urgently accelerate the widespread deployment of clean energy technologies. Key to achieving this ambition is to optimise and scale up the supply chain. The attendees were all sufficiently politically and economically aware to know that the transition must ensure the reliable delivery of energy required for strong national and regional economic performance and jobs growth. *Keep the lights on during the transition* was the mantra of the day. This was put to the test just one month later, when the Australian electricity grid nearly failed due to skyrocketing thermal power prices, ageing coal plants, under-investment in new capacity and a winter demand spike. At the same time, the measures taken to support the accelerated clean energy transition must ensure equitable access to energy and the best ethical, community and environmental outcomes.

In many ways, the Indo-Pacific is at the centre of the transition. It is the fastest growing economic region in the world. It represents more than 60% of total global energy consumption, almost 60% of global carbon emissions and most of the expected energy demand growth globally this decade. It represents approximately 65% of global rare earth element reserves, 89% of global solar PV module manufacturing and 86% of global lithium battery production.

The clean energy supply chain

One of the key insights from the Forum was that demand growth for clean energy is outstripping the rate at which the resources underpinning it are being mined, processed and transported. As Simon

Moores from market intelligence agency Benchmark Minerals said, 'We face a great raw material disconnect: upstream components take twice as long to establish as downstream components. This creates volatility as we scale up production.'

The clean energy supply chain starts with energy transition materials such as lithium, nickel, cobalt and copper. It includes solar panels, wind turbines and electrolysers to make the electricity and hydrogen to power our economies. It includes batteries for electric vehicles and stabilising the electricity grid. It includes transmission lines and shipping infrastructure for distribution and trade in clean energy commodities. It includes protection of human rights in Indigenous communities. It includes workforces that will need to be trained and retrained. To round out the list, it includes provision of credible certification schemes to ensure market transparency.

Clean energy supply chains consist of a sequence of interdependent elements. Let me illustrate this point with the production of lithium-ion batteries. The sequence starts with accessing the raw materials: lithium, manganese, nickel, cobalt and graphite for the batteries, copper for internal wiring, and bauxite and iron ore to make the aluminium and steel in the packaging. The new and expanded mines must respect the rights of Indigenous communities and other landholders and ensure that all workers are well trained and responsibly employed. Manufacturing the batteries requires large amounts of electricity, all of which should be zero emissions. Thus, the supply chain includes the solar-panel and wind-turbine factories that supply the capital equipment for the renewable electricity generator plants that in turn supply clean electricity to the battery factories. This electricity must be reliable. Thus, the supply chain includes batteries such as the type being manufactured and transmission lines to carry electricity within borders, across borders and even between continents. Finally, the supply chain includes the workforce to transport goods, and the pipelines and ships to transport sunshine between continents, in the form of hydrogen, ammonia or other energy carriers.

Global energy security

Speaking at the Sydney Energy Forum, the executive director of the International Energy Agency, Fatih Birol, said that 'the world has never witnessed such a major energy crisis in terms of its depth and its complexity'. He labelled it 'the first *global* energy crisis'.

The severe shortages and massively increased prices after the Russian invasion of Ukraine were exacerbated by a lack of diversity in the fossil-fuel supply chain to Europe. In their march to renewables in the twenty years prior to 2022, some European countries allowed their own domestic sources of fossil fuels to wane faster than they built up renewable alternatives, leaving themselves highly dependent on fossil-fuel imports.

Germany was particularly exposed, with more than half the natural gas it used as a chemical feedstock for industry, for heating and for electricity generation coming by pipeline from Russia. In retaliation against economic sanctions, in early September 2022 Russia reduced the supply and then, in mysterious circumstances, the undersea gas pipeline from Russia to Germany was blown up, as was the yet-to-be-commissioned companion pipeline. Prices went up and Germany and most European Union countries worried how they would get through the winter at the end of 2022. Commercial and domestic consumers became increasingly frustrated and angry at the soaring energy prices. These high prices were one of the significant contributors to the inflation spike in 2022.

Perversely, the well-intended sanctions against Russia delivered Russia hundreds of billions of dollars of additional revenue that helped it to finance its invasion of Ukraine. This windfall happened because Russia deliberately reduced its supply of gas to Europe and sold its excess gas to other countries, such as China and India, while massively increasing the price of the remaining gas it sold to Europe. The decline in volume was offset many times over by much higher prices.

This weaponising of gas supplies brought windfall revenue and profits to global oil and gas companies. For example, ExxonMobil's profits surged in the third quarter of 2022 to US$19.7 billion, up fourfold from US$4.7 billion in the first quarter.[14] Australia, Saudi Arabia and other countries enjoyed huge corporate taxes on profits as the international prices for oil, coal and gas skyrocketed.

European countries had to respond, and they did so in two ways. First, they shored up their conventional energy sources. They built LNG import terminals and encouraged other countries to increase their output of oil and gas. The European Union declared that use of natural gas would be classified as 'green' till 2035. They formulated plans for rationing, decided to keep coal-fired electricity generators going longer, and Germany even restarted mothballed coal-fired power plants. For its longer-term energy security, France decided to refresh its fleet of ageing nuclear power plants and perhaps build new ones. Germany decided to delay the closure of two of its last three nuclear power plants till the end of April 2023 to help its citizens get through the winter. The United States increased its gas exports and overtook Australia and Qatar to become the world's largest exporter of LNG.

Second, European countries doubled down on their investments in renewable electricity, in particular offshore and onshore wind, rooftop and large-scale solar, hydrogen production, transmission lines, batteries, heat pumps and energy efficiency.

This dual approach is inherently contradictory, but the hope is that it will be a short-term tactic. In the long term, we must focus on providing zero-emissions alternatives – to eliminate price volatility, to increase global energy security and to ultimately make fossil fuels obsolete.

The lesson from this experience is clear: diversity in the supply chain is essential. At the Sydney Energy Forum, while acknowledging with great respect the quality and competitive prices of China's products, participants warned of China's dominance in the manufacture and deployment of zero-emissions technologies, in the refining of rare earth elements and battery materials, and in the production of essential inputs such as polysilicon to make solar cells.

To ensure that our supply chains are robust and resilient, we need to diversify the sources of supply so that they are not too concentrated in one country – or indeed one manufacturer. For example, too much of the cobalt needed for lithium-ion batteries comes from a single, volatile, troubled nation – the Democratic Republic of the Congo. Feeling a little uncomfortable with that title, elsewhere in this book I simply refer to it as the Congo, but it should not be confused with the Republic of the Congo, a much smaller neighbouring country. Diversifying sources of cobalt by increasing production in other countries will be crucial to avoid the supply-chain disruptions and bottlenecks that can occur when resources are concentrated in a single region.

We need innovation, research and development to reduce costs, improve manufacturing and design out materials that are likely to cause supply bottlenecks. For example, can the next generation of lithium-ion batteries operate without cobalt?

We need large-scale financial investments and partnerships, globally, at the level of trillions of dollars per year.

We need consistency in government policy to attract the necessary investments.

We need competitive, open and rules-based markets.

We need demand for new decarbonised products such as green steel, green aluminium, hydrogen powered trucks, ammonia-powered ships and synthetic jet fuel for long-distance aeroplanes.

We need to build that demand through government procurement policies, government mandates and consumer demand for green products.

We need internationally agreed certification of the greenhouse gas emissions during production of commodities such as hydrogen, ammonia, fertiliser, steel, aluminium and cement, so that purchasers can make informed decisions.

Electrostates and the Electric Age

As the world takes the necessary steps to avoid adding to the already painful scourges of climate change, global energy security must be a constant consideration. If we get it right, there will be a shift in the world order away from petrostates to 'electrostates' – countries that are major exporters of clean energy or major exporters of energy transition materials.

Some of the electrostates will be democracies that will ensure local communities are well treated, that the rule of law is obeyed and that investors are given certainty about taxes, human-rights obligations and environmental regulations. Others will be autocracies and it will be up to international investors and customers to impose their expectations of proper practices.

Whether the electrostates benefit merely during the ramp up to a clean energy world or beyond will depend on factors difficult to predict, such as the contribution of recycling to producing the solar panels, wind turbines and batteries required for replenishment and the push to go beyond net zero to net negative.

Another shift will be that countries blessed with sunshine and wind and land and offshore locations will enjoy substantial or total energy independence, resulting in a major global geopolitical realignment.

The transition from a fossil-fuel-powered society to a clean-energy-powered society will be the toughest task deliberately undertaken by humanity since we tamed fire. If we get it right, future generations will look back on today as marking the end of the Industrial Age and the beginning of the Electric Age.

2.
Energy Transition Materials: Mining and Refining

The global clean energy transition is the most profound economic change to civilisation of all time. It will force us to dig more speciality minerals out of the ground than ever before to supply the huge resource requirements for the transformation of the global economy. The world will shift from burning fossil fuels to mining and refining energy transition materials, a shift described by American energy expert Daniel Yergin at the Sydney Energy Forum as 'moving from a world of big oil to a world of big shovels'. Australian treasurer Jim Chalmers made clear the Australian government's appreciation of this tectonic shift when he told a conference in November 2022, 'there is no net zero without mining'.[1]

The numbers are staggering. According to the World Bank, a single 3-megawatt wind turbine needs 355 tonnes of steel, 1,200 tonnes of concrete, 2 tonnes of rare earth elements, 4.7 tonnes of copper and 3 tonnes of aluminium.[2] In 2021, 94,000 megawatts of wind turbines were deployed, which would have been a little over 30,000 wind turbines if they were all the 3-megawatt variety. Multiply these tonnages by 30,000 to get a feel for the huge scale of the required resources, just for wind.[3] The answer is 11 million tonnes of steel, 36 million tonnes of concrete, 60,000 tonnes of rare earth elements, 140,000 tonnes of copper and 90,000 tonnes of aluminium. By 2030, the annual quantities will be much greater. While these quantities of concrete and steel are small compared with global production, the 60,000 tonnes of rare earth elements account for more than 20% of the global production in 2021.

A brief technical detour to consider the unit called the tonne. It is a metric unit used by scientists and most of the countries in the world. It is exactly equal to 1,000 kilograms; a kilogram is exactly equal to 1,000 grams. The tonne is sometimes referred to as a 'metric ton', to distinguish it from a 'US ton', a smaller weight also known as a 'short ton'. Throughout this book, weight measurements are exclusively given in kilograms and tonnes.

Resource extraction and supply is ground zero of the supply-chain battleground. Indeed, demand for clean energy is already outstripping the rate of resources extraction. The usual concern is directed at 'critical minerals'. However, there is no agreement on what this term includes. It generally refers to metals that are economically important and forward facing, but have a high potential for supply disruption, often because one country dominates production. Different lists are published by the governments of the United States, the European Union and Australia.

For clarity, in this book, we will refer to these important resources as the energy transition materials. They fall into five groups.

Group 1 contains traditional metals that are already mined in large volume for many purposes but face substantially increased demand to support the clean energy transition. The standout in this group is copper, used for most of the wiring in vehicles and wind turbines. Another is aluminium, used in wind turbine construction and the electric vehicles that are the future of transport.

Group 2 contains the battery materials: lithium, manganese, nickel, cobalt and graphite. Demand for these is increasing at breathtaking pace.

Group 3 is known as the rare earth elements. This is a family of seventeen metals used in high-power electronics and strong permanent magnets in wind turbine generators and electric vehicle motors.

Group 4 contains the solar photovoltaic materials, essentially two very common elements: silicon and silver. These are the two key ingredients of solar photovoltaic cells that are assembled to make solar panels.

Group 5 supports the hydrogen industry. The members of this group are the platinum group metals, mainly represented by platinum and its even more precious cousin, iridium. Platinum and iridium are used in the electrolysers that produce hydrogen from water, and platinum is used in the fuel cells that convert hydrogen and atmospheric oxygen into electricity.

Wherever you look, commentators are predicting huge growth in global demand for battery materials and rare earth elements. Markets for lithium and other battery metals, once used for niche applications, are becoming the lynchpins of the new global economy. The demand is significant already and will increase dramatically by 2030. In the International Energy Agency's 'stated policies scenario', which describes a conservative pathway based on current national policies, growth in battery materials will increase five to seven times. In the Agency's 'sustainable development scenario', which describes a more ambitious pathway that would enable the world to meet the Paris Agreement goals, the increase will be between 11 and 17 times; rare earth element demand could increase three to five times; large traditional markets such as nickel will quadruple and copper will double by 2030. Most remarkable of all, the energy transition materials market will be bigger than the global coal market by 2030.

There are two driving reasons for broadening the supply chain for energy transition materials.

First, most hard-rock lithium produced in Australia and lithium brine produced in South America is refined in China. The same goes for rare earth elements: they are refined in China. After rising geopolitical tensions, internal disruptions in China caused by their zero-Covid policy, concerns about forced labour in some provinces, and trade barriers imposed by the United States, international purchasers are investing now to diversify their supply chains.

Second, refining the mined ore to produce the metals or chemicals needed by manufacturers is energy intensive and must be decarbonised. Countries such as Australia, Chile and Canada are well positioned to use renewable electricity and thereby meet the international demand for chemicals such as lithium hydroxide ready to be used in electric car batteries.

Addressing the growing demand for energy transition materials will require global attention to three areas: diversification of supply; innovative design and deployment of substitutes; and improved re-use and recycling.

Group 1: traditional metals

Copper

A glint of sunlight must have caught the eye of an ancient romantic, because the first known use of copper was a pendant found in northern Iraq dating back to 8700 BC, the earliest period of the Mesopotamian civilisation.

Like gold, platinum and silver, copper is one of the few metals that can be found in the ground in pure form. For over 10,000 years it has arguably been the most useful metal in our society, and it continues to be incredibly important. In our domestic environment it is used in household piping and in every refrigerator, car, mobile phone and computer.

As we electrify our energy system, copper is making an essential contribution to electrification. We need ever more copper for cables in electric cars, the wire coils in wind turbine generators and electric motors, and the wiring to connect solar panels. For example, a midsize petrol car uses about 20 kilograms of copper, whereas a midsize battery electric car uses up to 80 kilograms.[4]

The preference for copper wiring is driven by the fact that copper has the second-highest conductivity – the ability to carry electric current – of any metal.[5] The only metal that is more conductive is silver, with approximately 5% higher conductivity, but silver is too expensive for large-scale applications. At recent prices of US$640,000 per tonne (US$20 per troy ounce), silver is 700 times more expensive than copper. Gold is the third best conductor, but there is no need to explain why it will not be used in bulk. Aluminium is the next best after gold, with 59% of the conductivity of copper. It is the conductor of choice for overhead transmission lines, where it has the advantage of lighter weight and lower price, but copper is preferred where space is at a premium, such as inside car motors and wind-turbine generators. Joanne Freeze, CEO of Candente Copper Corporation, says that 'gold is money, copper is life'.[6]

Global copper production in 2021 was 21 million tonnes of metal, up from 16 million tonnes ten years earlier. The top five producer countries, with 60% of the market between them, were Chile (27%), Peru (10%), Congo (9%), China (9%) and the United States (6%). The global copper market is forecast to more than double to about 50 million tonnes by 2035. If there is inadequate investment in new copper mines there could be a shortfall in supply of 10 million tonnes per year by 2035, according to a 2022 study by business analytics company S&P Global. This is much larger than the largest historical world copper deficit of nearly 1 million tonnes that occurred in 2014. Global scarcity of a high-volume, heavily used commodity such as copper could become a destabilising threat to international security.

Doubling production – or more – between now and 2035 will be difficult. The International Energy Agency has reported that it takes 16 years, on average, to develop a new copper mine because of the time taken to find the site, assess the quality, go through the permit process, work with local communities and undertake construction. Notably, the increasing difficulty of obtaining permits for new mines in the United States is one reason why US copper production has fallen by half in the last 25 years. Reducing regulatory overheads and designing regulations to facilitate development while maintaining high environmental standards and community protection should be the goal of all governments.

Other solutions, proposed in the S&P study, are to increase the output of existing mines and to optimise recycling. But even with these measures, the study predicts that there will be significant shortfalls in 2035. The gap between supply and demand will optimistically be closed by unexpected success in opening new mines more quickly than in the past, or by technology innovation. The latter would include innovation to increase the utilisation of existing copper mines even as ore quality deteriorates, and innovation to make recycling more cost-effective and therefore more attractive.

The S&P study predicts that the existing top five copper-supply countries will continue to increase their output and occupy similar rankings in the coming decade in percentage terms as the total output tonnage increases.

Aluminium

The most underappreciated characteristic of silvery white aluminium is that it quickly oxidises when exposed to atmospheric oxygen. Far from being a drawback, this is a desirable attribute because, unlike steel, the layer of 'rust' protects the aluminium from further oxidation. The oxidation can be deliberately accelerated at the aluminium fabrication facility in a process called anodising, with colourants added so that the aluminium is delivered with a hard, coloured, protective layer.

One of the enduring puzzles of this metal is why the Americans call it 'aluminum' despite the commonality of the Latin suffix -*ium* for naming metals. Some argue that it was the result of a spelling mistake in the advertising material created by American chemist Charles Martin Hall, who commercialised aluminium products, protected by his many patents. Others argue that it was an attempt to make aluminium seem more precious and alluring in the early days by likening it to platinum, the other exception to the rule.

The main steps in producing the pure metal are mining the bauxite ore, refining it into an intermediate product called alumina, the common name for aluminium oxide, and smelting the alumina into aluminium.

There is no shortage of aluminium on planet Earth. In fact, aluminium is the third most common element in the Earth's crust, after oxygen and silicon. It is mostly found in bauxite, a sedimentary rock, in which aluminium is chemically bound to oxygen and some hydrogen. Bauxite is often brown in colour because the aluminium hydroxides are mixed with iron oxides such as haematite.

Alumina in the crystalline form is rarely found in nature but when it is, there is cause to celebrate, because it is in the exotic forms admiringly called ruby and sapphire. Because alumina is lighter and smaller in volume than the bauxite used to produce it, refined alumina is the form commonly exported from bauxite-mining countries.

Aluminium metal is produced from alumina in a smelter, in which the alumina is dissolved in an electrolyte of molten sodium aluminium fluoride in a special vessel known as a pot. A very high electric current is passed through the electrolyte to break the bonds between the aluminium and oxygen atoms, leaving aluminium metal to sink to the bottom of the pot, from which it is siphoned off.[7]

The amount of electricity used in smelting is very large. For example, a single smelter at Tomago in Australia's most populous state, New South Wales, draws a continuous 850 megawatts of electricity from the network. This equates to about 10% of the state's annual generated electrical output and is the largest single user of electricity in Australia.[8]

It takes about 17 megawatt-hours of electricity to make one tonne of aluminium. That is enough electricity to power the average Australian home for nearly two years. Because so much electricity is used in aluminium smelting, the pure metal is sometimes referred to as congealed electricity.

Currently, the worldwide aluminium industry mostly uses fossil-fuel electricity, and its carbon dioxide emissions are therefore significant. At about 1.1 billion tonnes per year, the emissions are 3% of the 36 billion tonnes of carbon dioxide emitted in 2021.[9]

This places aluminium production third in the list of high-emitting materials. The highest is steel making, in which emissions of approximately 3 billion tonnes equate to 8% of annual carbon dioxide emissions.[10] The second-highest is cement making, in which emissions of 2.6 billion tonnes are 7% of the total.[11]

An aluminium part only weighs about a third as much as a steel part of the same dimensions. Pure aluminium is quite soft, but when alloyed with elements such as manganese, silicon, copper and magnesium it can be almost half as strong as steel. Aluminium is in high demand in the aerospace and vehicle industries, where its light weight and reasonably good strength are a highly valued combination.

Global aluminium production in 2021 was 68 million tonnes, up from 44 million tonnes ten years earlier.[12] The top five producer countries, with 77% of the market between them, were China (57%), India (6%), Russia (5%), Canada (5%) and the United Arab Emirates (4%). Note that China produces nearly ten times as much aluminium as the second-highest-producing country.

A 2021 report by Human Rights Watch and Inclusive Development International observed that the automobile industry uses nearly 20% of all the aluminium produced worldwide and that consumption in the automobile industry is set to double by 2050, mainly to maximise the range of battery electric vehicles by minimising the weight of the body, chassis and battery housing.[13] Worldwide demand for primary aluminium is expected to rise 60% to 108 million tonnes in 2050.[14]

There is no shortage of bauxite, with known reserves of 55 billion tonnes being more than sufficient to meet world demand well into the future. Thus, it is likely that the industry will be able to comfortably meet future demand. The existing worldwide smelter capacity is underutilised, with 77 million tonnes capacity for the 68 million tonnes produced in 2021. In the unlikely case that there is a future shortage of aluminium, there are many options.

In the first place, there are other materials to be considered for at least some of the uses of aluminium in the automobile industry.

For example, carbon fibre composites could be used more extensively for body panels, and magnesium alloys could be used where strength is a premium. Alternatively, manufacturers could simply continue to use steel and accept the weight penalty as a limitation on the achievable range for a given battery or hydrogen tank.

The main issue with aluminium is not supply, but unethical mining practices. Human Rights Watch and Inclusive Development International have identified practices including the destruction of community lands and damage to water sources. For example, bauxite mines in Guinea are spreading into agricultural lands without benefit to the farmers. The main recommendation in their report is for car companies to use their purchasing power to favour mining companies that can prove their ethical credentials.

Progress has already been made in that direction, and indeed Human Rights Watch and Inclusive Development International acknowledge that the leading car companies have publicly committed to addressing human rights abuses in their supply chains, although most companies have not yet sufficiently evaluated the impact of their commitments. To their credit, the companies have applied due diligence to other materials essential to the supply chain, such as cobalt for batteries.

Group 2: battery minerals

The biggest surprise of the clean energy technology boom is the success of batteries, on the back of stunning technological advances.

Batteries have, of course, been around for a long time. The first rechargeable battery, using lead and acid, was invented in 1859 by French physician Gaston Planté. Eventually, the lead-acid battery became ubiquitous, powering the starter motors and accessories in motorbikes, cars and trucks.

In the 1980s, interest turned to smaller rechargeable batteries to support personal products such as toys, mobile phones and laptop computers. This demand was met by nickel-based chemistries, initially nickel cadmium and then nickel metal hydride.

Compared to lead-acid rechargeable batteries, these nickel batteries had the advantage of being small, free of liquids and outgassing, and about twice the energy storage per kilogram of battery. However, they were far from ideal, discharging by as much as 20% each month even if they were disconnected from the circuit, and suffering reduced lifetimes if their owners did not know or care about the manufacturers' recommendation to alternate shallow discharging with deep discharging. Another problem was that cadmium is a toxic metal, thus careful disposal of used batteries was required.

Searching for alternative chemistries that would overcome these limitations, scientists Stanley Whittingham, John Goodenough and Akira Yoshino, working independently, developed lithium-ion batteries. They were jointly awarded the Nobel Prize in Chemistry in 2019 for their remarkable work.

I had the good fortune to give the opening speech at an international lithium-ion battery conference in 2022 at which Stanley Whittingham, aged 80, immediately followed me to present the major plenary speech of the conference. He thrilled the audience as he described his latest work and research strategies for lithium-ion battery performance improvement. He was animated and enthusiastic. It occurred to me that perhaps he was powered by lithium-ion batteries.

It was a vintage year for me, because I also spoke alongside Akira Yoshino at a conference on hydrogen supply chains between Australia and Japan. Yes, hydrogen, a chemical means of storing electrical energy in contrast to electrochemical storage in a battery. Yoshino was 74 years old and happily transitioning into a new field of research.

Ironically, the earliest work on lithium-ion batteries was pioneered by one of the world's biggest oil companies, Exxon Corporation. A half century ago, in 1972, Stanley Whittingham began working on lithium-ion batteries as an employee of Exxon Research &

Engineering. He discovered that lithium ions could be reversibly inserted into molecular gaps in an electrode. His initial electrodes were made from titanium disulphide and he showed that lithium ions could move through an electrolyte from one electrode to the other, creating current in an external circuit.

Exxon's vision was to use the new batteries in electric cars, but the company was definitely ahead of the market – nearly thirty years too early. Who knows if Exxon had it in mind back in 1972, but the product of the research it funded is now powering electric vehicles of all types. This will have a profound impact on oil consumption because nearly 50% of global oil consumption is for road transport.[15] Equally important, lithium-ion batteries are increasingly being deployed at large scale for backup and other services in national electricity grids, local networks and within buildings.

The first modern electric vehicle to use lithium-ion batteries was the tZero, from a Californian company named AC Propulsion. Only three tZeros were built, and only one of them was adapted to run on lithium-ion batteries, in 2003. It had a range of 480 kilometres and could sprint to 100 kilometres per hour in 3.6 seconds. It was a prototype, not registered for driving on the public roads.

The CEO of AC Propulsion, Tom Gage, showed it to Elon Musk and Martin Eberhard, who encouraged him to commercialise the tZero. But AC Propulsion balked, in favour of concentrating on other projects. So, Eberhard and a colleague, Marc Tarpenning, founded Tesla Motors to design their own vehicle, picking up funding from Musk and others. Eberhard, Tarpenning and Musk went to work to re-imagine the concept of an electric car.

The basic idea was not new. More than a century ago, in the 1890s and 1900s, electric cars were popular. Although they had short driving range, they were a much cleaner and simpler alternative to coal-fired steam cars. In any event, both these forms of propulsion were displaced by petrol-powered cars, especially after the commercialisation of the electric starter motor in 1912 eliminated the need for hand cranking.[16]

In the 1990s, General Motors and Toyota developed the next generation of electric cars, but the lead-acid batteries occupied too much space and the vehicles were deemed undesirable and impractical.

In the main, if asked to think about electric vehicles, most people at the turn of the present century thought about squat, ugly golf carts. The first Tesla, on the other hand, was dazzling and desirable. When it was released in 2008, the Tesla Roadster transformed the perception of electric vehicles and went a long way to defining their future. For starters, it looked great, being built on the body and chassis of the Lotus Elise two-seater convertible sports car, purchased under contract from the British manufacturer Lotus Cars. That company epitomises style and performance, and their Team Lotus division has won the Formula One World Championship seven times.

Not only was it good looking, but the Tesla Roadster was fast, using the high peak power of its lithium-ion batteries to leap out of the starting gate and get to 100 kilometres per hour in just 3.7 seconds. It was responsive. I recall being given the opportunity to test drive a Tesla Roadster in Sydney in 2011. I touched the accelerator and the bonnet rose against the horizon as the power surged into the rear wheels. My imagination was fired.

Tesla showed that an electric car could be elegant, fast, sporty and exciting. I was hooked. My wife and I purchased our first electric car, a Nissan LEAF, in 2013. Then we added a Tesla Model S to the stable, in 2015. Beyond helping to save the planet, the superb performance and convenience of charging at home is unbeatable. There is no looking back. To be clear, although the primary reason to purchase an electric car should be to help the environment by reducing one's personal transport emissions, a second definitive reason to purchase an electric car is that it performs so much better than the petrol-powered car it is replacing.

Returning to Stanley Whittingham and his pioneering work at Exxon Corporation, he recently reflected that, 'back then, Exxon wanted to be an energy company, far beyond oil and chemicals.'[17]

But the immediate profits in oil and chemicals and the lack of a large market for these new batteries led to Exxon discontinuing the lithium-ion battery project.

Later in the 1970s, John Goodenough at Oxford University demonstrated the use of lithium cobalt oxide as the cathode, substantially increasing the capacity and lowering the cost compared with Stanley Whittingham's titanium disulphide cathode. Soon after, in the early 1980s, initially at the National Centre for Scientific Research in France and then at the Asahi Kasei Corporation in Japan, Akira Yoshino demonstrated that lithium ions could be intercalated, or absorbed, into graphite, thereby pioneering the anode chemistry of modern lithium-ion batteries.[18]

These advances meant that a viable lithium-ion battery could potentially be commercialised. But what would be the killer app, the product that needed the rechargeability and high energy density of these newfangled batteries? Exxon had rightly concluded that it would not be electric cars, not back then. The answer turned out to be the portable video camera. Sony Corporation, a pioneer in the field, saw the importance and licensed the technology from Asahi Kasei. With Yoshino's help, Sony released the first commercial lithium-ion battery in 1991.

Video cameras were the most important application of lithium-ion batteries in the 1990s. In the 2000s, the most important application was laptop computers. In the next decade, it was smartphones, iPads and the early fleet of modern electric vehicles. In the current decade, the dominant application is the electric vehicle.

Separately, because of the performance improvements and price reductions in batteries designed for laptops, phones and vehicles, lithium-ion batteries have achieved the low price and high performance that make them the default choice for large utility-scale batteries and behind the meter batteries in homes, factories and commercial buildings.

While there are other prospective battery chemistries, lithium-ion dominates the market for now and the foreseeable future.

Growth in global lithium-ion battery demand has been estimated by management consultancy McKinsey & Company to rise more than eight-fold from 450 gigawatt-hours in 2020 to 3,900 gigawatt-hours in 2030, with two-thirds of that being for battery electric cars and the rest for stationary energy applications in the electricity grid and behind-the-meter storage.[19]

Before we proceed, let's think about a real-world example for a gigawatt-hour. The battery in the Tesla Model S sedan is 100 kilowatt-hours, good for about 600 kilometres driving range. Multiply by ten to get to one megawatt-hour. Multiply by a thousand to get to one gigawatt-hour. That is, a gigawatt-hour is the energy storage of ten thousand Tesla Model S sedans. With 3,900 gigawatt-hours of batteries, manufacturers would be able to produce nearly 40 million electric vehicles with a 100-kilowatt-hour battery in each car.[20]

These batteries will be produced in so-called 'gigafactories'. This term was coined by Elon Musk in 2013 to explain to investors the need to build a new factory to manufacture the batteries for the upcoming Tesla Model 3. The term is now widely adopted to refer to factories that produce batteries for electric vehicles on a scale that was inconceivable just a decade ago. In scientific jargon, the prefix 'giga' means a billion of whatever follows, but in Musk's descriptive context it is being used to represent something that is much bigger than normal. For this purpose, think of giga as deriving from the Greek word *gigas*, for 'giant'. There are nearly 300 gigafactories completed, under construction or planned worldwide.[21]

At present, China dominates battery manufacturing, making almost 80% of the annual global output. The supply chain issues that surfaced during the Covid-19 pandemic have highlighted to governments and vehicle manufacturers the need for localised supply. Europe and America are heavily investing, driven by their governments and their car manufacturers, but it is nevertheless expected that by the end of the decade China's share will only have fallen to 70%.[22]

There are four parts to a battery: anode, cathode, electrolyte, and separator. In the main, the important minerals are for the anode and the cathode. Lithium is always present in lithium-ion battery cathodes, alongside some combination of nickel, cobalt and manganese. By trading off some energy density and thus driving range, cathodes that use commonly available materials such as iron and phosphate can also be produced.

The most commonly used mineral for the anode is graphite.

As we will see, expanding supply to meet demand will involve investment in mining and process improvements. Of all the battery minerals, the one that faces most supply uncertainty is lithium. Occasionally, shortages have forced some manufacturers to cut production.

The surge in demand and increase in prices of most of the battery metals led to the price per kilowatt-hour for electric vehicle batteries rising slightly for the first time in 2022, despite the increased manufacturing volume.[23]

Graphite

Although most people might not think of graphite as a common substance in their world, it is not unusual. When your children sketch with black pencils, they are using graphite. If you need to loosen a stiff key lock, the best way to do so is a puff of graphite powder. Industrially, graphite is sometimes combined with oil to make lubricating grease, it is commonly used in vehicle brake pads, it is used to line crucibles that hold molten metal and it is one of the additives in steel.

Ironically, graphite, one of the minerals that will be recruited to the battle against climate change, is closely related to coal, one of the minerals most responsible for climate change. Metallurgical coal used in steel making is black coal containing about 90% or more carbon content by mass. Graphite is a more sophisticated cousin, being pure carbon, just like diamond. In graphite, the carbon atoms are arranged in hexagonal rings of six carbon atoms joined to each other to form flat sheets like a honeycomb. The individual sheets are called graphene. In the other crystalline form of carbon, diamond, the atoms are joined to each other in a three-dimensional tetrahedral structure.

Graphite is dark grey or black, opaque and very soft. It is soft because although the carbon atoms within each sheet are rigidly bonded to each other, the bonding between sheets is very weak. Graphite is not a metal, but like metals it is an excellent conductor of heat and electricity. Although, unlike metals, this conductivity has a directional preference. That is, in graphite the thermal and electrical conductivity are excellent in parallel with the sheets of hexagons but poor at right angles.

In the Earth's crust, graphite is formed from shale, coal or other carbon-containing minerals subjected to extreme heat and pressure.

When naturally occurring graphite is used for battery applications, the contaminants in flakes of natural graphite are removed, leaving behind an ultra pure form of 99.95% carbon or better, in small round particles between 10 and 25 millionths of a metre in diameter. This form is called spherical graphite and is widely used in the anodes of batteries.

Graphite can also be made synthetically by superheating coal or oil feedstocks to temperatures of 3,000°C or higher. Traditionally, the main uses of synthetic graphite are as the electrodes in electric arc furnaces used in steel making and in the electrolytic cells in aluminium smelting. Nowadays, there is growing interest in synthetic graphite for battery anodes because of its consistency and longer operational lifetime. The disadvantage of synthetic graphite is that it is more expensive. Nevertheless, more than half the graphite used in electric vehicle batteries is now the synthesised form.

The anode is the formal name for the external negative terminal of the battery. The formal name for the external positive terminal of the battery is the cathode.

When it is manufactured, the lithium-ion battery cell is in the fully discharged state. All the lithium ions are intercalated within

Figure 5: Basic structure and operation of a lithium-ion battery during discharge. The load is the device in the external circuit, such as a car motor, a toy or a computer.

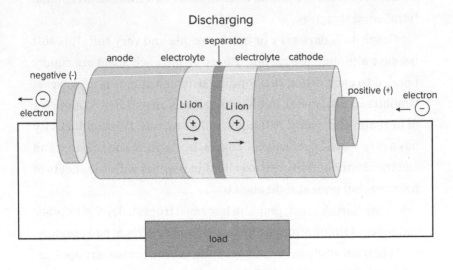

the cathode. During charging, the cathode loses electrons to the external charger circuit in a process that frees up an equal number of positively charged lithium ions that dissolve into the electrolyte solution. These travel across to the anode, where they are intercalated into the spaces between the graphite layers. With most battery designs, the ability of the cathode to hold lithium ions limits the charge rather than the ability of the anode to hold them.

During discharge, lithium ions disengage from the electrons that were tying them to the anode and travel internally through the electrolyte to the cathode. The electrons that were holding the lithium ions in the anode are released and flow into the external circuit, such as the vehicle motor controller and motor. At the other end of the battery, electrons from the external circuit flow into the cathode. Inside the battery, the circuit is completed by the flow of positively charged lithium ions from the anode reaching the cathode, where they associate with the electrons from the external circuit. When the cathode fills with lithium ions, the battery is flat. The electrical current flow during discharge is shown in Figure 5.

The electrolyte is commonly a solution of lithium salts, which means that the solution contains lots of lithium ions. The importance of this is that individual lithium ions during discharge don't have to travel the full way from the anode to the cathode to complete the circuit. As each lithium ion leaves the anode, a corresponding lithium ion that is already near the cathode surface can be intercalated into the cathode. The reverse is true during charging.

Graphite is ideal for the anode, due to its low cost, abundance, high energy density, high power density and excellent operational lifetime. Despite efforts to find alternatives with higher power or energy density while maintaining the operational lifetime, graphite continues to dominate as the anode material of choice. Silicon is the main alternative being investigated, but its problem is that it expands and contracts during charging and discharging, resulting in an accumulation of fractures that unacceptably shorten the operational lifetime.

Electric vehicle batteries are typically nearly 30%, and in some cases 50%, graphite by weight.

China does most of the processing to produce ready-to-use graphite. Market research firm S&P Global reports that China produces 100% of the ready-to-use spherical graphite, made from locally mined and imported natural graphite. It produces 85% of the global supply of refined battery-grade graphite. This extreme concentration of production is a significant global supply chain risk.

The processing from natural graphite to spherical graphite is very energy intensive, mostly powered by coal. Some companies are planning to use renewable electricity to refine graphite, but currently it is not cost competitive to do so, which is perhaps the main reason that economically advanced countries have been slow to develop domestic processing plants. Producing battery-grade synthetic graphite is also energy intensive. Countries that are leaders in extensively deploying low-cost renewable electricity will be well poised to build graphite processing plants.

For natural graphite, global mine production in 2021 was 1 million tonnes, up from 0.9 million tonnes ten years earlier. The top five producer countries, with 93% of the market between them, were China (79%), Brazil (7%), Mozambique (3%), Russia (3%) and Madagascar (2%).[24] Again, note that production in China is ten times the level of the second-highest-producer country.

For synthetic graphite, total global supply was estimated to be 1 million tonnes in 2021.[25] The top five exporters of synthetic graphite in 2019, with 68% of the market between them, were China (38%), Japan (10%), Germany (7%), South Korea (7%) and the United States (6%).[26]

The top five countries by estimated reserves of natural graphite are Turkey, China, Brazil, Madagascar and Mozambique.[27] Notably, the top country by reserves – Turkey – does not feature in the top five countries by production, so there is enormous potential for Turkey to become a producer country. Tanzania, India and Uzbekistan also have considerable reserves.

Expansion takes time. For example, Tanzania has at least five reasonably large graphite mining projects underway, some of which commenced planning early last decade, but none of them have reached the production stage.

Although global demand growth in the ten years leading to 2021 was slow, that is no longer the case. Demand for battery-grade graphite is now growing at 30% per year, and by 2030 it is expected that more than 80% of graphite produced worldwide will go towards making batteries.[28] The global demand for natural and synthetic graphite combined is expected to reach 5 million tonnes in 2030.[29] In light of the highly concentrated supply chain, prospecting in many countries has led to new mine sites being identified in Alaska, Australia, Sweden, Norway and Finland.

Lithium

Several years ago, I wrote an article contending that silicon is the king of computer circuits and lithium the queen of batteries.[30] Nothing has occurred since to reduce my esteem for either of these elements.

Lithium thoroughly dominates battery technology because it has properties that make it superior to all the alternatives.

It is special in the first instance because it is the lightest of all metals. Light weight is important for batteries used in mobile devices such as smartphones, computers and vehicles.

Equally important, lithium has the highest 'working voltage': up to 3.7 volts, being the voltage difference between the two terminals of the battery.

This combination of light weight and high working voltage ensures that batteries that use lithium as the ionised metal have the highest energy storage per kilogram. Commercial lithium-ion batteries have at least five times the energy density of lead-acid batteries. Thus, if an electric car with a 600-kilogram lithium-ion battery had to rely instead on lead-acid batteries, it would end up carrying three tonnes of batteries – clearly impractical.

Another advantage of lithium-ion batteries over lead-acid batteries, nickel cadmium batteries and nickel metal hydride batteries is that lithium-ion batteries can be discharged down to about 10% of their rated capacity without failure and can do so hundreds if not thousands of times. Furthermore, they do not suffer from the memory effect that reduces the working life of nickel cadmium and nickel metal hydride batteries. Equally important, lithium is very low on the toxicity scale. It is so safe that lithium carbonate is used as a medicine to treat bipolar disorder.

There are two major ways that lithium is mined. In Chile and Argentina, lithium is mined from salt deserts called salars. Lithium-rich salt water referred to as brine is pumped from deep aquifers to the surface, poured into large basins and allowed to evaporate. Lithium hydroxide and lithium carbonate can be produced from the concentrate that remains after evaporation.

In Australia, lithium is found in solid rocks, mostly in a form called spodumene, consisting of lithium, aluminium, silicon and oxygen. The theoretical lithium content is 3.7% by mass, which although it sounds low is actually one of the more concentrated forms of naturally occurring lithium. The spodumene can be processed into lithium hydroxide or lithium carbonate. Both lithium hydroxide and lithium carbonate are used as chemical feedstocks for the battery manufacturing process, with a growing preference for the hydroxide form. In any event, in most cases lithium carbonate is the precursor for lithium hydroxide.

The supply-chain journey is a long one. Take the battery pack in a Tesla Model S sedan. Much of the lithium is sourced from the Kidman Resources spodumene mine in Western Australia. The spodumene rock is sent to Ganfeng Lithium in China to be processed into lithium hydroxide. The hydroxide is then sent to Tesla facilities in Shanghai, New York, Nevada and California to be made into batteries. This kind of detour via China is not uncommon, because China refines nearly 70% of the world's lithium.

Outside of batteries, lithium is alloyed with aluminium and magnesium to improve their strength and make them lighter. These alloys are used for armour plating, aircraft and bicycle frames and high-speed trains. Various oxides of lithium are used in specialised glasses and ceramics, some air-conditioning systems and high-temperature lubricants.

Demand for these traditional uses changes slowly, but global demand for lithium is growing at an extremely rapid rate because of its use in batteries.

The countries with the largest known reserves of lithium are Chile (9.2 million tonnes of metal), Australia (5.7 million), Argentina (2.2 million), China (1.5 million) and the United States (0.75 million).[31]

Looking beyond reserves to production, global lithium mine production in 2021 was 100,000 tonnes of metal, up from 34,000 tonnes ten years earlier. The top five producer countries, with a very highly concentrated 98% of the market between them, were Australia (53%), Chile (25%), China (13%), Argentina (6%) and Zimbabwe (1%).[32]

The substantial growth rate in the last decade is set to accelerate. McKinsey & Company predicts that annual demand will grow meteorically from 100,000 tonnes to 650,000 tonnes in 2030.[33]

Of note, the United States is expected to become a significant producer of lithium, despite producing less than 1% of global output in 2021. Ironically, the United States was the world's leader in lithium production until about 1990, but, like many other industries, it was offshored.[34] Driven by demand from its domestic car manufacturers and stimulated by the incentives offered through the 2022 *Inflation Reduction Act*, several domestic lithium projects are in planning or underway in Nevada, North Carolina, California and Arkansas. The biggest risks to these projects are opposition from environmental activists, opposition from Native American tribes in the vicinity, and delays securing permits.

The soaring demand has put pressure on prices. In March 2022, lithium hydroxide was selling at US$65,000 per tonne, well above the average US$14,500 per tonne for the preceding five years. On the upside, these high prices are encouraging mining companies to invest at a rapid rate. As is often the case, the best cure for high prices is high prices.

To secure supply, most of the car manufacturers are signing long-term supply contracts and some, such as Tesla and Volkswagen, are investing in lithium mines. This investment by the car companies is reminiscent of the 1920s, when car companies bought up rubber plantations for tyres.

Manganese

After seeing how Britain's economy was almost starved of raw materials by Germany's submarine attacks on British and Allied vessels, at the end of World War II the United States government implemented a strategic reserve for selected commodities. In 1987, manganese was added to the list because of its essential role in steel production.[35]

Manganese is a hard, brittle, silvery metal. It is mostly found as the dull black manganese oxide known as pyrolusite or the pale pink manganese carbonate form known as rhodochrosite. Manganese is widely used as an ingredient of metal alloys, in particular stainless steel and aluminium.

Basic steel is a simple alloy of iron and a small amount of carbon. In modern times, many other elements such as manganese, chromium, nickel, molybdenum, titanium, cobalt and vanadium are added to improve steel's tensile strength, hardness, melting temperature, fatigue resistance and corrosion resistance. So much manganese is used in steel making that it is the fourth most traded metal in the world after aluminium, iron and copper.

When manganese is added in small quantities of up to 2% to aluminium, the alloyed aluminium exhibits improved resistance to corrosion. For this reason, aluminium alloyed with manganese is widely used for beverage cans.

Manganese is also an essential trace element for human health. In particular, it promotes bone strength and plays a key role in blood clotting. It is naturally present in many foods and sold as a dietary supplement.

Now, on top of its existing core industrial responsibility in steel and aluminium making, manganese is stepping up as a critically important energy transition material. It is already widely used in lithium manganese nickel cobalt batteries, and thus demand for the metal will increase rapidly in coming years. Furthermore, in their efforts to minimise the amount of cobalt, most of which comes from ethically unacceptable mining in the Congo, battery manufacturers are looking to reduce or eliminate the cobalt content by increasing the manganese content. Despite the performance reduction in terms of energy stored per kilogram when cobalt is reduced or eliminated, Tesla and Volkswagen have committed to eliminating cobalt from the batteries in their mid-performance vehicles.

Compared to nickel and cobalt, manganese is relatively plentiful. Global manganese mine production in 2021 was 20 million tonnes of metal, up from 16 million tonnes ten years earlier. The top five producer countries, with 83% of the market between them, were South Africa (38%), Gabon (18%), Australia (17%), China (7%) and Ukraine (3%).[36]

Although the use of manganese for batteries has increased dramatically in recent years, the tonnage required is small compared with the quantity used in steel making. About 2% of global consumption of manganese is for batteries while over 90% is used for steel production.[37] Most of the growth in manganese production in recent decades has been to meet the needs of steel production, which worldwide more than doubled from the year 2000 to 2021.

China is the largest importer of manganese ore and refines it to produce 90% of the world's manganese products, ranging from additives to alloy with steel, or ready to use battery compounds.[38]

Manganese demand is forecast to almost double to 39 million tonnes in 2030. Most of that increase will be for steel in the construction industry. Battery requirements will be small in comparison.[39]

Nickel

Say the word nickel to an American and the first thing that comes to their mind is the five-cent coin, endearingly nicknamed after the metal from which it is made – although the nickname might be at risk, given that in 2020 it cost the US mint seven cents to produce each diminutive five-cent coin.

Say the word nickel to anybody involved in the electric vehicle industry and the first thing that comes to their mind is one of the key metals used to make the cathodes in batteries.

Nickel is a hard, silvery white metal with a golden tinge. In the mineral deposits from which it is mined, it is found combined with sulphur, iron or arsenic. Nickel is also found in trace quantities in nuts, beans and chocolate. Its precise health benefits are not well understood, and although it is included in some vitamin supplements, there is no solid scientific evidence to support the claimed benefits.

The biggest global use of nickel by far is in the production of stainless steel, but this is set to change. In 2015, 97% of nickel was used to make stainless steel, other alloys and electroplating. The remaining 3% was for batteries, chemicals, catalysts and dyes.[40] Fast forward just six years to 2021 and 13% of global nickel consumption was for batteries.

The growth rate for batteries is so fast that nickel demand is forecast to outstrip supply by 2024.[41] Concern about pending shortages led to the United States adding nickel to its critical minerals list in 2021. This will encourage greater production in the United States as miners gain access to government subsidies.

Global nickel mine production in 2021 was 2.7 million tonnes, up from 1.9 million tonnes ten years earlier. The top five producer countries, with 71% of the market between them, were Indonesia (36%), Philippines (13%), Russia (9%), New Caledonia (7%) and Australia (6%).[42] China is by far the largest consumer of nickel, absorbing 66% of global production to supply its stainless steel and battery industries. China refines nearly 85% of the world's battery-grade nickel.

Nickel demand is forecast to rise from 2.7 million tonnes in 2021 to approximately 4 million tonnes in 2030. Most of that increase will be driven by rapidly growing demand from the battery industry, while demand for lower-grade nickel used for steel making is set to grow steadily but slowly.[43]

Much of the increased supply will come from Australia and Indonesia, although Canada and Russia are well positioned to increase their output.[44] BHP's December 2022 move to acquire Oz Minerals should underpin a significant step up in Australian copper and nickel production.[45]

Cobalt

During the Yan Dynasty in the 14th century, artists who travelled the Mongol Empire left a legacy of beautiful blue and white porcelain, coloured by cobalt-blue pigment. Cobalt blue used by the Chinese craftsmen is the natural but impure version of cobalt aluminium oxide. The pure form was discovered in the early 18th century and soon became a staple for artists intent on depicting glorious sky-scapes in their paintings. Today, cobalt blue is used to colour glass, ceramics and paints. However, it is toxic if ingested or inhaled and must be handled carefully.

Cobalt is a silvery-blue metal found in the Earth's crust compounded with other elements. It is most often refined as a by-product of copper and nickel mining. Indeed, in 2016 the National Renewable Energy Agency of the US government estimated that 67% of cobalt was mined as a by-product of copper mining and 32% as a by-product of nickel mining, with a mere 1% coming from primary cobalt mines.[46] Thirty-four different forms of cobalt ore have been identified.[47] Common forms found in the Congo include heterogenite, a compound of cobalt, copper and sulfur, and skut-terudite, also known as smaltite, a compound of cobalt and arsenic.

Other than its recent use in batteries, nearly half of cobalt con-sumption is to create superalloys used in aircraft jet engines and the rest to produce hardened machine tools and magnetic alloys. A tiny quantity is used in radiation therapy for cancer patients. Cobalt is also important for health as part of the structure of vitamin B12, one of the twelve essential vitamins identified by the United States government. Also known as cobalamin, vitamin B12 helps to make red blood cells and DNA. It is the only vitamin known to contain a heavy element.

The Congo dominates global cobalt mining. It has had very poor governance for decades and is plagued by a devastating armed conflict for control of its vast natural resources. The roots of its troubles lie in one of the world's most brutal examples of coloni-sation, led by King Leopold II of Belgium, starting more than 100 years ago.

About 15% of Congo's cobalt production is from artisanal min-ing, in which small-scale miners hand-dig the ore. This artisanal mining produces more than double the total cobalt output of Russia, the world's second-largest producer. 'Artisanal', the adjectival form of the noun artisan, literally refers to making things in a traditional or non-mechanised way. The advantage of this manual approach is that artisanal miners can focus on higher-grade ores, which are identified by their crystalline structure and occasional blue-green streaks, rather than the ores targeted by the large digging machines of the big mining companies.

However, artisanal mining in the Congo is fraught with unethical practices and personal risk for the nearly 200,000 practitioners.[48] The mines are dangerous, with frequent reports of miners being killed when tunnels and pits collapse or fires break out. Equally bad, if not worse, nongovernment organisations have reported that nearly 35,000 children, some as young as six, are being forced to dig for cobalt.[49] It is dirty work, and it has been reported that fathers in this line of business are more likely than average to have children with birth defects.

Corruption is widespread in the Congo, and artisanal miners have to pay bribes and unofficial taxes to state agencies, local chiefs, police and security guards. Bad as it is, the artisanal miners choose their livelihood because it yields returns averaging US$10 per day, in a country where most people earn less than US$2 per day.

The plight of the children and adult artisanal miners is unacceptable. Car manufacturers and their battery suppliers are looking for ethical alternatives and supply-chain accreditations, which are discussed at the end of this chapter.

Global cobalt mine production in 2021 was 170,000 tonnes of metal, up from 109,000 tonnes ten years earlier. The top five producer countries, with 87% of the market between them, were the Congo (73%), Russia (5%), Australia (3%), Philippines (3%) and Canada (3%). Note that production in the Congo is significantly more than ten times the level of the second-highest producer country.

The largest importer of cobalt in 2021 was China, taking in 52% of global exports, followed by the United States (8%), Japan (7%), the Netherlands (6%) and Singapore (4%). China refines 85% of the world's battery-grade cobalt.

Driven mostly by use in batteries, demand is expected to more than double to nearly 400,000 tonnes by 2030, despite the growing trend to reduce the use of cobalt in lithium-ion batteries.[50]

The Congo will continue to be the largest supplier country, but its share will likely fall from 73% to as low as 60% as other countries ramp up production. It has been estimated that Australia, Canada, Cuba, Madagascar, Philippines, Russia and Zambia will each account for between 2% and 6% of future production.

In terms of reserves, Australia, with 20% of known reserves, is a strong second to Congo, which has 50% of known reserves.[51] Given its heavyweight expertise in mining, Australia has significant potential to expand its cobalt mining. Much of the cobalt in Australia is produced alongside nickel, another in-demand energy transition material.

Major international mining companies Glencore and Vale operate cobalt mines in Canada. The US government's commitment to clean energy technologies favours production and sourcing in Canada, the United States and Mexico, so it is likely that cobalt production in North America will expand, although there is provision for supply from countries that have a free trade agreement with the United States, such as Australia. Further down the scale, Morocco, with the eleventh-largest reserves, is ramping up, encouraged by an agreement signed with BMW.

Summary projections for battery materials

The previous paragraphs have included projections from various sources of the demand and supply of battery materials in 2030. It is hard to keep track, so here we will summarise the projections. But first, a few words about modelling and predictions.

The only thing we know for sure is that 'prediction is very difficult, especially about the future.' This quote is attributed to the famous Danish physicist Niels Bohr, but has also been attributed to other Danes, including poet Piet Hein. Nevertheless, if we don't use

Table 1: Estimated demand for battery materials for 40 million new electric cars in 2030, not including heavy-duty vehicles. The 2021 production values and the 2030 mine-site production estimates are summarised from earlier sections. The estimated usage is based on NMC532 batteries and the indicated battery-pack energy capacity of 43 kilowatt-hours in 2021 and 100 kilowatt-hours in 2030.

	2021 battery and non-battery production (tonnes)	2021 estimated usage for 6 million new electric cars sold with 43 kilowatt-hours battery (tonnes)	2030 estimated mine production, battery and non-battery use combined (tonnes)	2030 estimated requirement for 40 million new electric cars with 100 kilowatt-hours battery (tonnes)
Graphite	1,000,000	310,000	5,000,000	4,800,000
Lithium	100,000	60,000	650,000	900,000
Nickel	2,700,000	260,000	4,000,000	4,000,000
Manganese	20,000,000	150,000	39,000,000	2,300,000
Cobalt	170,000	100,000	400,000	1,600,000

models to characterise economic systems and evaluate the impact of various scenarios, we will be flying blind. The trick is to be aware of the assumptions and constantly challenge the logic behind them and their conclusions.

Looking at numerous forecasts, on average the pundits are predicting that there will be 40 million electric vehicles sold in 2030. If the average battery pack at that time reaches 100 kilowatt-hours, the total requirement for new batteries in the year 2030 will be 4,000 gigawatt-hours.

The amount of cathode metals in a lithium-ion battery depends on the type of battery and the energy storage capacity. The Argonne National Laboratory in the United States reports that for a lithium-ion battery pack known as an NMC532 with 100 kilowatt-hour energy capacity, the cathode material content would be approximately 23 kilograms of lithium, 100 kilograms of nickel, 57 kilograms of manganese and 40 kilograms of cobalt.[52]

As a reality check, in Table 1 we summarise a scenario that assumes 40 million new electric car sales in 2030, with an average battery size of 100 kilowatt-hours (compared with 43 kilowatt-hours in 2021).[53] The table makes no provision for stationary battery demand because there are options in that market to use other battery chemistries that would not be suitable for the vehicle market because of their lower energy density. I repeat, this is not a model, just a scenario, to help summarise what we know so far.

We can see that cobalt is the battery material with the biggest gap between estimated mine production and demand, followed by lithium. The solutions will be diversification and expansion of the supply chain, and technology innovation to reduce demand, particularly for cobalt.

Group 3: rare earth elements

The rare earth elements are a family of seventeen heavy metals, silvery white in appearance. Despite their name, they are relatively abundant in the Earth's crust. In fact, one of them, cerium, is as abundant as copper. However, they are widely dispersed and only rarely found in concentrated mineral deposits.

The first discovery was in Ytterby, Sweden, in 1878. A miner found a black rock that was called 'rare' because it had never been seen before and 'earth' because that was the term for rocks that could be dissolved in acid. Hence the misnomer that has stuck ever since. Despite their name, the tonnage of 'rare' earth elements produced each year is about 100 times the annual tonnage of gold production.

There is no clue in the names of individual elements to identify them as rare earth elements; all have the suffix -*ium*, which is common to most metals. Perhaps they share an air of exotic mystery, with names reminiscent of Ancient Greek gods or planetary bodies. Here is the full list, worthy of a glance but most certainly not worthy of an attempt to memorise: cerium, dysprosium, erbium, europium, gadolinium, holmium, lanthanum, lutetium, neodymium, praseodymium, promethium, samarium, scandium, terbium, thulium, ytterbium (named after Ytterby in Sweden, where the first ore was found) and yttrium.

Rare earth elements have many uses, including in the electronics of smartphones and computers, and flat-panel television displays. In smartphones, neodymium, praseodymium and gadolinium are additives in the alloys for the magnets in the speaker and microphone. Terbium, dysprosium and neodymium are additives in the alloys in the vibration unit.[54] Rare earth elements provide special optical properties to glass, and lanthanum in particular is heavily used in the lenses of phone and digital cameras. Gadolinium-based contrast agents are widely used in medical imaging. In about a third of MRI procedures, they are injected into the patient's veins to enhance the contrast in the images, thereby improving the visibility of tumours, blood vessels and inflammation.

The revolution that is replacing incandescent light globes with light-emitting diodes depends on rare earth elements. The diodes central to the lamps that illuminate our homes and football stadiums emit blue light. To achieve the white and yellowish-white light we humans appreciate, coatings based on yttrium, cerium, terbium, europium or gadolinium shift the light from blue to the desired colour in a process known as scintillation.

By volume of rare earth elements consumed, the top two applications are in catalysts used in numerous industrial processes, and in powerful permanent magnets. It is the latter use that is of particular interest to the clean energy transition. Extremely strong permanent magnets made with rare earth elements are key to the efficiency of motors used in electric vehicles and the generators used in wind turbines. The use of neodymium to make ultra-strong permanent magnets was recognised by the award of the Queen

Elizabeth Prize for Engineering in 2022 to Dr Masato Sagawa of Japan 'for his work on the discovery, development and global commercialisation of the sintered neodymium-iron-boron permanent magnet.' The Queen Elizabeth Prize, awarded for ground-breaking engineering innovations of global benefit to humanity, is regarded by many as the equivalent of the Nobel Prize for engineering. I am proud to have been a member of the judging panel that awarded the prize to Dr Sagawa.

Extracting the metals from the ores is a complex process of more than 100 steps and repetitions.[55] The processing must be tightly managed because most rare earth element deposits are mixed with small quantities of radioactive thorium and uranium, requiring very careful separation and disposal. After decades of investment to build world-leading research, development and deployment skills, China has become the world's primary refiner, responsible for producing 90% of the global supply of the purified metals in 2021.[56]

The risks inherent in this concentration of supply were illustrated in 2010 during a disagreement over fishing rights. Japan had detained the captain of a Chinese fishing trawler after his boat collided with two Japanese coastguard ships while he was fishing in waters controlled by Japan but claimed by China. In response, China cut off exports of refined rare earth elements to Japan. At the time, Japan imported nearly all its rare earth elements from China and had to scramble to find alternative supplies to support its affected industries. These included glass making for solar panels and electric motors for hybrid cars.

Describing this incident at the Sydney Energy Forum, Japanese energy economics expert Tatsuya Terazawa observed that at the time Japan was not even aware that it was so dependent on Chinese rare earth elements. Fortunately for Japan, its companies had stockpiles, which gave Japan time to reduce its dependence on China. It did this by diversifying its supply chain through investing in projects around the world, and by engineering out some of its products' dependence on rare earth elements.

One of the major commitments that emerged from this effort was an agreement between Japanese trading company Sojitz to import US$250 million of rare earth concentrates from Australian company Lynas Rare Earths, which had commenced mining of rare earth minerals in 2008.[57] In 2021, Lynas was the leading supplier of neodymium praseodymium oxide to Japan, used in large quantities for the production of powerful permanent magnets.

The biggest rare earth element reserves are in China, Vietnam, Russia and Brazil, but of these only China is in the list of the top five mine production countries. Global mine production of rare earth elements in 2021 was 280,000 tonnes of metal, up from 111,000 tonnes ten years earlier. The top five producer countries, with a highly concentrated 96% of the market between them, were China (61%), the United States (16%), Myanmar (9%), Australia (8%) and Thailand (3%).[58]

The lack of diversity in rare earth elements supply is largely because China made it a strategic priority to develop its capacity to support its ever-growing manufacturing industry.[59] The lack of diversity in the supply chain has started to change in recent years. Responding to an executive order issued by President Trump in 2017, the Department of Defense has been issuing contracts to a variety of US-domiciled companies to establish domestic refining capabilities. The Biden administration is also investing in the rare earth elements supply chain.

Since making the decision in 2001 to focus on rare earth elements, Australian company Lynas Rare Earths has grown to become the largest miner and refiner of rare earth elements outside China.[60] It operates a mine and ore concentrator in Western Australia. The concentrate is sent to Lynas's refinery in Malaysia, where it is refined into pure oxides of cerium, lanthanum, neodymium and praseodymium.[61] That refinery is one of the world's largest. Nevertheless, it is limited to processing the lighter rare earth elements, those with atomic weight of 61 or lower. The heavier ones, such as terbium and dysprosium, are sent to China for processing.

In 2021, Lynas signed an agreement with the United States government to build a refinery in Texas to refine oxides of the heavy rare earth elements. Under the agreement, the Department of Defense is contributing US$120 million to finance the construction of the plant, which is due to be operational in 2025. This is a landmark agreement because there are currently no heavy rare earth element separation facilities outside China. This is of particular concern to the Department of Defense because some of the heavy elements are used in military lasers and guidance systems.

In 2022, Lynas committed to building Australia's first rare earth elements refinery in Western Australia, with public and private funding. The first production of oxides is expected in July 2023.[62] Elsewhere in Australia, mining companies Iluka Resources and Australian Strategic Materials are in the early stages of developing rare earth element production and refinery plants. Another promising company outside China is MP Materials, an American-led consortium, which resumed production in 2017 at the mothballed Mountain Pass mine in California.[63]

Demand continues to grow and will mostly need to be fed from new production, because the rare earth elements have a very low recycling rate.

Group 4: solar-panel materials

The clean energy transition is being driven by solar and wind electricity generation.

The wind-turbine industry uses huge amounts of concrete and steel, but these are not critically important energy transition materials. The large quantities of copper and rare earth elements required for turbines have already been discussed. In short, there are no other critical supply chain materials for wind turbines.

The solar-panel industry, on the other hand, is putting significant demands on two familiar materials. The first is quite obvious, being the processed silicon from which most solar cells are made.

The second is perhaps a surprise. It is silver, used to make electrodes in nearly every solar cell.

Polysilicon

Silicon is the king of semiconductor elements, and while other materials such as germanium, graphene, gallium nitride and silicon carbide have been touted as contenders for the throne, none has come close to overthrowing king silicon in its noble role as the substrate in computer chips.

Silicon is also the wafer material of choice for more than 95% of global production of solar photovoltaic cells. The remaining fraction of the solar photovoltaic market is made up of solar cells made from cadmium and telluride, which are by-products of zinc and copper mining.

The starting material for silicon photovoltaic cells is polysilicon, which is purified from silicon dioxide found as quartzite or quartz sand. The polysilicon is then either cast into multi-crystalline ingots or crystalised into mono-crystalline ingots. The ingots are sliced into thin wafers, which are transformed into solar cells by cleaning, doping, etching, texturing, coating and printing with metal conductors. The solar cells are arranged in a grid on mounting sheets, connected to each other, laminated, protected by a front glass sheet and mounted in an aluminium frame to form a solar panel.

In the early days, the silicon ingots were predominantly multi-crystalline, but in recent years the industry has shifted almost exclusively to mono-crystalline silicon. Although it is more expensive, the extra cost is compensated for by the mono-crystalline cells being several percentage points more efficient.

About 2.5 tonnes of polysilicon are used to manufacture one megawatt of solar cells. Global polysilicon consumption in 2021 was 600,000 tonnes, up from 280,000 tonnes in 2011.[64] It is forecast to expand dramatically to 4 million tonnes by 2030.[65] The top four producer countries, with an extremely concentrated 98% between them, were China (79%), Germany (10%), United States (5%) and Malaysia (4%).[66]

In one of the reports released by the International Energy Agency for consideration at the Sydney Energy Forum, the Agency warned that China's dominance of the global solar supply chain was a threat to the smooth transition to net zero emissions.[67] Before further considering the concerns raised in this report, it is worth repeating that at the Sydney Energy Forum, participants acknowledged that China achieved its dominant position by producing high-quality products, in ever-larger volumes at low prices. Indeed, China has made an instrumental contribution to bringing prices down by more than 80% in the last decade by an ongoing investment in new solar manufacturing capacity, thereby supporting the rapid global uptake of solar electricity and helping it to become the cheapest form of electricity in history. However, China's dominance leaves all countries vulnerable to supply-chain disruptions.

The IEA report pointed out that between 2010 and 2021, solar-panel manufacturing capacity increasingly moved out of Europe, Japan and the United States to China, which has taken the lead on investment and innovation. China's share of global polysilicon production capacity almost tripled during the 2000s, to 80% of the world supply, as can be seen dramatically in Figure 6. The remaining supply was split between Germany, Malaysia and the United States. The US Department of Energy notes that existing domestic polysilicon production facilities are either idle or supplying polysilicon to other industries.[68]

The IEA report further stated that with new manufacturing facilities under construction in China, the country is on track to increase its market share even further, to produce 95% of the world's polysilicon, wafers, solar cells and finished modules.

The investment in solar cell manufacturing in China was spurred by subsidised investment in domestic solar electricity generation, especially after the Global Financial Crisis of 2008. It was further fuelled by the opportunities for low-cost Chinese solar cell

Figure 6: Production in China of all segments in the solar-panel supply chain increased dramatically from 2010 to 2021, particularly the polysilicon and the wafers from which the solar cells are made. From the IEA Special Report on Solar PV Global Supply Chains released at the Sydney Energy Forum. (Source: www.iea.org/reports/solar-pv-global-supply-chains)

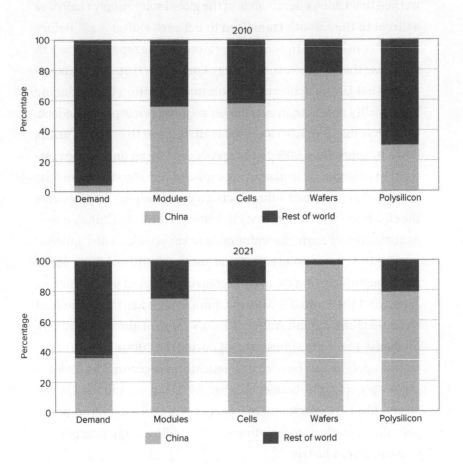

producers to sell into the subsidised markets of Germany and other European countries. Inside China, the domestic feed-in tariffs have led to it now having by far the greatest cumulative installed solar electricity generation capacity in the world.

The fact that China subsidised its solar electricity generation deployment is not unusual. What was unusual was the massive scale, and the fact that it developed an integrated domestic industry to supply the components. Because of this scale and the competitively low price of electricity for industry, the IEA estimates manufacturing costs in China for all solar components are 10% lower than in India, 20% lower than in the United States and 35% lower than in Europe.

A potential environmental concern is that the electricity used in Xinjiang and Jiangsu provinces, where most production of solar panels takes place, is 65% derived from coal-fired power plants. Nevertheless, the IEA calculated that it only takes between four and eight months to offset the manufacturing emissions, based on the average lifespan of a solar panel of 25 years or more.

Some international commentators are concerned that if the tensions between China and Taiwan were to escalate, there might be disruption to the supply of solar panels and components from China.[69] The potential for global supply chains to be disrupted was evident when regions in China went in and out of lockdown in response to Covid-19 outbreaks. Production of polysilicon became a bottleneck in 2021, leading to a quadrupling of prices. The price of finished panels increased by up to 40%, a rare upward blip in the overall downward trend of solar-panel prices for the last five decades. Such supply constraints are not compatible with the expected quadrupling of annual solar-panel deployment by 2030.

Another risk to supply is driven by concerns about forced labour in China. In June 2022, the *Uyghur Forced Labor Prevention Act* went into effect in the United States to prohibit imports of products made by forced labour.[70] The Xinjiang province, where 54% of Chinese polysilicon is produced, is specifically identified as a region of concern.

A third factor is the increasing trade tensions between the United States and China, and resulting import duties on solar modules from Chinese suppliers into the United States. In India, Prime Minister Modi has introduced solar-module import duties to accelerate the expansion of local manufacturing capacity as part of his government's 'Make in India' strategy, given the significant employment opportunities and diversification of supply chains this entails.

The Indian government and major corporates such as Reliance Industries Limited are committed to developing significant domestic solar-panel manufacturing capabilities.

The IEA has identified that one out of every seven solar panels produced worldwide is manufactured at a single integrated Chinese facility. Clearly, this level of concentration represents a supply-chain vulnerability that could be triggered just as easily by a fire or an earthquake as by geopolitics.

These supply constraints are a reminder and an opportunity for other countries to invest and diversify production to increase resilience. The IEA report states that new solar-panel manufacturing facilities could attract US$120 billion of investment by 2030 and create up to a million manufacturing jobs. The United States government in 2022 put in place policies to expand domestic solar-panel production capacity.

Silver

Mention silver and most people think of candlesticks and teapots, jewellery, investment coins and inflation-proof ingots of the pure metal. As a precious metal, silver is valued for its lustrous finish and its medium rarity.

But mention silver to a manufacturer in a solar-panel business and they will think of it as the metal in the electrodes that collect the sunshine-induced current from the top surface of the solar cells and convey it to the external circuits.

As a metal for electronic circuits, silver is valued because it has the highest electrical conductivity and the highest thermal conductivity. Half the annual production of silver is used in industrial applications such as solar panels, electronics, batteries and biocides.

Silver is found in small quantities as a pure metal, but more often alloyed with gold or as silver sulphide and silver chloride ores.

Mine production grew slowly over the last decade. Global silver mine production in 2021 was 24,000 tonnes (770 million troy ounces) of metal, up marginally from 23,000 tonnes (750 million troy ounces) ten years earlier. The top five producer countries, with 62% of the market between them, were Mexico (23%), China (14%), Peru (13%), Chile (7%) and Australia (5%).[71]

In 2021, just over 10% of the world's silver production was used to produce solar panels. This is expected to grow to 30% or more by 2030.[72] This is not as much growth as one might expect given the forecast quadrupling in annual solar deployment between 2021 and 2030. The reason for this modest growth is that solar-cell manufacturers are continually improving their processes to reduce the amount of silver in each cell.

The modest increases in supply between now and 2030 are expected to come from expansion at existing mines.

Group 5: hydrogen metals

Production of non-fossil hydrogen involves breaking water molecules into their constituent hydrogen and oxygen elements. This is done by an electric current in a process called electrolysis, in a machine called an electrolyser. There are two main types, an alkaline electrolyser and a proton-exchange membrane electrolyser. The former is mature technology that until recently has dominated electrolysis. Proton-exchange membrane electrolysers have been touted as the contender of choice because of their faster response and higher efficiency, but newer alkaline electrolyser designs are fighting back.

Alkaline electrolysers do not use precious-metal catalysts, but proton-exchange membrane electrolysers use platinum and iridium alloys to coat the cathode electrodes to minimise corrosion and speed up the reactions. For similar reasons, platinum is also used in fuel cells in hydrogen electric vehicles.

Platinum

Just like silver, what you think of when you hear the world platinum depends on your interests. To a regular person, platinum is a silvery white precious metal valued in fine jewellery because of its rarity and its resistance to wear and tarnish. To an investor, platinum is a precious metal that, like gold, is used as a hedge against inflation. To an industrialist, it is the metal used in catalytic converters in cars and trucks to minimise carbon monoxide and nitrogen oxide emissions from internal combustion engines; it is the metal used in electrical contacts, as a catalyst in the chemical industry for the production of nitric acid, silicone and benzene, and as an important ingredient of chemotherapy drugs used to treat cancers. Approximately 50% of the industrial demand is for vehicle catalytic converters.[73]

Because of its extremely high resistance to corrosion and low reactivity, platinum is referred to as a noble metal. When it is mined it is usually found as the pure metal, or alloyed with metals such as iron, copper, gold and nickel or with the other platinum group metals: iridium, osmium, palladium, rhodium and ruthenium.[74]

Platinum is rare in the Earth's crust, resulting in fairly small worldwide mine outputs of approximately 180 tonnes each year (5.8 million troy ounces), much lower than the 3,000 or more tonnes of gold mined most years.[75] The top five producers, with a very high 98% of the market between them, were South Africa (73%), Russia (11%), Zimbabwe (8%), Canada (4%) and the United States (2%).[76]

Some estimates are that the demand for platinum as a catalyst in electrolysers and fuel cells could reach 19 tonnes and 31 tonnes respectively by 2030.[77] This would be a significant but not overwhelming fraction of the 180 tonnes of annual platinum production. It could be that the increased demand will come from expanding the output of existing mines. It is also possible that new countries, such as Australia, might enter the fray.[78]

And of course, as battery electric and hydrogen fuel-cell electric vehicles displace internal combustion engine vehicles, the substantial demand for platinum in catalytic converters will ultimately be eliminated.

For all these reasons, while platinum availability to support the hydrogen economy is something to be watched, it is probably not a cause for concern.

Iridium

Platinum's cousin iridium is also silvery white, is even more rare in the Earth's crust, and typically sells for five times more per ounce. The prices of all these metals fluctuate, but at an arbitrary date – 10 October 2022 – the trading prices per troy ounce were approximately US$900 for platinum and US$4,300 for iridium, which could be compared with US$1,700 for gold and US$20 for silver.[79]

Iridium is even more corrosion resistant than platinum. Industrially, iridium is used in the electronics industry, in engine spark plugs and as a catalyst in chemical industries.

Both platinum and iridium are very dense. Whereas a cubic metre of water weighs exactly one tonne and a cubic metre of iron weighs 7.9 tonnes, a cubic metre of platinum weighs 21.5 tonnes and a cubic metre of iridium weighs 22.6 tonnes. Both platinum and iridium are even more dense than uranium, which at 19 tonnes per cubic metre is used in its depleted form by the US military in some bullets and armour because of its density.

Worldwide iridium mine production is tiny, about 7 tonnes (225,000 troy ounces) per year.[80] South Africa is the major producing country, followed a long way behind by Zimbabwe, Canada and Russia.[81]

The tiny production of iridium is a concern. In a 2020 report, the International Renewable Energy Agency (IRENA) calculated that based on current requirements per electrolyser, the annual production of iridium for use in proton-exchange membrane electrolysers will only support up to 7.5 gigawatts of annual manufacturing capacity, whereas IRENA estimates that there will be worldwide demand for 100 gigawatts of electrolyser production in 2030.[82]

It is unlikely that iridium mining can be scaled up to meet the needs of proton-exchange electrolysers if they become a substantial fraction of future supply. Either the quantity of iridium in proton-exchange membrane electrolysers must be reduced by design optimisations, or the market will favour alkaline electrolysers. Currently, proton-exchange membrane electrolysers use about 400 grams of iridium per megawatt, but the industry goal is to reduce this to about 100 grams per megawatt.[83]

Ethics and social licence

The rest of this chapter is about how to build the mining and refining industries for energy transition materials while minimising harm to communities and the environment. Quite appropriately, pressure is growing on manufacturers of batteries, vehicles, solar panels and wind turbines to ensure that their suppliers are following ethical practices, so that the clean energy transition is not achieved at the expense of local environments, communities or workforces.

As we have seen, a massive increase in mining of energy transition materials will be required to support the clean energy transition. More than 60% of new mines will be on or adjacent to the land of Traditional Owners. Whether they impinge on Traditional Owners' land, on privately held land or on government-owned land, mining companies and governments must ensure that communities are fully engaged in planning, and that they are financially rewarded and ethically treated.

Currently, this is often not the case. My niece and nephew Natalie Bugalski and David Pred, co-founders of non-governmental organisation Inclusive Development International, have devoted their lives to protecting the land rights and human rights of communities across the globe. Of their many interventions, here are two that illustrate the problems and some possible solutions.

The first started in late 2015, when an artisanal mining community in a remote part of the impoverished West African nation of Guinea was evicted at gunpoint and robbed of their land and livelihoods to make way for an open-pit gold mine owned by AngloGold Ashanti, one of the world's largest gold-mining companies.[84] Some four years later, through a concerted international advocacy strategy supported by Inclusive Development International and two Guinean NGOs, the community was able to bring company executives to the negotiating table and secure a series of agreements to begin to redress the harms the community had suffered.

The second involved community members living in remote forest towns in western Liberia, who believed a mining company's promises of a better life: functional roads, safe drinking water, electricity, education, healthcare and employment. But more than five years after Liberia's first and largest commercial gold mine went into full production, many community members found themselves worse off than before. With Inclusive Development International's assistance, the communities have had a ground-breaking complaint accepted, creating an opportunity to hold Bea Mountain Mining Corporation to its promises.[85]

The 2009 James Cameron epic science-fiction movie *Avatar* is an interstellar variation on this theme. The year is 2154 and Earth is fast running out of natural resources. Never daunted, humans travel the enormous distance to the Alpha Centauri star system to mine an incredibly valuable metal called unobtanium, on a fictional inhabited moon called Pandora. The richest deposit of unobtanium is underneath 'Giant Hometree', the most important edifice of the local civilisation, which houses community leaders and hundreds of clan members. Oblivious to the harm they will cause and without any respect for Pandora's rich culture, flora and fauna, the humans violently destroy the Giant Hometree and kill many clan members. In the movie, the clan members counterattack, overwhelming the humans and expelling them from Pandora.

That's the movie. In real life on Earth, injustice is rarely reversed so triumphantly.

Take artisanal cobalt mining. Following a 2016 report by Amnesty International, many phone and car companies pledged to stop using artisanal cobalt in their batteries and to help to ensure safety in small mines.[86] But in July 2022, *The Economist* magazine reported that six years on, little had changed.

There are pockets of excellent behaviour. For example, BMW now purchases its cobalt exclusively from certified mines in Australia and Morocco.[87] Major multinational mining companies publicly commit to respecting human rights in line with international standards, including the United Nations' *Guiding Principles on Business and Human Rights*.[88] These principles require companies to avoid infringing on the human rights of others, including by preventing and mitigating harms, for example through compensation for losses and other measures. In recognition of the negative impacts of mining on the natural resources and traditional economic base of affected communities, mining companies are expected to go beyond mere 'do no harm' standards and make positive contributions to the social and economic development of the local population.

Through a consortium called ReSource, a number of cobalt producers and users, including Tesla, mining company CMOC, battery-material supplier Umicore and chemical company Johnson Matthey, are seeking to implement a blockchain system to trace the origins of the cobalt they use. However, at the time of writing the system was still in the pilot phase, after three years of development.[89] The credibility of this voluntary consortium is inevitably called into question by the membership of Swiss mining giant Glencore. In 2018, Glencore paid US$180 million dollars to the Congo to settle claims of graft, corruption and bribing judges, and in 2022 it was fined more than US$1 billion for bribery and market abuse.[90]

The company has also been reported as having the worst human-rights record of any energy transition metals mining company.[91]

An alternative consortium, the Responsible Sourcing Blockchain Network, is using IBM blockchain technology to verifiably trace cobalt supply lines. Information is tracked from the mine site to the battery factory. All participating producers are large mining companies. They must agree to follow the standards and best practices established by the OECD[92] Members include car companies Ford, Volkswagen, Volvo and Fiat Chrysler, and battery manufacturer LG Chem. The system is fully deployed. It does not help with the artisanal and small-site mining sector, but it does, in principle, allow participating manufacturers to limit their cobalt purchases to members of the network.

Through another organisation called the Fair Cobalt Alliance, some firms are taking a more nuanced approach than avoiding supply. Instead of refusing to purchase artisanal cobalt, the Alliance recognises that although artisanal mining is extremely hazardous and depends on child labour and unfair, unregulated trading practices, at the same time it provides a livelihood to thousands of people in a country where many have no job at all. The challenge, therefore, is to dramatically improve working conditions and ensure a continued income stream for workers.

The stated aim of the Fair Cobalt Alliance is to support 'the professionalisation of artisanal and small-scale' mining by promoting responsible mining practices and investment. The Alliance specifically addresses child labour by working with local community cooperatives to make it more practical for children to go to school or attend vocational training programs. In recognition of the causative effect of widespread poverty on safety shortcuts and child labour in artisanal mining, the Alliance is investing in community development programs outside mining. Members of the Alliance include Glencore, Google, LG Energy Solution, Save the Children and Tesla.[93] The Alliance launched in 2020, and it is not yet clear if it has been successful; it is probably too early to tell. In March 2022, an executive from the Alliance, David Sturmes, observed that the industry as a whole had not yet taken meaningful steps to ensure responsible cobalt production in the Congo and that substantial investment would be needed to reduce hazardous working conditions and prevent accidents.

Like other schemes, the Fair Cobalt Alliance is voluntary and industry led. Given that some of its member companies have been implicated in human rights violations, environmental destruction and corruption, the onus is on the Alliance to prove its credibility through independent auditing and compliance mechanisms, both of which are yet to be implemented.

In 2019, the World Bank launched an initiative called Climate-Smart Mining.[94] Its stated purpose is to 'work with developing countries and emerging economies to implement sustainable and responsible strategies and practices across the mineral value chain'. However, the support provided is only US$50 million over five years, so it is difficult to imagine that it will have much impact.

In considering corporate commitments to ethical production, an illustrative analogy is provided by the Nike scandal. In 1991, the US-based company was accused of operating factories in Indonesia where workers were paid below the minimum wage and expected to work long hours, children were put to work in hazardous conditions and workers were housed in slums near open sewers. In the wake of a public lashing, Nike pledged to take action. But in 2018, a Netherlands-based rights advocacy group, the Clean Clothes Campaign, published a report claiming that Nike continued to pay poverty-level wages to its factory workers around the world.[95] Two years later, bad practices were still being discovered. A 2020 report by the Australian Strategic Policy Institute found that a factory in eastern China that manufactured shoes for Nike employed Uyghur workers under forced labour conditions in a facility equipped with watchtowers, barbed-wire fences and guard boxes.[96]

Mining projects are frequently subject to criticism, whether it is evidence-based or not. For example, locals in the vicinity of the salt deserts of Chile and Argentina where lithium is mined complain about increasing droughts threatening livestock farming. However, it is not clear that evaporation from the salt ponds is a drought-inducing factor beyond the global climate change that is already altering weather patterns in most regions of our planet. Although no fresh water is used in evaporative mining of lithium, concerns have been expressed that freshwater from adjacent aquifers will flow into the saltwater aquifers to replace the salt water that has been extracted. Whether or not this is happening is unknown because there has not been sufficient research.[97]

Responsible car manufacturers work with their suppliers to ensure the use of sustainably mined battery materials. Volkswagen states that it has signed memoranda of understanding with some of its lithium suppliers, including the Chinese company Ganfeng Lithium, which obtains much of its raw materials from Australia. However, laudable as this is, it is not an enforceable commitment because a memorandum of understanding is not legally binding.

Throughout 2021 and 2022, European legislators were developing the European Battery Regulation, commonly known as the 'battery passport', the details of which are still being negotiated. Under this proposal, batteries and other consumer goods will be individually tracked with a digital identification number. The passport will trace the emissions intensity during production and will track the operating history and performance of the battery to assist with subsequent recycling.[98]

In New Caledonia, Tesla has taken a novel approach to securing its nickel supplies while simultaneously investing in environmentally friendly and ethical mining. An overseas French territory, New Caledonia is an archipelago in the Pacific Ocean. The capital, Nouméa, is 1,500 kilometres from Brisbane, Australia, and 17,000 kilometres from Paris, France. The population of 270,000 consists mostly of the indigenous Kanak people, but also of Europeans and Polynesians. All are French citizens.

As well as being a tropical paradise, New Caledonia also happens to be the fourth-largest producer of nickel in the world. However, the production from the Goro mine, located on the southern tip of the main island near Prony Bay, has been plagued by environmental problems. There have been five recorded acid leaks into pristine bays and reefs since the mine started in 2010. The local Kanak community objected to the development of the mine in the first place because of concerns about the environmental impact and an inadequate plan for training a locally sourced workforce. The mine was owned and operated by Vale, a major international mining company.

In early 2021, Vale sold its interests in the Goro mine to Prony Resources, a locally led consortium, with more than half the shares owned by New Caledonian shareholders, including local Kanak communities. Tesla is a minority investor in Prony Resources and has committed to being the largest customer of the mine's nickel output, buying 42,000 tonnes per year.[99]

Tesla says its approach to ethical mining follows two tracks: direct sourcing from mining companies and direct engagement with affected local communities. Tesla signed a memorandum of understanding with Prony Resources to act as a technical advisor to increase production capacity and incorporate sustainability standards while securing the mineral supply for its car production facilities. Being a high-profile listed public company, Tesla will be accountable to its shareholders and customers and subject to the scrutiny of environmental and human rights organisations to ensure the supply is ethical and environmentally friendly.

In summary, the responsible and sustainable mining record is mixed, and the voluntary schemes have variable credibility. There is a base, but much work to be done and there is most likely a role for governments.

Purchasing power

There is one overriding prerequisite for success that every producer needs: customers.

Despite the antics of Elon Musk as the new owner of Twitter, Tesla's commitment is an example of a principled customer requirement constructively influencing the environmental and community responsibilities at the mine site. This approach is a form of activism that has been described as ethical purchasing, ethical consumerism or ethical sourcing.

Customers, be they individuals who purchase cars or home batteries, or car and truck companies that purchase batteries or raw ingredients, can and do influence upstream producers. If every car buyer uses their purchasing power to demand that products originate from ethical and socially responsible mining operations, car companies and hence mining companies will respond.

Purchasing power is popping up everywhere. The latest Barbie doll from Mattel is made of recycled plastic waste collected in Mexico. The Matchbox Tesla Roadster from the same company is made from 99% recycled materials and certified as carbon neutral. Why? The company says it is responding to surveys of parents showing that 80% of them rate the sustainability of toys as important.[100]

Without a coordinated effort at the purchasing end of the supply chain, many of our solar panels, wind-turbine generators and vehicle batteries could be tainted by modern slavery, child labour or displaced communities. New South Wales became the first state in Australia to introduce legislation to address modern slavery through the appointment of an anti-slavery commissioner. The commissioner has oversight of the state's procurements to ensure that products of modern slavery are eliminated from supply chains.

The expansion of mining under the watchful eye of manufacturers and customers should be seen as an opportunity: new jobs for the poor, infrastructure to bring electricity and water to the needy, a boost to government revenue in developing countries. The challenge is to make it so despite the chequered history of the global mining industry.

Buyers don't always know the origins of the energy transition materials in the goods they purchase. To shine a light on the investment and supply chain, Inclusive Development International has been deploying a ground-breaking model to hold multinational corporations accountable. Launched in 2016, their Follow the Money to Justice initiative investigates the investment and supply chains behind projects that are causing harm to local communities.[101] The premise is that the mining companies are backed by a mostly invisible web of global actors, including banks, buyers, investors, trading houses and sometimes even global financial institutions (such as the World Bank Group and the Asian Development Bank). Many of these actors are bound by policies that require them to respect human rights and the environment. But because affected communities are often unaware of the involvement of these actors, they are unable to enlist them in their efforts to prevent or remediate harms caused by poorly designed investment projects.

The principle of Follow the Money is that making the investors and consumers who fund these projects aware of where their money is going opens up a range of opportunities for accountability. Many investors and buyers are committed organisationally to ethical investments and purchases and are therefore responsive to advocacy. Inclusive Development International investigates these investment and supply chains, identifies pressure points for advocacy, and shares that information with impacted communities. These advocacy opportunities have helped tens of thousands of affected people to secure redress for harms they have endured.

• • •

We have accepted the inevitability that 'there is no net zero without mining'. The resource extraction and refining to support the clean energy transition will be massive, as we have seen in this rundown of the key energy transmission materials. In exchange for this investment, we gain the global benefit of eliminating nearly three-quarters of greenhouse gas emissions. Governments and companies can and must ensure that the mining and refining are responsibly undertaken. Even with the best of intentions, however, such an expansion will not be without consequences. Thus, to the maximum extent possible, as described in the next chapter, we should look to recycling, re-use and innovation to make sure that we do no more mining than necessary.

3.
Energy Transition Materials: Minimising Future Demand

Are there ways the clean energy transition can proceed at the fastest possible pace with reduced mining and refining requirements, if only by a small percentage? This chapter explores a number of innovations that address this question.

Recycling and re-use

Recycling and re-use are two alternatives to mining for meeting a portion of future demand.

Recycling is common for some of the energy transition materials that have been used at large scale for a long time. For example, in addition to the 770 million troy ounces of silver mined in 2021, a further 170 million troy ounces were recycled.[1] In addition to the 21 million tonnes of copper mined that year, 5 million tonnes were recycled.[2] Aluminium can be recycled almost without limit. Already, nearly 70% of aluminium waste is recycled, and it is conceivable that this could be increased to a higher rate, thereby substantially reducing demand for primary aluminium production.[3]

When it comes to the battery materials lithium, manganese, cobalt, nickel and graphite, and the rare earth elements, recycling is elusive. There are two challenges to be overcome.

The first is availability. Because electric vehicles are still a small part of the market and growing from a tiny base, and given the lifetime of a battery is ten years or more, there are simply not nearly enough old batteries to recycle to meet manufacturing needs. The growth numbers are striking. From 2011 to 2021, global electric vehicle sales rose from 55,000 per year to 6.6 million.[4] In principle, if all 55,000 batteries in the vehicles sold in 2011 had been recycled for use in new cars sold in 2021, they would have been sufficient for just 0.8% of the new vehicles. But it would not even have been as much as that, because recycling is never perfectly efficient, and batteries back in 2011 were smaller. Sales in 2011 were dominated by the Nissan LEAF, which had a 24-kilowatt-hour battery, whereas in 2021 the average battery size was 43 kilowatt-hours.[5]

Perhaps from the mid-2030s onwards the supply of old batteries will become sufficient to allow recycling to become a substantial contributor to the supply of materials. To use them effectively, it will be necessary to resolve the second challenge – immature recycling technologies. Now is the time to develop recycling technologies to ensure that they will be practical and cost-effective once the number of available batteries starts to climb.

Several companies are developing recycling processes for lithium-ion batteries. Mostly, they use high temperatures to vaporise impurities and recover the cobalt, nickel and copper. The lithium and aluminium are usually lost, inseparable from the slag that remains. The processing is expensive and energy intensive and the rate of recovery of the energy transition materials is low.

Some new battery gigafactories are being designed with recycling in mind, although perhaps with unrealistic ambitions.[6] Swedish battery maker Northvolt aims to be one of the largest manufacturers in the world, hoping to produce 150 gigawatt-hours of batteries in 2030. It also intends to source 50% of its required battery metals, such as lithium, manganese, nickel and cobalt, by recycling batteries.[7] This is surprising, given the company also points out that battery production in Europe is expected to grow 20-fold by 2030. Northvolt is equally ambitious about reducing the carbon dioxide emitted during battery manufacturing: its goal is to reduce the typical 150 kilograms of carbon dioxide manufacturing emissions per kilowatt-hour in 2022 to 10 kilograms per kilowatt-hour by 2030.[8]

Redwood Materials, a Nevada-based start-up co-founded and led by Tesla co-founder J.B. Straubel, has announced a collecting and recycling program, with a respected list of recycling partners that includes Volkswagen and Panasonic. However, the company is only in the earliest stages of its genesis.

Despite the inherent high cost and inefficiency of recycling, it will be required by legislation if the market fails to deliver, as has already happened with lead-acid batteries. It is clear that more innovation will be required.

The silicon solar-cell market is more mature than the lithium-ion battery market, but there is no significant recycling of solar-panel ingredients due to the cost, the energy requirements and the difficulty of achieving the original performance from the recycled products.

When it comes to rare earth elements, recycling is, well, rare. At most, about 3% of rare earth elements in today's consumer products are recycled.[9] The limiting factors are cost and efficiency in collection and processing. Collection involves mandating that electronic waste be separately handled. Processing is difficult because rare earth elements are spread at molecular scale throughout the smartphone, television or computer. To recycle smartphones, they are typically ground into a powder, and then the materials are separated out for disposal or recycling by chemical means.

The difficulty is that there are around 65 elements in a smartphone, making the powder a very complex mixture to process, with the added problem that the recycling processes might produce hazardous waste.[10] It is much easier to separate rare earth elements from the mineral deposits in which they are found than from the powder derived from the electronic products in which they have been used.

When it comes to batteries, an attractive alternative to disposal or recycling is to continue to use them in a second-life application. Electric vehicle batteries cease to be useful in their first-life application either because they have fallen below the vehicle manufacturer's performance guarantee, usually 80% of the range when new, or because the vehicle has reached the end of its life.

The second-life opportunities will be in stationary storage applications that are less demanding than powering a vehicle. It is anticipated that used vehicle batteries could be used for home storage with solar panels, or even for utility-scale storage once enough used batteries become available. If it becomes practical to extend the life of electric vehicle batteries by another six, eight or ten years through re-use, that would reduce the pressure on mining and manufacturing.

There are many challenges, however. One is that the economics and performance of new batteries continue to improve. The cost to manufacture new batteries in 2021 was less than a sixth of what it was in 2011, and the batteries in new vehicles are highly integrated. This means that the cost to remove, test and reconfigure the batteries for second-life applications starts to meet or exceed the cost of making new batteries for those same applications. The batteries taken out of the electric vehicles must be examined for obvious damage and tested for performance. It is mostly not practical to use the batteries as they are packaged, so in most cases the battery cells will have to be removed and repackaged. Finally, the reconfigured or ready-to-use battery must be certified as being suitable for its intended use.[11]

Some early trials are taking place. A New Zealand electricity and gas company, Vector, is working with an Australian battery-control company, Relectrify, to test the re-use of electric vehicle batteries for stationary electricity storage.[12] Car manufacturer Jaguar Land Rover is similarly working with a power electronics company, Off-Grid Energy Australia, to use old batteries from its IPACE electric car.[13] However, the quantities re-used to date are minuscule.

Innovation to reduce demand

Another way to minimise future mining for some energy transition materials is to minimise the quantity used in batteries, electrolysers and other manufactured products. For example, because of the concerns about how cobalt is supplied, entrepreneurs, engineers and scientists are working to develop innovative battery designs that use less or even no cobalt. The cathode in lithium-ion batteries is usually a combination of manganese, nickel and cobalt. By sacrificing range, car manufacturers can use batteries in which nickel and cobalt are reduced or replaced by cheaper and more plentiful cathode metals such as manganese, or by iron and phosphate.

Manganese is alluringly safe and stable. But when it is used instead of nickel and cobalt, the energy density of the battery is considerably lower and the operational lifetime is shorter. As I mentioned earlier, the first electric car my wife and I bought in 2013 was a Nissan LEAF, basically the same as the 2011 launch version. At the time there were no suppliers willing or able to deliver batteries in the necessary quantities, so Nissan developed its own. For simplicity, the company chose a lithium manganese oxide cathode material. We loved the car, but the small original range of about 150 kilometres degraded to about 100 kilometres over six years of suburban commuting, at which point the need to recharge was so frequent it became frustrating. We eventually replaced the car with a 2019 Nissan LEAF that uses a lithium manganese nickel cobalt battery and, thankfully, we have not noticed any deterioration of range in four years of driving.

What seems to be an emerging pattern is that car manufacturers will use lithium manganese nickel cobalt for premium cars, where speed and range are highly valued, but forego the cobalt for mid-range cars. A combination of lots of manganese, less nickel and zero cobalt should be cheaper than the regular cobalt-intensive formulations and avoid the challenges inherent in the nickel and cobalt supply chains.

Other combinations abound. The 'Ultium' battery cells introduced for the first time in 2020 by General Motors in the GMC Hummer EV add aluminium to enable a reduction in cobalt-use by 70% compared with conventional high-performance batteries.[14]

The battery in the Hummer EV has a staggering 200-kilowatt-hours capacity, twice that of the largest Tesla battery. But while the driving range in the Hummer EV is good, it is not better than the range of the high-end Tesla because the Hummer itself is so heavy and non-aerodynamic.

Manufacturers are worried by their dependence on nickel, mainly for price reasons. In the month after Russia invaded Ukraine, nickel prices spiked to US$100,000 per tonne from the historical average of about US$15,000, before settling down for the rest of the year at around US$25,000 per tonne.

To reduce costs and avoid cobalt, Tesla, VW, Ford and Chinese car manufacturers are switching to lithium iron phosphate batteries, commonly referred to as LFP batteries. Other benefits of the LFP battery are longer operational lifetimes and reduced risk of thermal runaway and catching fire. That is, they are safer. The trade-off is reduced range. For a given weight of battery in a car, the premium nickel manganese cobalt batteries will provide about 30% more range than the LFP variety. Tesla is using cobalt-free LFP batteries for its vehicles produced in China for the Chinese market, and has shifted to nickel-rich nickel cobalt aluminium cathode chemistries to reduce the cobalt content of its high-performance batteries produced outside China.[15]

In stationary applications, where battery volume and weight are not issues, other inexpensive, plentiful materials can be used, such as zinc and bromine in zinc-bromine batteries, and vanadium in vanadium redox batteries.

A radically different approach to reducing the need for battery materials is to encourage more hydrogen fuel-cell vehicles. These are electric vehicles, but the energy is stored in the chemical-bond energy of hydrogen rather than the ion-separation energy of batteries.

There are two advantages of hydrogen electric vehicles. First, they avoid what has been called 'mass compounding', which affects battery electric vehicles.[16] This term refers to the fact that as the storage capacity of the battery increases, the battery gets bigger and heavier, and an ever-increasing fraction of that storage capacity is used to move the battery itself rather than the vehicle and its cargo. In contrast, in a hydrogen electric vehicle, an increase in vehicle range requires a larger or additional storage tank, with only a small impact on vehicle mass. For this reason, hydrogen is likely to have a significant role in long-haul, heavy-duty vehicles.

The second advantage of hydrogen electric vehicles is that they are much less dependent on battery materials. It is true that hydrogen electric vehicles use lithium-ion batteries to overcome the few hundred milliseconds of lag while the fuel-cell system responds to the throttle and to absorb kinetic energy during deceleration. However, the battery in a hydrogen electric vehicle is less than 2% of the size used in a battery electric vehicle of comparable range.

A downside of hydrogen electric vehicles is the low efficiency. For example, with 100 kilowatt-hours of solar electricity supplied to a battery electric vehicle, it might be able to drive 600 kilometres. Starting with 100 kilowatt-hours of solar electricity, a similar-sized hydrogen electric vehicle will likely drive only 250 kilometres. For this reason, as well as the convenience of charging at home, battery electric vehicles are the electric passenger car of choice.

Nevertheless, hydrogen electric passenger cars might be preferred by drivers who do not have off-street parking where they can charge their car. Routine public charging of a battery electric car takes between 20 and 60 minutes, depending on the type of car and the charger.[17] Routine refilling of a hydrogen car takes three to five minutes.[18] There is a problem, however, in that there are not nearly enough hydrogen refuelling stations. Another potential problem is that hydrogen fuel cells today use between 30 and 60 grams of platinum to accelerate the hydrogen and oxygen recombination reaction. Fortunately, it is likely that mining output will be able to scale up to accommodate the demand.[19]

In any event, there is ongoing work to find alternatives to platinum in fuel cells. One team from Imperial College London has developed a fuel cell that uses a catalyst made from iron, carbon and nitrogen instead of platinum, but it is early days, and it is not clear that the lifetime and performance will equal those of the platinum catalyst version.[20] Other teams around the world are undertaking similar searches.

We saw earlier that it is unlikely that iridium mining will be able to scale up to meet the expected requirements of proton-exchange electrolysers for hydrogen production. An innovative alternative is the high-efficiency alkaline electrolyser in development by Australian start-up Hysata.[21] It uses platinum but no iridium.[22] Other groups around the world are trying to develop proton-exchange membrane fuel cells that do not use platinum or other platinum group metals, but they are still in the laboratory research phase.[23]

The solar-panel industry has made great headway in reducing the amount of costly silver used in solar cells. In 2009, each solar cell on average used 520 milligrams of silver but by 2019 that had fallen to 110 milligrams.[24] This process of innovation to reduce the amount of silver is called 'thrifting' and is expected to continue. A potential breakthrough comes from Australian company SunDrive Solar, which proposes to eliminate silver entirely by replacing it with electroplated copper electrodes.[25] If SunDrive is successful at commercialising its approach, it will revolutionise solar-panel production and eliminate the expense and supply constraints of silver.

The benefits do not stop there. Because SunDrive deposits its copper electrodes using a technique called electroplating, the conductivity is that of the pure metal. In contrast, the silver electrodes in a conventional solar cell are deposited by screen printing a silver paste, which has lower conductivity than pure silver. The electrodes are therefore made wider than they would be if they were pure silver. In both cases, the electrodes are placed on the surface of the solar cell, where they unavoidably block some of the photons in the sunlight from penetrating into the silicon. The narrower copper electrodes used by SunDrive Solar block fewer of the photons, helping the SunDrive cells to achieve an efficiency of over 26%.

This compares favourably with the best commercially available silver-based cells at just under 23% and is not far short of the practical maximum for a silicon solar cell of 29%.

An important innovation in solar cells is the thin film technology from American company First Solar. It is commercially producing solar cells that use cadmium telluride instead of polysilicon, and these have attracted the attention of investors and project developers seeking to reduce their dependence on polysilicon supplies. First Solar's commercial cells have reached 19% efficiency and degrade less in the field than polysilicon-based solar cells. First Solar is continuing to invest in improving efficiency and building multi-gigawatt production facilities.[26]

Stockpiling

Sometimes, supply-chain challenges are caused by lumpiness in the supply rather than by the average of the supply. Maintaining a stockpile can help to minimise the impact of temporary or sudden shortages. For example, after the oil crisis in the 1970s, all member countries of the International Energy Agency committed to keeping a 90-day stockpile of crude oil or petrol on hand to withstand sudden supply shocks.

A similar approach could be applied to energy transition materials. As we saw earlier, Japan would have suffered extreme economic harm when China stopped supplying rare earth elements in 2010 were it not for the fact that its major companies had been stockpiling during the prior two years. The United States maintains a stockpile as a matter of routine practice. Its National Defense Stockpile includes some, but not all, of the energy transition materials, including platinum and iridium, as well as a wide range of other materials, such as zinc, chromium, beryllium, tantalum and palladium. In February 2022, the Pentagon announced that it would boost the stockpile of cobalt and lithium, but at the time of writing the details are unclear. The severe limitation of the National

Defense Stockpile is that it has not been properly funded. At the beginning of the Cold War in 1952, its contents were valued at US$42 billion in today's dollars, but the value of the contents nose-dived to less than US$1 billion in 2021.[27]

This neglect by the US government of its stockpile probably reflects the reality that a meaningful stockpile of energy transition materials and other metals would simply cost too much. The better alternative is for governments to support robust international and domestic markets for these materials.

Innovation in mining

While I was Australia's Chief Scientist, I was constantly asked why Australia scores so poorly on various innovation indices. In particular, CEOs of digital start-ups would lament that mining companies were doing nothing more than digging rocks out of the ground. Matt Barrie, the founder and CEO of the highly successful web company Freelancer.com, said at a conference in 2017, at which we both spoke, that 'mines are and always will be wasting assets'.

In contrast, I contended back then, and now, that the mining industry has been brilliantly innovative, in Australia and elsewhere. And besides, we will need the output from the mining industry to build the computers and electricity supply that will support the digital technology revolution indefinitely into the future. The problem is that from the point of view of global innovation metrics, products such as iron ore are not themselves high-tech. To put it bluntly, iron ore is iron ore is iron ore and has been so since before human beings first walked the surface of the Earth. Innovation in the mining industry – called process innovation – is not visible in the product itself, which at first glance is indistinguishable from one producer to another.

Classic innovation is measured many ways, including by the newness of the product. Consider one of the world's major innovation reports, the Global Innovation Index, produced by the World

Intellectual Property Organization. Quite rightly, the Global Innovation Index is a composite of many metrics, but I take issue with one: the 'knowledge diffusion' metric, which measures high-tech exports. It is a ratio derived from high-tech exports on the top line, divided by total exports on the bottom line, where high-tech exports are things like semiconductors, software, pharmaceuticals and medical devices.

Domestic smartphone manufacturers advance a country up the Global Innovation Index because the smartphones made and sold count towards the high-tech exports above the line. Iron-ore production, on the other hand, pushes a country down, because iron-ore exports only count towards the total exports figure below the line. That is, the more iron ore a country exports, the bigger its bottom line, while the top line stays constant, so the worse the country looks.

To address the fact that much of the innovation in mining is missed in such national performance metrics, as well as other problems with these calculations, in 2018 Mark Cully, the Chief Economist in the Department of Industry, Science and Resources, and I were asked by the Australian government to co-chair a review of innovation metrics. The final report, engagingly titled *Improving Innovation Indicators*, is available on the department's website.[28]

The recommendations are based on the insight that most of the existing national innovation metrics focus on measuring research and development (R&D) activities, whereas much innovation does not involve conventional R&D. Examples include digital activities and revised processes that lead to improved outcomes. It is our hope and anticipation that the recommendations from this review will be adopted in coming years by the Australian government and ultimately by other national governments.

If one knows where to look, the substantial innovation in Australian iron-ore mines is readily visible. I think of Rio Tinto's 'mine of the future' in Western Australia. I got a good taste of the extraordinary innovative technology used by Rio Tinto when my wife and

I visited the Perth control room in 2016. From there, the operators supervise mines in the Pilbara 1,500 kilometres to the north. That mining region includes the world's longest private railroad, much of it automated, and the world's largest fleet of autonomous trucks. More than 400 control-room operators, working around the clock, track 3D visualisations of every piece of capital equipment. The innovation is visible in the remote-control systems, the quality-assurance algorithms at the crushing and separation plants and the autonomous vehicles. This automation and quality control contributes strongly to Australian iron ore being internationally cost competitive despite Australian mine operators paying the highest salaries in the world.

Some of the innovation is unexpected. I remember visiting the Solomon Mines operated by Fortescue Metals Group in the Pilbara. My family was with me because we were en route to a vacation on the northwest coast. All of us were impressed with the vastness of the facilities. The trains were up to 2.8 kilometres long, hauling more than 30,000 tonnes of iron ore nearly 400 kilometres to Port Headland to be unloaded into ships that take the iron ore to customers in Asia.[29]

As impressive as the trains and the filling gantry at the mine site were, the outstanding innovation was in the unloading. The obvious way to unload the trains would have been to open side doors on each of the 244 ore cars and let the ore pour out. But that would have left a pile of iron-ore residue on the floor of each car. Instead, giant arms decoupled two ore cars at a time, each carrying 140 tonnes of ore, lifted them and flipped them upside down so that the contents poured down a chute to a conveyor belt and off to the port.

The mines operated by BHP and Rio Tinto are no slouches either. If our mining industry didn't invest in innovation, Australia would not be the iron-ore export powerhouse it is today. In 2021, for example, BHP concluded that it would be able to extend the life of one of its iron-ore mines by five years by applying newly created algorithms to interpret hyperspectral images of the surrounding surfaces to determine which patches contained enough iron ore to warrant mining.[30] (For the technically inclined, hyperspectral imaging analyses all the colours in visible light, rather than just the three primary colours red, blue and green.)

Silver mining

Demand for silver will grow in the next decade, and some observers forecast that supply will not keep up with the growing demand because not enough new mines are in development. Instead of starting new mines, operators are turning to digitalisation to improve the output of existing silver mines. This is especially the case with deep and remote mines, particularly where the silver deposits are low grade. Monitoring and analysis are being integrated with automated and remote-controlled mining equipment to improve efficiency and lower costs.[31] At the same time, many of the large silver miners are shifting to electric machinery to save costs and improve their environmental footprint.

Copper mining

In copper mining, BHP has turned to seawater desalination for its giant Escondida copper mine in Chile, with the intention of eliminating freshwater use entirely by 2030.[32] Elsewhere in Chile, the Codelco mining company, which happens to be the largest copper producer in the world, is facing the dual challenge of rising costs and declining ore grades. In response, it is investing in automation, predictive analytics and artificial intelligence at its facilities.[33] In addition, Codelco has started the process of converting its vehicles and underground mining equipment to be electric rather than diesel-powered.

Lithium mining

In lithium mining, the two commercial production sources to date are hard-rock spodumene, which is the dominant source in Australia, and brine.[34] Some recent innovations should simplify the extraction of lithium from brine and reduce the time it takes to develop new supplies.

Conventionally, brine pumped from aquifers under the salt flats is spread out into evaporation ponds. It takes about a year to evaporate, and the material left behind needs multiple purification steps. These include filtration, treatment by a series of chemical solvents and reagents, further filtration and finally a reagent such as sodium carbonate to form lithium carbonate.[35]

'Direct lithium extraction' is a new approach being developed by a number of start-up, emerging and established companies, in a surge of interest not dissimilar to a Silicon Valley boom. In direct lithium extraction, the lithium is immediately extracted from the brine brought up from the aquifers, using a highly selective absorbent material, after which the brine is returned to the aquifers.[36] There are key environmental benefits. One is that the mine-site processing plants are small and the overall environmental footprint is much lower than traditional brine evaporation. Another is that because most of the brine is rapidly returned to the aquifer, there is no risk of fresh water from adjacent aquifers flowing into the brine aquifers, potentially depleting the freshwater sources used by adjacent communities. The key quality advantage of direct lithium extraction is that there is less than one part per million of impurities in the lithium carbonate output, which is battery-grade material ready to be delivered to battery manufacturers for use as is or for conversion into lithium hydroxide.

In a variation called 'direct lithium to product', pioneered by British company IBC, battery-grade lithium hydroxide is produced from brine, ore or even recycled batteries without the need to first produce lithium carbonate.[37] The technology is in the pilot phase, currently being demonstrated in Chile. As in direct lithium extraction, there is no net water extraction from the salt flats and no need for evaporation ponds.

If successful, direct lithium extraction and direct lithium to product will help the mining industry respond more quickly to rising demand.

Aluminium mining

The key innovation challenge for aluminium production is to reduce emissions at all three stages – bauxite mining, alumina refining and aluminium smelting – and to minimise environmental impact.

Most bauxite mining is open-pit mining using huge excavation machines and conveyer belts. From the carbon dioxide emissions point of view, where they are running off electricity the companies must invest in renewable sources to replace the diesel-fired or gas-fired electricity commonly used. Where the vehicles or equipment use diesel engines, the companies must work with suppliers to implement battery-powered and hydrogen-powered replacements. These challenges are shared with iron-ore and other mining operations. The companies know what to do. The challenges are installing the battery recharging and hydrogen refuelling facilities, the cost of the new equipment and the useful lifetime of the existing equipment.

In open-pit mining, large areas of land are impacted. Mines are often located near areas of high conservation value such as tropical forests, or adjacent to or on indigenous lands.[38] The International Aluminium Institute reports that more than two-thirds of bauxite mine operators have land-use rehabilitation plans in place that have been agreed with Traditional Owners, landholders, regulators, local communities and non-government organisations.[39] Companies that purchase bauxite or the downstream refined aluminium products should require that such plans and best practices cover 100% of their purchases.

As it happens, the emissions from bauxite mining are tiny compared with the emissions from alumina refining and aluminium smelting.[40] Of the average 16.6 tonnes of carbon dioxide emitted per tonne of aluminium produced, only 0.05 tonnes is attributable to bauxite production, with 3.2 tonnes coming from alumina refining and 13.4 tonnes from smelting and casting.

Conventional alumina refining uses large quantities of natural gas to achieve the required high temperatures. Rio Tinto is investigating the possibility of using green hydrogen instead. The immediate challenge is the high cost of this substitution.[41] Separately, Alcoa is investigating the use of renewable electricity in a process known as mechanical vapour recompression. In this process, renewable electricity is used instead of fossil-fuel-produced steam in a key part of the alumina refining process.[42]

The biggest challenge is smelting. Significant progress has been made in a partnership between Rio Tinto and Alcoa in Canada. The bulk of the emissions in aluminium smelting come from the use of coal-fired electricity, but in Canada the two companies are using zero-emissions hydropower. This leaves the final challenge, related to the electrodes in the electrolysis process. Made from graphite, the electrodes are slowly consumed and converted into carbon dioxide during smelting. The partnership between Rio Tinto and Alcoa will demonstrate the use of inert electrodes developed by their joint-venture company, Elysis. The combination of renewable electricity and inert electrodes will enable zero-emissions smelting. In a practical example of responsible purchasing, American technology company Apple, with a view to greening the aluminium used in its smartphones and computers, is an investor in the project.[43]

The constant output from hydropower is an advantage of this Canadian project. Conversely, the variable output from solar and wind electricity is a problem for aluminium smelting, because if the electricity supply to the smelter fails for more than four hours, the result is a disaster. The molten aluminium in the pots and pipes freezes, the plant has to be shut down, and repairs take months, costing hundreds of millions of dollars in addition to the value of lost production. Thus, where solar and wind electricity are to be used for aluminium smelting in future, firming the variable supply to guarantee constant operation will be essential.

Platinum mining

Innovation in platinum mining will come from several sources. On the leading edge, the Platinum Consortium comprising universities, government survey institutions and industries in Europe is committed to developing new survey technologies such as laser-induced breakdown spectroscopy pioneered on the NASA Curiosity Rover that explored Mars in 2012.

Reducing mining's emissions

Currently, mining accounts for nearly 11% of global energy use.[44] To achieve our global net-zero goal, both new and existing mines must use renewable energy instead of diesel and natural gas to power their operations.

The intention to make this transition has been declared by many major mining companies. Fortescue Mining Group, the fifth-largest iron-ore mining company in the world, is committed to decarbonising its operations by 2030. Others, such as giant mining companies BHP and Rio Tinto, are also committed to fully decarbonising their operations. British miner Anglo American is committed to decarbonising its operations by 2040. All of them have climate transition plans, but it is early days in terms of progress.[45]

In their determination to decarbonise mining operations, in 2022, BHP, Rio Tinto and Brazilian miner Vale collaboratively ran a competition to develop charging solutions for large electric haul trucks. These trucks are enormous, and the big batteries would take too long to charge using even the most powerful conventional quick-charging stations. One of the selected solutions combines stationary charging and charging the trucks while they are in motion, one is a battery-swap solution, and another uses overhead wires like for city trams.[46]

Lots more innovation in the mining industry will be required in coming years as the industry starts to value decarbonisation, driven by purchasing power and by the looming carbon border adjustment mechanism (CBAM) being introduced by the European Union. Both these factors will expand the mining industry's focus on low-emissions mining and low-emissions refining.

Avoiding the peak

If it were not for innovation, we would run out of most essential resources. Take oil. In 1956, M. King Hubbert, a geophysicist at the Shell oil company, predicted there would be a global peak in crude oil production around the year 2000. The predicted peak was 34 million barrels of oil per day, with output falling every year there-after.[47] Hubbert's modelling was probably fine, but the underlying assumptions were based on what was known then about pros-pecting, drilling and production technologies, which limited his estimate of recoverable oil reserves.

His prediction proved wrong. The peak still hasn't happened. Global production keeps on rising, and in 2022 was 101 million bar-rels of oil per day.[48] Production has been able to rise so high to meet demand thanks to a plethora of innovative technological improve-ments. These include deep-ocean oil rigs, enhanced oil recovery by pumping carbon dioxide into ageing oil wells to push out the remaining oil, and oil extraction by fracking from shale deposits.

It is almost a universal rule: modelling gets it wrong because it underestimates human ingenuity. Thankfully, human ingenuity is a resource we will never run out of.

A quixotic approach to expanding the proven resources for man-ganese, nickel, cobalt and copper is deep-sea mining. The ocean floor is covered with tennis-ball-sized rocks called nodules that are rich in manganese and also contain nickel, cobalt and copper. Of course, the environmental impact of mining the ocean floor is unknown, as is the cost and practicality. To answer some of these questions, the international body responsible for overseeing deep-sea mining operations, the International Seabed Authority, in September 2022 granted the first approval for a mining trial in the Pacific Ocean, 2,000 kilometres west of the Mexican coast.[49] The target zone is deep, more than four kilometres, so the costs and difficulties will be substantial. It is something to watch, not unlike fictional mining of unobtanium on Pandora, and not of immediate transformational value.

Innovation in mining can help with social licence by reducing mining's environmental impact. For example, the piles of tailings from a copper mine often contain copper and cobalt in concentrations that could be recovered if the economics could be improved. A project at the University of Lubumbashi in the Congo is studying the economics. If it can be shown to work, it will increase the lifespan of the mines and minimise their environmental footprint.[50]

●   ●   ●

Innovation will continue to revolutionise the industry. It is easy to fall into the trap of believing that we have all we need, but continued investment in innovation is essential to reduce costs, accelerate the transition and ensure social justice. Innovation will improve the efficiency of mining, extend the life of existing mines and assist with prospecting. Innovation is how we will avoid the doomsday scenario of running out of necessary materials, and it is how we will wean mining off its heavy dependence on diesel fuel and coal-fired electricity. A crucial part of this process will be converting fully to renewable electricity, a challenge that I explore further in the next chapter.

4.
Renewable Electricity

Zero-emissions electricity will completely replace our existing fossil-fuel-generated electricity and largely replace fossil fuels where they are used directly in transport, heating and industry. It will decarbonise key elements of the supply chain, such as mine sites and the factories that make solar panels, wind turbines, batteries and electrolysers.

With the exception of nuclear power, that zero-emissions electricity will be renewable. Two important features that define renewable electricity are that it has zero emissions, and that it is powered by an energy source that is constantly replenished and never runs out.

Significantly, this definition does not specify that the input energy is continuously available, just that over time it never runs out. Thus, solar, wind and hydropower electricity are all renewable even though the energy that powers them is not always available. The full name for solar and wind electricity is variable renewable electricity, in deference to the variability in the availability of sun and wind.

Hydropower reservoirs can run out of water from time to time, but this happens infrequently and until it does the power station can generate on demand, so the adjective 'variable' is not applied to hydropower. In some countries with exceptionally high hydropower generation, such as New Zealand and Brazil, droughts require dry-year solutions.

Although in principle geothermal energy reservoirs might become depleted, many have been operating reliably for over 100 years and geothermal is regarded as renewable.[1] It has the benefit over solar, wind and hydropower of continuous operation 365 days per year. Its big limitation is that there are not enough sites.

There are other renewable electricity sources, and there are ways to use renewable sources other than by making electricity. For example, geothermal energy can be used directly as heat. About 25% of Iceland's electricity is geothermal, with most of the balance being hydropower. Hardly any of this electricity is used for heating. Instead, 90% of the building heating and hot water is provided by geothermal direct heating. But Iceland has a population of only 370,000, and it is atypical; no other country has such ready access to geothermal energy.

Ocean energy, in the form of waves, tides and currents, can be used to produce electricity and is both zero-emissions and renewable. However, ocean energy makes only a miniscule contribution despite decades of development.

Biomass is a renewable energy source, but its emissions status is more complicated than the other renewable energy sources such as solar and wind. If the biomass is solid waste or biogas from waste that is then burned to produce electricity, it is clearly an excellent alternative to allowing the methane from decomposition to be released into the atmosphere. If the biomass is from sustainable cropping or forestry, it is renewable, but it is not a truly zero-emissions source because of emissions that occur during collection and processing. Further, there are concerns about potential negative impacts on biodiversity and competition with agricultural crops. Given its finite availability, biomass use should arguably be focused on hard-to-abate areas, such as jet fuel for long-distance aviation. Another consideration is that the biomass might be put to better use in non-energy applications. Because biomass contains organic molecules, it will be of value in chemical industries that currently depend on oil and natural gas as their input ingredients.

The outputs of the renewable and zero-emissions energy-generation technologies worldwide are best compared in terms of energy quantities such as terawatt-hours, shown in Table 2.[2]

Table 2: Biomass in this table is the sum of solid biofuels, municipal waste, liquid biofuels and biogas. Wind is the sum of onshore and offshore. All data other than nuclear power is from the International Renewable Energy Agency (IRENA). Nuclear power data is from the BP Statistical Review of World Energy collated by OurWorldInData.

Source	2010 global generation in terawatt-hours	2020 global generation in terawatt-hours	Percentage increase in 10 years
Hydropower	3,426	4,356	27%
Nuclear power	2,769	2,693	-3%
Wind (onshore and offshore)	343	1,589	360%
Solar photo-voltaic	32	831	2,500%
Biomass (all sources)	312	584	87%
Geothermal	68	95	40%
Solar thermal	1.7	13	670%
Ocean energy	0.51	0.95	86%
World total from all sources	21,570	26,900	25%

Hydropower is currently the largest source of zero-emissions electricity. However, its rate of growth has been modest for reasons to do with permitting, environmental impact, site availability, social licence and the cost of transmission lines.

Nuclear power is the next-largest source of zero-emissions electricity. Worldwide, the output has been more or less static for nearly two decades for reasons of cost, waste management and community aversion.

Wind power from onshore and offshore facilities is large and rising rapidly. There is every reason to be excited by its growing contribution to displacing fossil fuels.

Solar photovoltaic is just over half of wind but growing at an explosive rate and, like wind, will make a huge contribution to displacing fossil fuels. Its growth rate is outstripping that of its sibling, solar thermal.

Looking at the size of the generation sources in 2020 and the rate of growth, the top two to focus on are clearly solar photovoltaic and wind. Hydropower and nuclear power are and will continue to be globally very important contributors, but they lack the extraordinary rate of growth of solar and wind.

Magic that works

The novelist Kurt Vonnegut said, 'Science is magic that works', and electricity is a prime example.

Electricity is by far the most versatile form of energy ever discovered. Like coal, it can provide intense heat for industrial processes. Like oil, it can power cars and trucks. Like natural gas, it can heat buildings and cook our food. Electricity powers our computers and smartphones, enables the internet and lights up our televisions.

Electricity came into prominence after a decisive battle at the 1893 Chicago World Fair. On one side, the celebrated inventor Thomas Edison. On the other, his former employee Nikola Tesla, after whom the car company is aptly named. What were they fighting over – love, religion, territory? None of the above. They were fighting over alternating current versus direct current.

To understand their argument, we need to know that current in metal wires is the flow of electrons, pushed along by a voltage. If the driving voltage is a constant value, the electrons flow in one direction only. We call this direct current (DC). Batteries and solar panels are DC voltage sources.

If the driving voltage alternates between positive and negative many times per second, the direction in which the electrons flow rapidly alternates. We call this alternating current (AC). Traditional generators such as coal, gas, oil, hydro and nuclear are AC voltage sources.

Starting in the late 1880s, Thomas Edison developed a suite of DC generators, motors and meters. To be safe for use in homes and factories, the DC generators were designed to produce electricity at low voltage. The downside was that at low voltage much of the electricity was lost during transmission from the generator to the consumer, which limited the distance between the generator and consumers to less than two kilometres. Edison had no way to convert the DC voltage to higher or lower values during transmission.

In the other camp, Nikola Tesla had a secret weapon known as the AC transformer. It is a simple arrangement of iron cores and copper windings that allows the voltage to be easily converted up or down. With transformers, Tesla could boost the generator output to thousands of volts during transmission, resulting in less loss and allowing transmission over long distances. A transformer could then be used to cut the voltage back to a safe level when it reached the consumer. The limitation was that these transformers only worked with AC electricity.

There was a lot at stake, including patent royalties and the right to electrify the cities of the United States.

Feeling the tide of battle swinging against him, Edison changed tactics and launched a misinformation campaign, claiming that AC current was dangerous. To prove his point, he used AC current to publicly electrocute stray dogs, cats and horses!

These skirmishes continued during the lead-up to the 1893 Chicago World's Fair, where victory was declared for the Tesla AC camp. They were awarded the contract to electrify the Fair. From there it was all AC. In 1896 the city of Buffalo in New York electrified its streetlights with AC power supplied by hydropower generators 500 kilometres away at Niagara Falls.

AC was the correct decision, because it enabled the far and wide distribution of electricity safely and efficiently. The consequence, however, is that system operators must closely manage frequency so that all generators operate at exactly the same frequency and in synchrony with each other. But more about that later.

Today, electricity is everywhere. It increasingly powers everything we do. As well as powering our cars, machines, appliances and electronic devices, electricity is important behind the scenes, as part of the supply chain for the clean energy transition. We need zero-emissions electricity to power the factories that build the batteries for our electric cars and the electric cars themselves. We need zero-emissions electricity to power the mine sites that extract the energy transition materials and all the other resources used across the economy. We need zero-emissions electricity for smelting alumina into aluminium and to make the hydrogen that will be key to producing the green steel of the future.

Whichever way you look at it, there is nothing more important for decarbonisation than having an abundant, zero-emissions, low-cost electricity supply.

Electricity is the ultimate supply-chain enabler and end product.

The rest of this chapter is devoted to a deep dive into the four main sources of zero-emissions electricity, starting with solar.

Solar power

The earliest experimental work with solar electricity generation was performed in 1839 by a budding 19-year-old French physicist, Edmond Becquerel, who discovered the photovoltaic effect in an electrolytic cell he had constructed that generated voltage and current when the electrodes were exposed to sunlight. The theoretical understanding derived from Albert Einstein's 1905 work on the photoelectric effect, for which he won the Nobel Prize in 1921. The first practical solar photovoltaic cell was developed in 1954 at Bell Laboratories, the extraordinary research arm of the Bell Telephone

Company. The Bell Laboratories were the birthplace of radio astronomy, the transistor, the laser, digital camera chips, the Unix operating system and the C programming language. A few years later, solar cells were further developed for use in Earth-orbiting satellites, and they very quickly became the standard energy source for space applications. Commercial production began in the late 1970s, by which time the efficiency of solar cells had reached 14%.

The efficiency of a solar cell refers to the percentage of the solar energy hitting the surface that is converted into electrical energy. The theoretical maximum for a silicon solar cell in direct sunlight is 32%. However, various loss mechanisms within the silicon structure are regarded as unavoidable, and the standard conjecture is that 29% efficiency is the upper limit.[3]

In 1977, worldwide production of solar photovoltaic cells exceeded 0.5 megawatts for the first time. If we take this milestone as the beginning of the modern solar industry, you could say that the industry is just a few years short of fifty years old.

Seminal developments took place in the 1980s at the University of New South Wales laboratories of Professor Martin Green. In 1985, Green and his student Andrew Blakers produced the first solar cells to reach 20% efficiency.[4] By the end of the decade, Green and his colleagues had developed passivated emitter and rear cell (PERC) technology, which is now used in 90% of solar panels manufactured worldwide, for which they were awarded the 2023 Queen Elizabeth Prize for Engineering, which recognises 'bold, ground-breaking engineering innovation which is of global benefit to humanity'.

Progress to improve efficiency and durability and cut costs was steady, and in 1999 the worldwide production of solar photovoltaic cells exceeded 1,000 megawatts for the first time. Things have been getting better and better ever since.

The empirically observed rule of thumb is that for every doubling of cumulative production, the solar price per watt falls by about 20%, as shown in Figure 7.[5] The curve is stunningly steep, with the price declining 99.6% from 1976 to 2019, and by 90% from 2010 to 2019.

Figure 7: Dramatic price reductions resulting from economies of scale. The vertical axis is the price per watt of the solar cells. The dotted line joins the end points and has a slope of approximately 20% decline per doubling of capacity. (Graph compiled from multiple sources by OurWorldInData.)

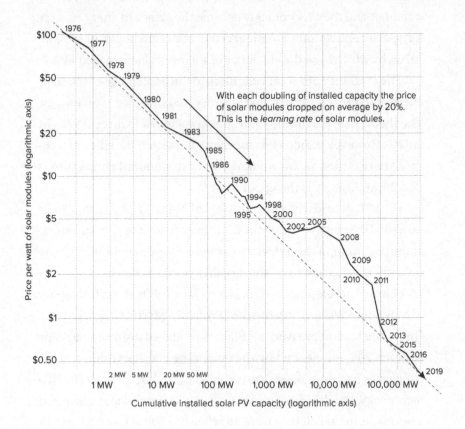

Cumulative installed solar PV capacity (logarithmic axis)

This rapid progress was driven by government policies aimed in part at battling climate change and in part at building domestic manufacturing capacity. In Japan, from 1994 to 2006, the New Energy Foundation provided subsidies for residential solar rooftops.[6] This was followed by subsidies for businesses installing solar generation systems of 1 megawatt or larger. Germany, building on its residential rooftop-solar subsidy program, in 2004 offered an unbounded program that purchased solar electricity for US$567 per megawatt-hour, about five times the price of coal-fired electricity.

Investor interest took off like a rocket, fuelled by US$250 billion paid out by the German government between 2004 and 2012. Unfortunately for Germany, Chinese manufacturers were the ones who flew highest.

In Australia, the Renewable Energy Target and various state and federal programs to incentivise large-scale and rooftop solar installations were so effective that by 2021 Australia had achieved the highest level of installed solar capacity per person in the world. In that year, the Australian Renewable Energy Agency (ARENA) launched its Solar 30/30/30 objective, an ambitious program to improve solar efficiency to 30% and reduce the cost of solar modules to 30 cents per watt by 2030.

Globally, new solar capacity deployed in 2021 was 168 gigawatts, seven times more than a decade earlier. The International Energy Agency's *Net Zero 2050* report forecasts a further increase to 630 gigawatts in the year 2030.[7] That is a remarkably fast rate of increase, but there is good reason to think it will be exceeded. Solar has consistently outperformed predictions. The IEA forecasts are based on wide consultation and are, quite rightly, highly respected, but even they have struggled to predict the extraordinary uptake of solar. In November 2020, the IEA forecast total worldwide solar installations for 2022 would reach 150 gigawatts.[8] This proved conservative, with global installations for 2022 in fact reaching 270 gigawatts.[9] According to research and analysis company BloombergNEF, planned global polysilicon manufacturing capacity is sufficient for 940 gigawatts of solar panels every year, indicating that the industry is confident of exceeding current forecasts.[10]

The 2030 forecast of 630 gigawatts installed capacity is such a big number that is difficult to visualise the enormity of the task. Let's look at it from the bottom up. The panels used in solar farms produce about 500 watts each. To install 630 gigawatts in a year will require the worldwide deployment of 3.5 million solar panels *every day*.

A significant challenge is the labour cost of installing panels at such a scale. Australian company 5B has developed an approach in which pre-connected solar panels are hinged together at the factory to form a concertina package of many panels, which can then be folded into a shipping container. In the field, the panels are simply unfolded and laid out on the pre-prepared ground, dramatically increasing the number of kilowatts of solar panels that can be deployed per worker per day. I haven't seen them in the field, but I had the pleasure of seeing a tractor unfold a full set of concertinaed panels in 5B's company car park in Sydney. It was quick, simple and robust. In May 2022, the company self-proclaimed a global speed record of 110 kilowatts per person per day for a project in the Atacama Desert in Chile.[11]

Currently, more than 80% of the world's solar panels are made in China. There is a good reason for this: China is excellent at solar-panel production at scale and at low cost. All nations have benefited from the achievement of Chinese manufacturers, but we need to increase the diversity of supply to avoid future bottlenecks and to mitigate the single-point-of-failure risk. There is an opportunity for India and other low-cost manufacturing countries to become major global suppliers. For example, India's solar panel manufacturing capacity is expected to exceed 40 gigawatts per year by the end of 2025, meaning it is well on its way to becoming a significant supplier.[12]

Wind power

The principle behind wind-powered electricity generation is simple. Rotor blades convert the kinetic energy of wind into rotational kinetic energy in a generator that converts the rotational kinetic energy into electrical energy.

The industry keeps getting bigger and bigger, literally. The power in the wind increases with the wind's speed, and wind speed increases with height. The amount of energy gathered by a wind-turbine rotor also scales with the diameter of the rotor. There is therefore a massive economy of scale to be gained from making wind turbines larger and taller.

In 1980, a big commercial rotor was 15 metres in diameter and the rated power was about 0.1 megawatts. Today, there are offshore wind turbines rated at 12 megawatts with rotors 220 metres in diameter towering 260 metres above the sea surface. For comparison, the wingspan of the Airbus A380, the largest passenger aeroplane in the world, is 80 metres; the towers of the Golden Gate Bridge soar 227 metres above the water.

Offshore wind has become popular for several important reasons. Unlike onshore wind, which is commonly strongest at night, offshore wind is commonly strongest in the afternoons and evenings, when consumer demand is highest.[13] Offshore wind tends to be faster than wind on land and blows more consistently. Finally, offshore wind farms can be located close to big cities or industrial sites, minimising the length of the transmission lines needed to connect them to the network.

In counterpoise to the growth in size, there has been a reduction in cost, albeit more slowly than for solar. From 2010 to 2019 the capital cost of onshore wind turbines installed in the United States declined by 44%.[14]

Interestingly, in terms of their rated power output, the wind turbines of the 1980s were a step back from the early prototypes. From 1943 to 1945, an experimental 1.25-megawatt turbine in the United States, known as the Smith-Putnam, intermittently delivered power to the Vermont electricity grid. In France, another experimental wind turbine, known as the Nogent-le-Roi, operated on and off from 1958 to 1962 at an output power of 0.65 megawatts.

While there was considerable commercial development in the United States in the 1970s, wind turbines made their major leap forward in Denmark, where the three-blade design common to all modern commercial wind turbines was pioneered by Henrik Stiesdal and colleagues and became known as 'the Danish concept'. The

Danes also introduced the standard that all turbines should rotate clockwise, from the perspective of looking at the turbine with the wind behind you. This simplified manufacturing, but it also means there is a certain elegance to a field of wind turbines rotating in harmony, like couples waltzing round the dance floor, rather than a cacophony of turbines rotating in arbitrary directions.

Although the first offshore wind farm was installed off the coast of Denmark in 1991, the commercialisation was driven by the United Kingdom, starting in the 2000s. The United Kingdom led the world in offshore wind installed capacity until 2020, when China took the lead. If we take the mid-1970s as the start of the modern wind-turbine era, then, just like solar, the industry is approaching fifty years old.

Wind capacity added worldwide in 2010 was 31 gigawatts; the capacity added worldwide in 2020 was 110 gigawatts, a nearly fourfold increase in a decade.[15] The International Energy Agency's *Net Zero 2050* report forecasts a similarly rapid increase in the next decade, to 390 gigawatts in 2030. Using wind turbines of 3-megawatt capacity, this will require the deployment of 356 turbines every day.

Wind-turbine manufacturing is much more diverse than solar panels. The largest manufacturer is Vestas in Denmark, followed by GE in the United States, Goldwind in China, Envision in Japan and Siemens Gamesa in Spain.[16]

For onshore wind farms, much of the innovation in deployment is visible in the novel ways being found to transport ever larger turbine blades. Extraordinary trucks have been developed to transport blades of up to 80 metres long. These trucks have steerable rear wheels that are essential for anything beyond the most mild turns. For steep mountain roads with switchback turns, a class of truck has been developed that holds only the base of the rotor blade and allows the full length of the blade to cantilever out over the mountain valleys as the truck negotiates sharp turns on the way to the installation site. The longest rotor blade ever to be transported by road was 88 metres long. It was taken 218 kilometres along the highways of Denmark from the factory to the seashore, suspended between two trucks and accompanied by a small army of support personnel and vehicles with flashing lights.[17]

At the time of writing, the longest rotor blade ever transported by any means was a Siemens Gamesa rotor blade of 108 metres weighing 66 tonnes, intended for a prototype 14-megawatt offshore wind turbine. The blade was manufactured at the company's facility on the banks of the Humber River in the United Kingdom, from where it was directly transported to the North Sea by ship.

If you have been asking yourself why onshore wind turbines are not as gigantic as offshore wind turbines, the answer mainly comes down to the difficulties of transporting blades by road. Because of the tremendous stress blades are under during operation, the accepted wisdom is that they must be delivered from the factory to the site in one piece, rather than in segments.[18] For blades transported by road to onshore wind farms, the practical limit has been reached. For blades transported by ship, size is not a limiting factor, provided they are manufactured at coastal facilities.

Offshore wind turbines are installed using specially developed ships. One class of ship is used to install the tall foundations, called monopiles, that are driven deep into the seabed. To ensure precision during this process the ship jacks itself up on the seafloor until it is firmly suspended in the air and to all practical purposes is immovable while the cranes and impactors get to work.

A second class of ship installs the tower that projects high above the water, the housing that holds the generator, the rotor hub to which the rotor blades are anchored, and finally the rotor blades themselves. The ships and their installation equipment have been refined so much that a large offshore wind turbine can be fully installed in a day.

Installation is completed by laying undersea cables from each turbine to an offshore substation from where the electricity is sent by a high-voltage undersea cable to the onshore network.

The largest offshore wind project in the world is the Hornsea Project 1 and 2 wind farm, with a total capacity of 2,600 megawatts. It is located in the North Sea, 120 kilometres off the east coast of England. The largest Dutch offshore wind farm is the Borssele cluster, rated at 1,500 megawatts, 22 kilometres off the coast of Zeeland province. The largest operational Danish offshore wind farm is the 600-megawatt Horns Rev facility in the North Sea, 14 kilometres west of the Danish coastline.

Visibility of offshore wind farms from the coast is an issue in many locations. The usual goal is to reduce the visual impact in order to minimise stakeholder opposition. Although large wind turbines are visible as far as 35 kilometres from the coast, they are generally not regarded as having a significant visual impact if they are at least 15 kilometres offshore.[19]

In general, conventional offshore wind turbines cannot be installed in water more than about 60 metres deep.[20] In some locations they can be positioned as far as 120 kilometres from shore and still be anchored to the seabed. Some coastal waters, however, get deep very quickly. For example, the coastal waters off the east coast of the United States are relatively shallow, but coastal waters off the west coast are deep close to shore.[21]

In cases where the ocean becomes deep close to shore, floating wind turbines can be installed. Their designs have evolved from deep-sea oil and gas rigs, which use mooring lines anchored to the sea bed to maintain their horizontal location.[22] Because they can be moored in water a thousand metres deep or more, there are many more options as to where to put them. It is early days for floating offshore wind farms, with the first operational facility of 30 megawatts commissioned by the Norwegian energy company Equinor in 2017. By the end of 2021 there were two more, one in Scotland and another in Portugal; together these three wind farms produced a total of 105 megawatts.[23] This is a tiny amount compared with the 56,000 megawatts of offshore wind in operation in 2021. One of the US Department of Energy's Energy Earthshots Initiatives is the

Floating Offshore Wind Shot. Its ambitious goal is to reduce the cost of floating offshore wind electricity to US$45 per megawatt-hour by 2035.[24]

Nuclear power

There is no doubt that nuclear power plants are superb zero-emissions electricity generators. From an electrical performance point of view, they have the advantage of contributing inherently desirable electrical generation and transmission characteristics known as inertia, fast frequency response and system strength. Like solar and wind, nuclear power generators produce no emissions during operation and have a low carbon footprint on a lifecycle analysis. They have the big advantage of not requiring much in the way of specialised energy transition materials.

Despite these useful characteristics, there are three formidable challenges for nuclear power.

The first is purely technical. Traditional large nuclear power plants are unlikely to integrate well with an electricity grid dominated by solar and wind because they are very slow in adjusting their generated output power. It may be that this limitation will be overcome in the next-generation small modular reactors (SMRs), which are discussed below. Although no SMRs have yet been built, it is claimed they will be able to increase or decrease their output by 80% in less than 30 minutes, thereby providing modestly good load-following and firming capabilities.[25]

The second formidable challenge is lack of broad public approval, because of a failure in most countries to implement long-term plans for disposal of radioactive waste, and because of the potential consequences of an accident or an attack by terrorists or foreign armies.

The third is a lack of private investor interest because of the inordinately long time it takes to approve and build large-scale nuclear power plants, the high costs driven by ever-increasing licensing obligations, and the length of time capital is tied up before revenue begins to flow.

Nevertheless, in some countries the argument for nuclear power is persuasive. Take Poland, which has no nuclear power plants. In November 2022, the Polish government approved the construction of a large, 3.8-gigawatt nuclear power plant to be supplied by the American company Westinghouse. The decision was motivated by a desire to reduce Poland's dependence on coal-fired electricity generation and a determination to be independent of Russian oil and gas despite the high cost.[26] Prime Minister Mateusz Morawiecki said when announcing the commitment, 'We assume the overall cost at around US\$20 billion. The upfront capital investment is big, but once a nuclear power plant is operational, the cost of generating electricity is relatively low.' The project duration is not short; construction is expected to start in 2026 and the first of three generator units should start producing electricity in 2033. Based on recent experience in the UK and Finland and cancelled projects in the United States, it would not be surprising for that cost estimate to more than double, especially if it is delivered a decade later than planned.

Next consider Japan, which imports more than 90% of its energy requirements as coal, oil and natural gas. To transition its economy to net zero, Japan has to replace those imports with zero-emissions alternatives or build up its domestic zero-emission electricity generation. However, Japan has very few natural energy resources. Its landmass is small relative to its population. Mountainous forests cover 66% of the land and much of the rest is used for agriculture or the built environment.[27] Thus, Japan does not have enough available land to build extensive solar and onshore wind farms. Its most promising renewable energy option is offshore wind, always more expensive than onshore wind and in Japan's case even more so because its coastal waters are deep, making it difficult to construct conventional, fixed-bottom offshore turbines. About three-quarters of Japan's prospective offshore wind turbines will likely be floating turbines, which are even more expensive.[28]

Nuclear power plants have a small real-estate footprint and can help Japan become self-sufficient. Japan commissioned its first nuclear power reactor in 1966. Prior to the Great East Japan Earthquake of 2011 that resulted in the Fukushima disaster, the country had 54 nuclear power reactors operating at 17 sites, providing 30% of its electricity.[29] Since the Fukushima disaster, some have been decommissioned and there are now 33 operable reactors, of which 10, following a careful and slow process, had been restarted by the end of 2022.[30] In September 2022, Prime Minster Fumio Kishida instructed officials to review Japan's nuclear power policy. He specifically tasked them with considering the merits of restarting a further 17 reactors, extending the operating life of the existing reactors from 40 years to 60 years and constructing a new generation of advanced reactors.

For Japan, excluding the hundreds of billions of dollars for Fukushima clean-up costs, nuclear power from its existing nuclear power reactors is economically competitive with imported clean hydrogen and hydrogen derivatives and the construction of offshore wind turbines. Without a contribution from nuclear power, it will be difficult for Japan to achieve net zero emissions. What is unknown is whether new nuclear power plants will be economically competitive given that new facilities will be subject to much more stringent design and safety requirements than their predecessors.

The time taken to build large reactors in developed countries is extreme. For example, the 3.2-gigawatt Hinkley Point C nuclear power plant in the UK was first approved in principle by the government in 2008 and the latest estimate is that it will be completed in 2028. The capital cost of Hinkley Point C is enormous, most recently estimated at £26 (A$47) billion. The projected wholesale price of the electricity is also very high. The designers initially estimated that the electricity price would be £24 (A$43) per megawatt-hour, but ultimately the operator negotiated a guaranteed price from the British government that after adjustment for inflation in 2021 was £106 (A$191) per megawatt-hour.[31] This uncompetitively high price will continue to be adjusted for inflation during the construction period and for 35 years following commencement of operations, and ultimately it will be worn by consumers.[32]

In terms of resource requirements, a modern 1-gigawatt nuclear power plant uses about 40,000 tonnes of steel and 200,000 tonnes of concrete.[33] It may sound a lot, but on a global scale that is small. Nuclear power plants do not use battery materials or rare earth elements in significant quantities. Wherever a nuclear power plant is used to produce zero-emissions electrical power, that obviates the need to build equivalent solar and wind electricity generators and battery backup systems, with huge savings on energy transition material requirements.

As we have seen, despite the high cost of building new nuclear plants, the UK and Poland are committing to new nuclear power generation, as are China, Russia and India, driven by their ambition to achieve net zero and their simultaneous determination to minimise their dependence on imported energy sources. Against this trend, Germany decided at the start of this century to close its once large nuclear power fleet, with the phase-out now in its final stages.

Globally, nuclear power generation is slowing down. Annual generated output grew steadily from 26 terawatt-hours in 1965 to 2,720 terawatt-hours in 2006 but has been more or less flat since then and was only 2,740 terawatt-hours in 2021.[34] Because of closures, the total number of 429 operable reactors at the end of 2021 was down from the total of 439 operable reactors at the end of 2017.[35] For the first time, in 2021 the combined worldwide solar and wind electricity generation overtook worldwide nuclear power generation.[36]

In response to the soaring costs and protracted construction, attention in recent years has been drawn to a new configuration of nuclear reactors called small modular reactors (SMRs). The idea behind SMRs is that unlike large conventional reactors, they will be made in a factory using a single, highly optimised design. This will result in lower costs, quicker deployment and higher operating reliability. SMRs are small in comparison to conventional reactors, but far from tiny. For example, the 77-megawatt modular reactor from the US company NuScale Power is 23 metres long and 4.6 metres in diameter, weighing approximately 700 tons.[37] It can be shipped from the factory in three segments, by truck, rail, barge or ship.

Progress in the nuclear industry takes time. NuScale was founded in 2007, made its first submission for design approval to the Nuclear Regulatory Commission (NRC) in the United States in 2017 and is now pending final NRC approval, anticipated in March 2023.[38]

In competition with NuScale, an alliance between global engineering firms GE and Hitachi is developing a reactor of 300-megawatt capacity. Although it is not small and it is not modular, it is still referred to as an SMR in recognition of the intention to deploy it repeatedly using a single design format. Its capital costs will be lower than a conventional reactor because it uses only half the amount of concrete and building volume per megawatt.[39] It is not yet approved in the United States or Canada, but the Ontario Power Generation company has a licensed site for new nuclear power generation not far from Toronto, on the shores of Lake Ontario. The decision to proceed is pending regulatory approval from the Canadian Nuclear Safety Commission.

Both NuScale and the GE and Hitachi Alliance originally predicted that their small modular reactors would be able to produce electricity at US$60 (A$90) per megawatt-hour. However, in January 2023, NuScale lifted their estimate to a less competitive US$89 (A$130) per megawatt-hour.[40] Based on the experience of large-scale nuclear power plants, budget and timetable overruns could easily lead to the actual price of electricity being much higher than these early estimates.

There are two other, more exotic approaches to nuclear power in development that deserve to be mentioned.

The first is controlled nuclear fusion. In fusion, enormous

quantities of energy are released by fusing two hydrogen atoms together to produce helium. The difficulty is that it takes temperatures of the order of 100 million degrees centigrade and high pressures to squeeze the hydrogen nuclei close to each other. Many inventive approaches to doing this in a controlled fashion are being actively explored, but all of them are far from achieving net power output or continuous operation. The closest is the laser-driven fusion device at the US National Ignition Facility, which in December 2022 reported a single event in which the energy produced was greater than the laser energy that heated the fuel pellet. But even then, the fusion-energy output was only 1% of the grid electrical energy drawn to energise the lasers.[41] It is worth noting that controlled hydrogen fusion for electricity production has been an aspiration that has attracted substantial funding for more than sixty years.

The second is nuclear fission using thorium instead of uranium. Thorium is a weakly radioactive metal. By itself it cannot sustain a continuous chain reaction, which means that it can never suffer a meltdown, even after a reactor failure. To produce heat, sustained fission can be triggered by neutrons from a small quantity of radioactive uranium or plutonium. While there are multiple projects underway in China and India, they are preceded by fifty years of research and development that has failed to deliver an operating power plant.[42]

The commercial relevance of nuclear fusion and thorium nuclear power plants is highly speculative and will not be further explored in this book.

Nuclear power in Australia

I am often asked to comment on nuclear power for Australia. Back in 2013, as president of the Australian Academy of Technology and Engineering, I supported an Academy symposium that called for robust debate on the potential for nuclear power to contribute to

Australia's clean energy transition. Ten years later, with zero progress on this matter, I am not optimistic about the prospects for nuclear power in Australia.

The challenges for nuclear power generation in Australia are timing and community acceptance.

On timing, nothing can be done quickly even if there were a will to do so because there is a legislated block on nuclear power, dating back to 1998. The current government has been clear that it is not inclined to unravel the legislation, and in my opinion no government would try to do so without an election mandate, so we are probably two election cycles away from the possibility of undoing the legislative block. That takes us to 2028.

Now add the time it would take to debate and pass the supporting legislation and design the regulatory system, the time to identify processes and sites for storing nuclear waste, the time for developers to work their way through regulatory hurdles, the time to overcome court challenges from activists and the time to build and commission. All up, it is hard to see a nuclear power plant being commissioned in Australia before 2040.

Community acceptance of nuclear power has been growing in Australia, on the back of broader concerns about greenhouse gas emissions and climate change. A poll by the Lowy Institute found that in 2022, 52% of Australians would support removing the existing ban on nuclear power, a five-point increase on 2021, whereas 45% would oppose removing the ban.[43] However, it is likely that if the issue were presented for real to the electorate, the minority would be animated in their opposition. Many people are fearful of the potential for a nuclear power accident and have little confidence in the likelihood that nuclear waste material will be responsibly managed and disposed. Furthermore, the fact that Russian troops have been using Ukraine's Zaporizhzhia nuclear power plant for shelter during a war has been a reminder of the potential security risks.

If Australia were to establish a nuclear power industry,

communities would be right to demand that the government implement a long-term waste-management plan. The trouble is, with few exceptions, governments around the world have not done so. Two exceptions are Finland and Sweden, and even in these cases the planned repositories are not yet operational.[44] Both countries plan to encapsulate high-level waste in copper canisters and bury them deep underground, below a 400-metre-thick layer of bedrock. The copper canisters, the water-absorbing clay in which they are buried and the thick layer of bedrock above will provide three layers of protection for people and the environment. The intention is for the canisters to remain undisturbed for at least 100,000 years.

Setting up a long-term storage facility like that takes time. The process in Finland has been an extraordinary example of patience and community consultation. Planning and consultation began in 1987 and now, after steady but slow progress, the facility in Onkalo is set to commence operations in 2025. That's 38 years from consultation to commencement. The repository is expected to be filled to capacity around 2120, at which time all surface facilities, including the encapsulation plant, will be demolished and the surface restored to its original state, including grasses and trees. Nothing will remain, not even a warning sign.

The Swedish facility in Forsmark received government approval in 2022 after three decades of planning, consultation and research.[45] It must now go through further review by district courts and the Swedish Radiation Safety Authority before excavation and construction can begin. Expect another decade on top of the three decades so far, and it, too, will be nudging 40 years from consultation to commencement of operations.

Contrast the slow deployment speed of nuclear power with the speed of projects in the renewable electricity industry. In the Australian state of Victoria, a 300-megawatt, 450-megawatt-hour battery was switched on in December 2021. That's a big battery, but even more remarkable is that the decision to build it was made in

November 2020 and construction commenced in January 2021.[46] That is, it took only 11 months from turning the first sod of soil to commencement of operation, despite a two-month break to respond to a fire in one of the battery packs.

By 2040, the earliest date nuclear-powered electrons might conceivably enter the Australian electricity network, our electricity supply will already be an almost fully zero-emissions system, powered by solar and wind firmed by batteries, pumped hydro and hydrogen storage, with the occasional use of natural gas as the firming source of last resort. Given the trajectory of price reductions for solar, wind and batteries, it is likely that the cost per megawatt-hour in 2040 will be lower than the historical average to date. Thus, any nuclear power plant switched on in 2040 will be competing against an established, low-cost, reliable renewable electricity system. It will be a case of too little, too late.

Hydropower

There are two types of hydropower. The traditional form goes by many names, such as catchment hydropower, renewable hydropower, reservoir hydropower and large-scale hydropower. Rainfall in the catchment area flows into the river that fills the reservoir impounded by the dam. When electricity is called for, the reservoir water is sent downhill through pipes or tunnels to turbine generators that convert its gravitational potential energy into electrical energy. If the reservoirs start full, electricity can be continuously generated for several months.

A variation on the large-scale hydropower concept is run-of-river hydropower. Instead of building a dam and creating a large reservoir, river water is diverted to a pipe or tunnel and races downhill to a turbine, where it generates electricity and is immediately returned to the river. The advantage is minimised impact on the local environment. The significant disadvantage is that generation is seasonal, with higher output in spring and reduced or no output in dry summers or frozen winters.

A third form of hydropower is pumped hydropower, called 'pumped hydro' for short. It is important to note, however, that pumped hydro is *not* a source of renewable electricity. Unlike large-scale hydropower and run-of-river hydropower, pumped hydro is a storage system. Instead of rainfall being used to fill the reservoir or river flow being diverted into a tunnel, a pumped hydro system relies on electricity produced elsewhere to pump water from a lower reservoir to an upper reservoir, thus storing the electrical energy as gravitational potential energy. When electricity is needed, the water from the upper reservoir flows downhill and the gravitational potential energy is converted by turbine generators into electrical energy. In this section, our focus is on large-scale hydropower or run-of-river hydropower.

The supply-chain limitations of hydropower are not the materials used for construction. Yes, dams require a lot of concrete, but massive as the amount might be it is nevertheless small compared with total worldwide usage. The generators themselves are light on materials. Hydropower systems do not use battery materials or rare earth elements at any significant level. Maximising the use of hydropower, either as a primary energy source or to provide firming services (which I will discuss in the next chapter), could therefore greatly reduce the resources required for solar and wind electricity and put less pressure on the supply chain.

The main supply-chain limitations of hydropower are community acceptance of flooding valleys and changing river flows, obtaining permits for reservoirs and transmission lines, and the time it takes to study the negative impacts on fish and birds. Large numbers of people have been displaced in the past by reservoirs and their surrounds. The same approaches to ethical engagement with communities as have already been discussed for mining apply to hydropower projects.

Natural-gas-fired electricity

Gas-fired electricity is not a zero-emissions source, but it is important to consider it here because it will have a role supporting solar and wind electricity long after coal-fired generation is discontinued. Natural gas is a fossil fuel, and when it is burned to produce electricity there are carbon dioxide emissions. Were natural-gas generation to be used to replace coal-fired generation for so-called 'baseload power', the reduction in carbon dioxide emissions would be up to 50%, even taking into account upstream methane leakage – but the emissions from new natural gas generators would be locked in for thirty years or so.[47] This has happened in some countries, such as in the 'dash for gas' that preceded the race for renewables in the UK and some states of the United States.

In Australia, there is no intention for such substitution to occur. To the contrary, there has been a downward trend in the percentage of electricity generation from gas since its share of total electricity generation peaked at 14% in 2014. By 2022, the share of gas generation had fallen to 9% of the national total. Instead of using natural gas to replace coal-fired generation, in Australia solar and wind electricity are doing the job.

Natural gas does, however, have the potential to be used for 'firming' and storage, providing backup power in case of disruptions to the supply from solar and wind. I will discuss this potential in the next chapter.

The main materials needed for natural-gas electricity generators are steel, copper, magnesium, aluminium and nickel. These generators do not use battery materials, except for some nickel, for the obvious reason that they do not have batteries, and they do not use rare earth elements for the less obvious reason that the magnets in most natural gas turbines are electromagnets rather than permanent magnets; that is, they are current-carrying coils of copper rather than magnets built from rare earth elements. In summary, the total resource requirements for a large gas turbine are trivial.

Solar and wind electricity, backed up by batteries, transmission lines and other measures, stand out as the two electricity-generation sources that will do the heavy lifting for the clean energy transition.

The good news is that solar and wind are on a roll. Of the new electricity generation capacity installed globally in 2021, 50% was solar and 25% was wind. The ever-increasing interest in solar and wind can be seen in the number of countries busy with new installations. Between 2012 and 2021, the number of countries that constructed solar farms more than doubled, from 55 to 112, and the number of countries that constructed wind farms increased from 48 to 53. In contrast, the number of countries that constructed large-scale hydropower facilities fell from 70 to 47.[48]

Australia is in a privileged position, blessed with sunshine, wind, land aplenty, a relatively small population and a strong determination to fully decarbonise its electricity system some time in the 2030s. The legislated commitment is for the National Electricity Market to be 82% renewables by 2030. As we move towards using solar and wind electricity for nearly all our energy needs, the biggest challenge will be ensuring that supply can continuously meet demand. The process by which we achieve this is known as 'firming' – a crucial part of the clean energy supply chain, which we turn to in the next chapter.

5.
Firming: Unlocking the Full Potential of Renewables

For more than a century, to balance supply and demand, the engineers and planners who ran our electricity systems forecast the expected demand hours, days, weeks, months and years in advance. If demand was expected to increase in two hours, they warmed up the idle coal-fired generators or sent more coal into the furnaces of those already operating. If demand was forecast to increase in two years, they put out a tender for the supply and installation of more generators, poles and wires.

That comfortable world is gone. Instead, as we embrace solar and wind electricity, the biggest challenge is for these variable sources to be 'firmed' so that planning is meaningful. 'Firming' is the process by which the discontinuous outputs of solar and wind generation are converted into the steady, reliable supply that electricity users expect. As Daniel Westerman, the CEO of the Australian Electricity Market Operator (AEMO), says, 'firming unlocks renewables'.[1]

One way to provide firming is by adding electricity storage to the system. Lots of it. The idea is to store electricity when it is cheap, then re-generate it from the storage facility when electricity is expensive or inadequate to meet demand.

There are many ways to store electrical energy. The rarest way to do so is to store it as electricity itself, as electrons. That can be done, in capacitors, but capacitors are only suitable for very specialised applications with short durations of a few seconds. All other storage involves converting the electrical energy into a different form of energy. The energy can be converted and stored as electro-chemical energy in batteries, as chemical energy in hydrogen and ammonia and synthetic fuels, as gravitational potential energy in pumped hydro and elevated weights, as kinetic energy in spinning flywheels, as mechanical energy in compressed air storage, or as heat energy in thermal storage.

Another way to provide firming is to call upon low-emissions, rapid-response generators, such as those provided by natural gas, biomass, biogas and geothermal generation, small modular nuclear power and large-scale hydropower. Collectively, these flexible sources are sometimes referred to as dispatchable low-emissions sources. The word 'dispatchable' is a standard term in the electricity industry to describe generators or batteries whose electrical output can be called upon – dispatched – by the system operator at any time, in contrast to solar and wind generators, which can only be called upon when the sun is shining and the wind is blowing.

A third way to provide firming is by overbuilding solar and wind generation. By building more solar and wind generation than is required to meet the annual demand, the need for long-duration storage and rapid-response generation could be minimised, although we might need to invest in more transmission lines, depending on where the extra capacity is built.

Under the worst extremes, firming can be achieved by rationing demand, but this has societal and political risks that should not be underestimated.

A final way to provide firming is through system design. One approach is load-shifting, by which the timing of certain activities is adjusted to match the availability of the electricity supply. Pool filters, for example, might be instructed to operate late at night when there is plenty of wind. Another system-design approach is to use transmissions lines to move solar and wind electricity long distances across time zones or from regions with different weather patterns, from where it is generated to where it is needed.

Realistically, surety of supply in a well-designed electricity grid of the future will be a balance between storage, dispatchable low-emissions sources, overbuilding and system design.

To start our discussion of firming, let's look at storage.

Storage

Storage duration is defined as the length of time a facility can operate at its rated peak power output. Of course, at reduced power, storage facilities can contribute for much longer. For example, a large network battery rated at 200-megawatt peak power with 600 megawatt-hours of storage could run for three hours at its peak output or for 60 hours at 10 megawatts.

The duration of any storage option is important and should always be specified. Think about the small cylindrical batteries you might use in a flashlight or a television remote control. They are available in sizes AAA, AA, C and D. These four sizes all have the same 1.5-volt output but are progressively bigger and store more energy. You wouldn't ask your friend to pick up a 1.5-volt battery for you from the local shop without specifying the size. The same applies to utility-scale batteries: both power and energy are important. The next time you see an article that mentions a 100-megawatt battery being connected to the grid and says nothing about its storage duration, please write to the editor to criticise the oversight.

The US Department of Energy defines two durations of storage. Short-duration storage is up to 10 hours; long-duration storage is 10 hours or more. The Australian Energy Market Operator (AEMO) divides storage duration into three categories: less than four hours, between four and 12 hours, and more than 12 hours. The main reason for the extra category is to distinguish between short-duration and medium-duration batteries.

Short-duration storage (usually in the form of batteries) supports a limited amount of firming. It also offers fast ramping and frequency-control services, to ensure that the frequency of the AC system is accurate and uniform. In a system with a large contribution from solar electricity, short-duration storage is called upon routinely once a day, and more frequently when weather conditions affect the solar and wind output.

Medium-duration storage (again usually provided by batteries) offers the same system services as short-duration storage but also provides sufficient storage to support 24-hour operation.

Long-duration storage facilities are not restricted to operating for long periods. They can be used for minutes or hours, in the same way as short-duration and medium-duration storage. But they can also supply power during multi-day shortages caused by sustained low solar output or low wind. Such weather events are called *dunkelflaute*, a German word meaning 'dark doldrums'. Long-duration storage can also cover anticipated seasonal variability.

Just how bad *dunkelflaute* events might be is difficult to predict, and it is made more difficult by the fact that historical solar and wind data sets are all relatively recent and geographically limited. In 2022, Joel Gilmore, Tim Nelson and Tahlia Nolan of Griffith University quantified the risks in Australia's National Electricity Market using 42 years of real-world weather data to simulate the electrical output from solar and wind that would have been generated had the systems been in place. Surprisingly, they found that the worst two-week period in the historical time sequence still delivered 54% of the National Electricity Market's average output. Their conclusion was that *dunkelflaute* events might not be as concerning as has been suggested. Nevertheless, they are real, and they might get worse with climate change, which is already causing unusual weather patterns. In 2022 alone, there were three 'one-in-100-year' floods in New South Wales.

System operators must plan for extremes and ensure that the electricity system can manage all reasonably foreseeable interruptions. In 2021, Tony Wood and James Ha from the Grattan Institute analysed how best to deal with *dunkelflaute* events and concluded that gas-fired generation alongside battery storage would be needed.[2]

An important parameter of all storage systems is round-trip efficiency. Basically, this is a measure of how much electrical energy can be discharged into the network from the storage facility as a percentage of the amount of electrical energy that was used to charge it. This is always less than 100% because of thermal losses in the conversion electronics, in chemical conversions and in the pumps and generators of a pumped hydro facility.

For example, if 50 megawatt-hours of electrical energy is used to charge a storage facility but only 45 megawatt-hours of that can be discharged back into the network, the facility is said to have 90% round-trip efficiency.

A quirk in the Australian electricity market, and in other markets that do not price emissions, is that while we still have coal-fired generation in the system, coal-fired electricity may be used to charge storage facilities. This is because coal-fired generators are designed to operate continuously. If they are switched on and off too frequently, their operational lifetime is shortened and their maintenance costs go up. So, when they cannot compete with cheap solar, for example when the sun is high during the afternoon or when demand is low at night, it is to the advantage of the operators of coal-fired generators to offer their electricity at no cost to the storage operators, or even to pay them to take it. This is a perverse outcome from the emissions perspective. However, this quirk is not a long-term problem: it will self-correct as coal-fired generators exit the system.

With these general notes about storage in mind, let's consider the key storage options currently available.

Battery storage

Batteries are ideal for storage of several hours. They are being rapidly installed in networks in which wind and solar generation are a large percentage of the total and the network is not strongly connected to other jurisdictions. Hence the surging rate of installation of utility-scale batteries in California and Australia.

Homeowners are installing batteries to increase their independence from network-supplied electricity, while hospitals, commercial buildings and factories will increasingly use batteries for emergency backup in lieu of diesel generators. These batteries are commonly referred to as behind-the-meter storage.

The rate of uptake of utility-scale batteries is stunning. Worldwide, Bloomberg NEF reported that the by the end of 2021 the cumulative installed battery capacity was 26 gigawatts with 56 gigawatt-hours of energy storage, for an average duration of 2.3 hours.[3] The annual installation rate nearly doubled compared to the year before. Bloomberg forecasts that by 2030 the cumulative storage capacity will increase 16-fold to 410 gigawatts, with an average duration of 2.9 hours. Data analysis company Clean Power Technologies reported that the new battery capacity installed in the United States in 2021 was 2.7 gigawatts for an average of 2.9 hours duration. This was three times the amount of battery storage installed in 2020. In Australia in 2021, new utility-scale battery capacity installed was approximately 500 megawatts for an average 1.5 hours duration.[4]

In addition to behind-the-meter batteries and utility-scale batteries, there is a third kind of large-scale battery, but at the moment it is theoretical. This third kind of battery consists of the batteries in electric vehicles. The total storage capacity of these batteries will be massive, and many system planners hope that they will be available to assist with utility-scale storage. However, it is not a sure thing. To be useful, the cars must be fitted with 'vehicle to grid' inverters so they can supply power to the outside world. In addition, the external chargers into which they are plugged must have bi-directional capability. Both these requirements add costs and complexity. Most importantly, the vehicle must be plugged in. Expecting drivers to plug in whenever they are not driving is a big call. It amounts to asking them to plug in several times a day, instead of once or twice a week.

Returning to utility-scale batteries, because of their dominance in the electric vehicle market and the availability of supply from gigafactories, most stationary utility-scale battery installations so far have been lithium manganese nickel cobalt designs. To reduce the long-term dependence on nickel and cobalt, some manufacturers are turning to lithium iron phosphate (LFP) chemistries. The other advantage of LFP batteries is that they have very little risk of thermal runaway that could lead to a battery fire. The round-trip efficiency of lithium-ion batteries is high, approximately 85%.[5] Their estimated operating lifetime is 10 years, although that is likely to improve with design and manufacturing refinements.

According to the US Department of Energy, the capital cost of batteries in the United States, including the balance of plant for a 100-megawatt four-hour duration system, was about US$400 per kilowatt-hour in 2020, forecast to fall to about US$280 per kilowatt-hour by 2030.

Other battery chemistries are making modest progress. One such alternative is called a vanadium redox flow battery. A milestone was reached in 2022 when the world's largest vanadium redox flow battery was switched on in China. Made by Rongke Power and taking six years from commencement of planning to commencement of operation, it is a 100-megawatt, 400-megawatt-hour battery.[6] The intention is to expand it to double this size in coming years. Although this is an impressively big battery, it is a rarity in the vanadium redox flow battery world. The round-trip efficiency of vanadium redox flow batteries is modest, at approximately 70%. The estimated operating lifetime is 15 years.

A challenge for vanadium redox flow batteries is that vanadium is expensive. Zinc is an alternative, abundant, low-cost material. In 2021, Australian company Redflow supplied the world's largest zinc-bromine flow battery, of 0.6-megawatt, 2-megawatt-hour capacity, to fertiliser company Anaergia for use at their Rialto Bioenergy Facility in California.[7] It should be noted, however, that this battery was very small compared with the utility-scale lithium-ion batteries being widely deployed.

Neither of these two battery types uses any of the battery energy transition materials in high demand for lithium-ion batteries. The main impediment to their use in stationary energy storage is competition from the amazingly low manufacturing costs of lithium-ion batteries, driven by the high production volumes for the electric vehicle market.

Pumped-hydro storage

Pumped hydro is by far the largest form of electrical energy storage worldwide to date. The International Energy Agency (IEA) reports that the total installed capacity in 2021 was 160 gigawatts, with 8,500 gigawatt-hours of stored energy, sufficient for 53 hours of continuous operation at the full rated power.[8] This was six times the installed utility-scale battery capacity of 26 gigawatts in 2021 mentioned above and more than 20 times longer continuous operation. However, the growth rate for battery storage is such that the installed capacity is expected to exceed the pumped-hydro capacity by 2030, although pumped hydro will still be ahead in terms of hours of continuous operation.

Undertaking a pumped-hydro project can be economically challenging. Some pumped-hydro systems can operate at their full rated output power for a week or more. However, they might only be called upon to do this rarely, as little as once a year. The annual sales of stored energy back into the market might therefore not be sufficient to pay for the investment. Instead, the investment case could come from the pumped-hydro storage providing support to contracts from generators that attract a higher price because they have an 'availability-to-run' commitment. Equally, or more likely, the investment case is strengthened by direct government support or by special market mechanisms known as capacity markets, discussed later.

Another problem is that in many countries, it takes years to obtain regulatory and community approval to build the reservoirs and transmission lines to connect the electrical output to the network. This slowness increases investment risk and costs.

In many instances, governments step in directly to encourage the investment. The biggest example of this in Australia is the Snowy 2.0 pumped-hydro scheme under construction in New South Wales. It is an enormous civil-engineering project, delivering a very substantial storage facility of 2-gigawatt power capacity that can run flat-out for seven days. Two more large, pumped-hydro projects were announced in Queensland in 2022. Between them they will have 7 gigawatts of power output with sufficient storage to operate for 24 hours at full power.[9]

Another supply-chain limitation is that these big civil-engineering projects often encounter unexpected difficulties, leading to delays and price blowouts. When the Snowy 2.0 storage project was announced by then prime minister Malcolm Turnbull in 2017, it was expected to cost A\$2 billion and to be commissioned by 2021. It did not meet either of those goals. In early 2023, tunnelling was proceeding at a glacial pace and construction of the transmission lines to connect to networks in New South Wales, Victoria and South Australia had not started. It was estimated that the final cost for the underground generators, tunnels and transmission lines might be A\$20 billion, ten times the original estimate. The project is unlikely to begin its storage operations before the end of the decade.[10]

On the plus side, pumped hydro is dispatchable, offers long-duration storage, is highly suitable for an AC electricity grid, and has an expected operational lifetime of more than 50 years. The round-trip efficiency of pumped hydro is generally good, at approximately 80%. For Snowy 2.0 the round-trip efficiency is marginally lower than that, because of friction losses in the long tunnels within the project and electrical losses in the long transmission lines between it and the major load centres in Sydney and Melbourne.

On balance, where governments and investors are willing to co-invest and overcome the hurdles to construct pumped-hydro facilities, the fact that they perform so well and last so long makes pumped hydro a highly useful storage option.

The total cost for a 100-megawatt, four-hour duration pumped-hydro system in the United States was in the vicinity of US$510 per kilowatt-hour in 2020, forecast to fall slightly to about US$430 per kilowatt-hour in 2030. The cost comes down significantly for 10 hours' duration, to US$260 per kilowatt-hour in 2020, forecast to fall to about US$220 per kilowatt-hour in 2030. The reason for the substantial decline in cost for 10 hours' duration is that achieving this longer storage duration is simply a matter of finding the topography that allows for larger reservoirs.

However, it is important to note that for pumped hydro there will nearly always be a significant additional capital expenditure for transmission lines to connect it to the electricity grid. The exact cost will depend on the location and can be considerable.

Hydrogen storage

Hydrogen storage is an example of electricity storage via a chemical system. Electricity is used in the well-known process of electrolysis to split water into hydrogen and oxygen. The oxygen is released to the atmosphere and the hydrogen is stored as a gas or liquid. The hydrogen is used as a fuel in gas turbines or fuel cells to regenerate electricity when needed. The overall system offers the means to store large quantities of electrical energy.

The main capital expense is storing the hydrogen. Some countries' geology allows relatively inexpensive storage of large quantities of hydrogen underground in giant salt caverns. In Australia, the geological opportunities for salt caverns are few and mostly far away from existing industrial or mining centres, so we will need above-ground or below-ground tanks. These are currently expensive, thus a lot of innovation will be required.

Australian start-up Ardent Underground uses vertical boring technology to create cylindrical shafts 5 metres in diameter and up to 500 metres deep.[11] The shaft is lined with cylindrical steel sections. These sections do not have to be particularly strong, because it is the surrounding rock that withstands the compressed hydrogen pressure. Up to 500 tonnes of compressed hydrogen can be stored per shaft. The storage cost per tonne is expected to be low, and these shafts can be bored and lined just about anywhere.

The round-trip efficiency of hydrogen storage is poor, at approximately 35%. If the electricity to be stored were expensive, this low round-trip efficiency would be a serious problem. However, if the hydrogen storage facility is intended for long-duration storage, it is reasonable to expect that there will be excess electricity from solar and wind generators from time to time that would otherwise be curtailed. These periods of extremely low-cost electricity can be used to slowly fill the hydrogen storage. There is no practical limit to how long the hydrogen gas can be kept in storage.

The total installed cost for a 100-megawatt, 10-hour duration system with hydrogen salt-cavern storage in the United States was in the vicinity of US$310 per kilowatt-hour in 2020, but was forecast to fall to about US$161 per kilowatt-hour in 2030.

Depending on their type, the electrolysers and fuel cells use platinum and iridium as catalysts, so hydrogen storage of electrical energy competes for these precious metals. The need for platinum in fuel cells can be avoided by using hydrogen-gas turbines instead.

Compressed-air storage

An old but still promising technology is compressed-air energy storage, in which electricity is used to compress air and store it in underground caverns. When electricity is needed, air is released and expands to drive a turbine to generate the electricity. Deployment is limited by the availability of caverns. Although it is old technology that has not enjoyed wide uptake, it is looking increasingly attractive for long-duration storage in networks with high penetration levels of solar and wind electricity, especially with the shift to so-called 'advanced' compressed-air storage systems in which heat generated during compression is saved for subsequent re-use during discharge, thereby improving efficiency.

The round-trip efficiency of compressed-air energy storage is modest, at approximately 50%. The estimated operating lifetime is 30 years.

The total cost to install a 100-megawatt, 10-hour duration compressed-air system in the United States was in the vicinity of US$120 per kilowatt-hour in 2020, forecast to remain the same in 2030.

Gravity-battery storage

While a pumped-hydro storage system relies on gravitational potential energy, the term 'gravity battery' is reserved for systems that use electricity to power motors to raise solid masses of concrete or metal. When electricity is needed, the mass is allowed to drop, and via a mechanical or cable linkage it turns a shaft to drive a generator that produces electricity. Some of these systems raise the masses using railway cars on steep hills. Others use specially constructed towers. A recent proposal from Australian company Green Gravity would lower and raise metal blocks in abandoned vertical mine shafts.

The round-trip efficiency of gravity batteries is good, at approximately 85%. There have been insufficient deployments to reliably comment on costs.

Thermal-electrical storage

Thermal-energy storage is another alternative to battery storage, in which electricity is used to heat a solid or liquid material. Hours, days or weeks later, when electricity is needed, the heat is used to drive a generator of some kind. An advantage of thermal energy storage systems is that they can be easily scaled and built close to where they will be used. This is distinct from solar thermal generation, where the heat of sunlight is directly used to heat the solid or liquid.

The round-trip efficiency of thermal-energy storage systems depends on the operating temperature: the higher the better. Based on analogy with coal-fired steam generators, it is likely to be poor, at about 40%.

Firming using dispatchable low-emissions sources

The common features of all these storage technologies are that excess solar and wind electricity must be used to charge them, and they have a limited discharge duration of hours or a few days. In contrast, dispatchable sources do not need to be charged and can run for days, weeks or longer.

Natural gas

As we saw in the previous chapter, natural-gas electricity generation is unlikely to be a major source of power to any significant degree in the future. It will play an important role, however, as a dispatchable, low-emissions source of energy to provide firming in systems dominated by solar and wind.

Natural-gas 'peaking' generators are useful in this role because their output can ramp up and down quite quickly, certainly much faster than coal-fired generators. Modern gas turbines based on jet-engine designs can ramp from idle to full power in two minutes; conventional single-stage gas turbines can do so in about five minutes, and the large-format, so-called combined-cycle gas turbines can do so in about 10 minutes.[12] These ramp rates are fast enough to compensate for rises and falls in solar and wind electricity output. As long as a source of natural gas is available, the generators can activate without needing to be charged in advance like a battery, and they can operate for as long as necessary without running flat like a battery.

To be very clear, there is no reason for jurisdictions with lots of solar and wind capacity to use natural-gas generators as a replacement for coal-fired electricity. The value of this dispatchable, low-emissions source of electricity is for firming, to unlock the potential of solar and wind and avoid interruptions of supply that have economic, personal and political ramifications.

Importantly, rapid-response natural-gas generators need only operate as a last resort, to keep the lights on. The average number of operating hours per year is therefore small, and so their contribution to overall emissions is also small.

In the long term, measured in decades, the cost of hydrogen production and storage will have fallen to the level that it will be possible to use stored hydrogen in modified or new peaking generators instead of gas.

The crucially important role of natural-gas electricity generation in supporting the transition to renewable energy was recognised by the European Union in July 2022, when the European Commission agreed to classify natural gas as a 'green' fuel until 2035. Natural-gas generators are the firming option of choice in Germany.[13]

Natural-gas storage in geological formations is relatively cheap to build and can be built on a large scale. The Iona Gas Storage Facility in Victoria uses a depleted gas field to store 26 petajoules, equivalent to 7,200 gigawatt-hours in electrical units.[14] If used to generate firming electricity at 40% efficiency, this would provide 2,880 gigawatt-hours of dispatchable electricity. This is eight times the stored energy of the Snowy 2.0 pumped-hydro storage project, by far the largest electricity storage project underway or even contemplated in Australia.

Other dispatchable sources

Another dispatchable source is large-scale hydropower. Already widely adopted as a zero-emissions primary source of electricity, it also works well to firm solar and wind electricity. In some cases, large-scale hydropower can fundamentally improve the economics of an integrated system. For example, aluminium smelting in Canada and green steel making in Sweden are both combining wind and hydropower to provide the necessary constant supply of electricity. Wind is always used as the first choice and hydropower fills the gaps.

Other dispatchable low-emissions sources include biomass electricity generation, geothermal electricity and nuclear power, but there are limits to their practical availability and flexibility. For example, in Denmark in 2020, biomass and biogas were used to fuel 21% of the total electricity production, while in Australia they fuelled a mere 0.13%.[15] In New Zealand, shallow geothermal heat provides about 15% of the total electricity generation, but in Australia generation from deep 'hot rock' geothermal is non-existent despite decades of investment.[16] In France in 2021, nuclear power provided 69% of the total electricity generation; in Australia it is non-existent.[17]

Capacity mechanisms and capacity markets

The biggest challenge in market-driven electricity systems is to ensure that supply and demand are matched. Millisecond by millisecond, the amount of electricity being generated must be similar to the amount of electricity being directly consumed or sent to storage. If this balance is not preserved, severe disruptions such as brownouts and blackouts may occur.

Unlike natural-gas distribution pipelines, there is no sponginess in the electricity transmission lines. In the case of gas, if the amount being introduced exceeds the amount being used – not a problem. The pressure in the pipeline starts to rise and more gas is stored in the pipeline itself. In most gas distribution networks, the pipelines can hold several days' worth of gas. In electricity poles and wires, by contrast, the tolerance for mismatch is a fraction of a second.

Although there is no tolerance for mismatch in the transmission lines, if the generated output exceeds requirements, the frequency output of the generators will naturally start to increase, which triggers technology-based responses and price signals to reduce the generator outputs. If the system demand increases, similar technology-based responses and pricing signals act to increase the generator outputs. Ordinarily, these mechanisms keep the system in balance every second of every minute of every day. But what if there is insufficient generation capacity in the system to meet increases in system demand?

In the old days, the electricity system typically belonged to a state government and was operated by a wholly owned corporation. Whether motivated by a desire to make money for state coffers or by a genuine conviction that the private sector would be able to operate the electricity system more efficiently, many governments throughout the world auctioned off their electricity systems – and they sold them off in pieces. That is, they sold the poles and wires under one set of rules, the generators under another, and the retail function under a third.

For a while, this worked well. Most state-owned systems had an excess of gas and coal generators, and the new owners did indeed operate them more efficiently. Statutory bodies were put in place to design and continuously update the market rules. Regulators were established to ensure that the generator owners did not collude or otherwise manipulate the market, to determine the rate of financial return for the owners of transmission and distribution networks, and to ensure that retailers provided fair and transparent offerings to consumers.

To encourage new investment and ensure the efficient dispatch of the lowest-cost electricity, so-called spot markets were established, under the management of independent systems operators. In a spot market, generators submit offers to supply electricity during upcoming trading intervals, which are usually 5 or 30 minutes in duration. A software program called a dispatch engine progressively schedules the generators into production, starting with the lowest-cost generator. When demand is high, expensive generators such as gas generators enter the bidding and are dispatched. At the end of the payment interval, all the generators are paid the highest price, even though most of them bid at a lower price. The standard unit traded in the spot market is the megawatt-hour. Because the only thing valued in the spot market is energy, it is called an energy-only market.

There has been an increasing tendency for generators to pre-sell their electricity under fixed contracts, but they are still required to use the spot market to bid and register their intention to supply. By selling under a contract, generators are assured of secure, long-term income. A side benefit is that they can get a better contract price if they install batteries or other firming means to reduce the variability of their supply. This is good for the generator company, good for large industrial customers, good for retailers and good for the stability of the overall electricity grid. It is a market-driven approach to ensuring that all new facilities include firming.

Periods of sustained high prices send a signal to investors that if they invest in building a new generator, they will receive an attractive return on their investment.

Perhaps.

There are several confounding factors.

The first is related to the essential nature of the product. Electricity is special. Let's contrast the electricity market with the avocado market. If there is a shortage of avocados, farmers put up their prices and retailers pass this increase on to consumers. Some consumers withdraw entirely from the avocado market and others eat fewer avocados. Demand reduces to match the supply. If there is a period of bad weather and the supply ceases entirely, so be it: consumers simply eat something else. A cliff has been reached, the market has gone to the brink, but instead of a disaster, alternatives fill the void. In the meantime, the combination of consumer demand and high prices convinces wholesalers to import avocados and local farmers to plant more and install irrigation. Eventually the supply resumes and everybody is happy.

With electrons, it isn't so. If the supply to your home stops, it is called a blackout. Nobody likes that, and if it happens repeatedly or for long durations, consumers remember that they are voters and blame the government. Governments don't like to be blamed, so they intervene and the proper operation of the market is undermined forever. Stating this is not to criticise any particular government. All governments, in all countries, will intervene in such circumstances.

The second confounding factor is the rampant pace of technological change. Governments, regulators, investors and operators have to work together to ensure that the electricity system is a well-oiled machine, but things are changing so fast that it is almost impossible for all players to share the same vision for the necessary next steps.

The third is uncertainty. Climate-change policy directly affects the opportunities and rules in the electricity market. Historically, in countries such as the United States and Australia, climate policy has twisted and turned depending on the government of the day, meaning market conditions are unpredictable.

As a result of these factors, in Australia we have a National Electricity Market that is still serviceable, but which is under tremendous strain. Something has to change.

Increasingly there is a move away from market-driven investment. Instead, we have a hybrid system in which governments intervene to incentivise certain investments. This goes by the name 'capacity mechanism', describing attempts by governments to ensure investment in new capacity to generate the electrical energy that we will need in future. But not just any capacity: they want the right type – renewables, or dispatchable gas, or storage – at the right time and place. The trouble with these interventions in the market is that they undermine the case for future investments by industry.

The first capacity mechanism in Australia was the Renewable Energy Target, which incentivised investment in solar and wind. For solar, the scheme existed in two streams, one for large-scale solar farms and the other for small rooftop installations. It was very effective and contributed to Australia's enviable position of holding the world record for the most installed solar capacity per person. However, it has a downside. Because it was neither integrated with the electricity spot market nor focused on geographical regions of need, the Renewable Energy Target led to over-investment in some regions and under-investment in others.

In 2016 and 2017, as Chief Scientist of Australia, I led the Independent Review into the Future Security of the National Energy Market, which came to be known as the Finkel Review. Our review made 50 recommendations. Of these, 49 were agreed to by the states and the federal government, but the fiftieth was rejected by the federal government. This rejected recommendation was the creation of a Clean Energy Target, an expanded version of the Renewable Energy Target, which would have integrated better with the market. Even though it would have replaced uncertainty for coal-fired electricity companies with a clear path to an orderly exit, it was opposed by the coal lobby, represented by the Minerals Council of Australia.

Ultimately, despite the prime minister at the time, Malcolm Turnbull, and his energy minister, Josh Frydenberg, supporting the Clean Energy Target, a considerable number of their colleagues in cabinet and on the backbench fought against it, either because they doubted the climate science, because they sensed political advantage in voting against their leadership, or because they saw their role as defending the status quo instead of helping their electorates to prepare for the future.

The prime minister proposed an alternative, called the National Energy Guarantee, which was strategically similar to the Clean Energy Target but very different in detail. It was much more complex, so much so that its complexity may have obscured the fact that one of its key intentions was to drive down emissions by increasing the percentage of renewables at the expense of coal-fired generation. It, too, went down like a ton of bricks. Former prime minister Tony Abbott, then sitting on the backbench, said that if prices came down while the deployment of renewables went up, as predicted by the Energy Security Board's modelling, 'pigs might fly'. The rumblings against the National Energy Guarantee contributed to the Liberal party rebelling against Turnbull and overthrowing him as prime minister. Such were the climate wars in Australia in 2018.

At the same time, state governments were determined to reduce emissions by increasing the percentage of renewable electricity. They implemented mechanisms to achieve this, including feed-in tariffs, contracts for difference and reverse auctions.

Internationally, instead of, or in addition to, such schemes, most jurisdictions have introduced fully competitive capacity *markets* rather than capacity *mechanisms*. Capacity markets are managed by the system operator, without political interventions. Basically, once a year the operator runs an auction to encourage generator companies to contractually commit to having a certain amount of dispatchable capacity ready to operate in three years' time. The cheapest bidders are paid a lump sum for committing to that capacity. They also agree to pay a significant penalty if they do not deliver. This approach has worked very well for the large New York and PJM (Pennsylvania, New Jersey and Maryland) markets in the United States, and in the UK. In the Finkel Review, we saw merit in these systems, but after consultations we decided that a capacity market would be too big a change for the Australian system, given all the other modernisations required, so we included a substantial discussion of the topic but left it for future consideration.

The Australian entity charged with coordinating the evolution of the National Electricity Market is the Energy Security Board, established on the recommendation of the Finkel Review. The Board spent a couple of years designing a capacity market, but when it was released as a final proposal in August 2022 it failed to garner support from industry, the community or governments. It was technology-neutral, and thus allowed coal-fired and gas-fired electricity generation to bid into the market, which proved unacceptable to some state governments and to climate-advocacy groups. When a capacity mechanism was finally agreed to in principle by the federal, state and territory governments in December 2022, it was limited to 'dispatchable renewables'. In the Australian context, this means solar and wind, supported by storage such as pumped hydro or batteries.

Perhaps the final design will have something in common with the suggestion from Bruce Mountain and his colleagues at Victoria University for a Renewable Electricity Storage Target (REST), conceptually an extension of the successful Renewable Energy Target.[18] The REST would provide financial incentives for the provision of electricity storage from distributed small-battery systems behind the meter, and from large, grid-connected storage systems.

Perhaps it will be based on the proposal by Tim Nelson and colleagues at renewable energy company Iberdrola for a capacity reserve in which funding would be available for new storage capacity to be brought into a 'waiting room' and held until it is needed.[19] If the usual market operates well, the reserve would only be called upon in extreme cases. Prominent Australian economist Ross Garnaut, seeing merit in that approach, has proposed a variation in which the Commonwealth of Australia would own reserve electricity-generation capacity and demand, sufficient to deal with extremes.

Overbuilding

Overbuilding to firm an electricity system powered primarily by solar and wind might sound crazy or be dismissed as too expensive. But hold on – it is well worth exploring.

If, for example, the wind generation in the system has a peak capacity of double what is needed but it happens to be operating at 20% of peak because of persistent low wind, it will be providing 40% of the system's requirements, obviating the need for a considerable amount of storage. Yes, it sounds expensive to overbuild, but the cost of building solar and wind farms continues to decline.

Furthermore, surplus electricity can be used to supply flexible loads such as hydrogen production or the recharging of electric vehicles, providing extra income to the generation companies.

The idea is obvious, but someone had to think of it first and do the formal analysis. In 2012, researchers from the University of Delaware and Delaware Technical College put two and two together. That is, acknowledging the intermittency of solar and wind generation while also acknowledging their rapidly falling cost.[20] They built a computer model of the largest electricity jurisdiction in the United States, the PJM Interconnection, which spans 13 eastern states. They ran 28 billion combinations of storage, solar, wind, the size of the geographic area of renewable generation, and dispatchable low-emissions generation. They found that the lowest-cost system was when the combined solar and wind capacity was about three times higher than peak demand. Of course, the specific combinations will be unique for each jurisdiction.

This approach has been embraced, and in Australia we are powering towards this outcome. The Step Change scenario of the Australia Energy Market Operator (AEMO) hypothesises that our National Electricity Market will have more than 210 gigawatts of solar and wind capacity to meet the growing demand out to 2050, about four times higher than peak demand.

A side effect of overbuilding, as explained by Tony Wood and James Ha of the Grattan Institute, is that there will be times when the system has surplus capacity that will be wasted in the absence of a flexible buyer. Nevertheless, they concluded that overbuilding would still be a cost-effective way to reduce the risk of shortfalls when wind and sunlight are scarce and demand is high.

Firming using system design

Firming using storage, dispatchable low-emission sources and overbuilding relies on the brawn of the system. Firming using system design calls on the brains. Transmission lines, frequency management, demand response, sector coupling and digitalisation are not themselves sources of energy, but they ensure that the installed energy sources operate optimally and reliably.

Transmission

Transmission lines are the very long overhead lines or, in special circumstances, underground cables that connect one or more large generators to areas where consumers live. The energy transmission materials required for transmission lines are small, consisting mostly of aluminium for the cables and rare earth elements in the high-voltage electronics required if the transmission lines operate on DC instead of AC. The time it takes to build new transmission lines, however, is currently limiting how quickly we can scale up the renewable electricity supply. Hence the industry saying: *there's no transition without transmission.*

At a macro level, there are two types of transmission lines. Those that hook up generators to consumers are local transmission lines, even if they are long. The second type – interconnectors – join two economic regions, such as adjacent states or provinces.

To avoid transmission lines criss-crossing the countryside, state governments are identifying and supporting renewable energy zones (REZs) – places where multiple solar and wind projects can be located, with the state government ensuring that sufficient local transmission lines will be deployed to connect the projects to metropolitan and regional centres. In general, these will need to be new transmission lines, because most REZs will be far from the old coal and gas electricity generators they are replacing.

In 2017, I travelled with members of the Finkel Review to visit leading regulators and operators in Europe and America. One of the most impressive transmission-line initiatives was the Competitive Renewable Energy Zones (CREZ) project in Texas. The irony of finding this project in a state famous for its oil production was not lost on us.

The importance of planning was evident. In the early 2000s, developers had starting building wind farms in Texas, but they struggled to gain permission to connect them to the state-wide electricity grid. The investors did not want to continue to build wind farms until new transmission lines were built. In 2005, the Texas legislature instructed the authorities to begin identifying REZs and their transmission requirements. This review was completed by 2007. Construction of transmission lines capable of carrying up to 18.5 gigawatts of generation capacity commenced at the beginning of 2009 and was completed in five years. The CREZ project was an excellent example of government, regulators and industry working together to develop local resources that benefited the public interest, the economy and the environment.

Unlike local transmission lines, which generally must be built to meet demand, interconnectors are optional and are built to optimise the system. There is not much value in interconnectors if they simply connect two economic regions that both use solar or wind energy and have similar weather patterns. Instead, interconnectors should be built to enable the supply of dispatchable low-emissions generation from one economic zone to another that does not have that particular source of dispatchable generation. For example, as part of the Snowy 2.0 project, interconnectors will be built to ensure that the massive storage capacity of the project benefits consumers in New South Wales, Victoria and South Australia.

Consistent with this, there is a formal proposal to build a 1.5 gigawatt undersea cable to connect the island state of Tasmania to the Australian mainland via the state of Victoria. Although the justifications are complex and disputed, one of the benefits is that Tasmania has large-scale hydropower ready to dispatch when needed. Indeed, Tasmania has so much hydropower and wind electricity that its annual electricity generation from these sources is already hovering near 100% of demand.

Another proposal, this time informal, put forward in Australia for interconnectors in a renewable electricity future is to build ultra-long-distance east–west interconnectors to supply solar electricity from the west to the east of Australia for about two extra hours into the eastern evening. However, such long-distance east–west lines have never been built, despite their technical appeal, for the simple reason that they are too expensive. For example, a transmission line from the west coast of Western Australia to the east coast of New South Wales would be over 3,000 kilometres long. At 2-gigawatt capacity, it would cost much more than A$10 billion and take years to be permitted, then many more years to construct. Instead, adding two-hour batteries to existing and new east-coast solar farms would be equally effective, much cheaper and quicker to deploy. For example, a 2-gigawatt two-hour duration battery built near the population centres in the eastern regions to provide the same extension of supply into the evening would cost about A$2 billion and could be built in less than two years from financial commitment to activation.

It takes many years to design, plan, obtain approvals, gain agreement from landowners and, finally, construct transmission lines. While it can also take several years to plan and build a large-scale wind or solar farm, it is generally considerably quicker to do so. Construction of new transmission lines must therefore start early, sometimes in advance of knowing the specific plans for the new solar and wind farms that will connect to them.

The main factor slowing down the deployment of transmission lines is sociological, not technological. Transmission-line technology is mature and costs are unlikely to change rapidly in either direction. The problem is that it takes many years to navigate the thicket of regulatory approvals and obtain permissions from landholders, neighbours and communities. Investor money is available, social licence less so.

In Australia and all developed countries, the morass of vertically and horizontally interacting and overlapping regulations should be rationalised, so that the necessary permissions can be secured more quickly, ideally in one or two years.

The way the industry interacts with landholders, be they Traditional Owners, private owners or government, must be improved. That will require major government-led coordination. Landholders must be treated fairly and respectfully and given clear and consistent information about what activities they would be able to undertake on their properties under the proposed transmission lines. The growing trend to make sure landholders are financially compensated for transmission lines crossing their properties obviously helps.

Another way to improve acceptance of new transmission lines by local communities is to build them underground instead of overhead.[21] The trouble is, underground high-voltage cables can be four to ten times more expensive.[22] Underground lines are also not practical in hilly or mountainous areas. They can take longer to construct than overhead lines, particularly in difficult terrain. The cost of maintaining them is also much higher, sometimes five or ten times so. Eventually, because of internally generated thermal cycles dependent on power flows in the cable, the insulation weakens to the point that a fault occurs. When that happens in underground transmission lines, there are the added costs of finding the fault, digging down to it, repairing it and restoring the site.[23]

Underground transmission lines will continue to be used only when communities are willing to bear these added costs and complexities. In Germany, they are building the 'SuedLink DC3' project, a 700-kilometre-long, 525-kilovolt DC underground transmission line to carry wind-powered electricity from northern Germany to the cities and industrial zones in the south. It is due to commence operations in 2027. The projected cost is US$11 billion.[24]

While the main reason for going underground is to avoid compromising the aesthetics and utility of the property where above-ground transmission lines would otherwise be built, there can be other advantages. In California, above-ground transmission lines have occasionally been linked to wildfires during hot and gusty conditions, but there is little evidence of such events in Australia.[25]

In hurricane-prone and tornado-prone zones in the United States, where overhead transmission lines are sometimes destroyed by ferocious winds or wind-borne tree branches, underground transmission lines are obviously much more resilient.

To get a head start on the lengthy process for constructing new transmission lines in Australia, some of the key recommendations from the Finkel Review were for the establishment of a long-term planning process to look at system-wide benefits and in particular to 'develop an integrated grid plan to facilitate the efficient development and connection of renewable energy zones across the National Electricity Market'. These recommendations were adopted, and since then, AEMO has produced two generations of the Integrated System Plan.

The expense, effort and time it takes to build new transmission lines influences major decisions on where to build solar and wind farms. In Australia there is plenty of land for onshore wind generation, yet there are plans afoot to build higher-cost offshore wind farms, in part because the requirements for new transmission lines can be minimised. For example, there is a proposal to build an offshore wind farm to supply an existing aluminium smelter on the coast at Portland in Victoria. This would require no more than a kilometre of onshore cabling to connect to the smelter and, via the smelter, to the existing electricity grid.

Another proposal is for an offshore wind farm off the Gippsland coast, not far from the Latrobe Valley, historically the home of Victoria's brown-coal-fired generators. This would require approximately 100 kilometres of new transmission lines from the Gippsland shore to the centre of the Latrobe Valley, where they will connect to the existing high-voltage transmission network to Melbourne and across Victoria.

Minimising or eliminating the need for transmission lines is one of the advantages of using batteries to strengthen the system rather than interconnectors. In most cases, large utility-scale batteries don't require new transmission lines because they are usually built on existing solar and wind farms or at existing load centres, decommissioned coal-power plants or otherwise located near an existing transmission line.

Finally, it is worth mentioning a quirk. The time it takes to build local transmission lines has led to a surprising acceleration in the uptake of rooftop solar installations ahead of large-scale solar. If you had asked me twenty years ago whether rooftop solar would contribute a significant fraction of our total solar generation, I would have said no! Obviously not! My reason was that rooftop solar cannot benefit from the economies of scale enjoyed by large-scale generation. But in Australia in 2021, more than 3 gigawatts of rooftop solar was installed, which exceeded the installation of 1.7 gigawatts of large-scale solar.[26] This trend is likely to continue. AEMO forecasts Australia's 15 gigawatts of cumulative installed rooftop solar in 2021 will more than double by 2030.[27]

There are many reasons for the dominance of rooftop solar, like the individual incentive to save on your household electricity bill by generating electricity at home. However, arguably the main reason for the comparative success of rooftop solar is that it does not have to wait for new transmission and distribution lines to be built. The typical process from quotation to completed installation is just a few weeks, including time for approvals.

Furthermore, the higher per-kilowatt-hour cost of rooftop solar compared with the wholesale price of electricity generated at a utility-scale solar farm is more than compensated for by the fact that by the time the utility-scale solar electricity gets to a domestic consumer it is significantly more expensive than the wholesale price because of transmission, distribution and retailer costs.

Frequency management

All major electricity systems are AC systems. In AC systems, it is crucially important to preserve synchronous operation, meaning that all generators, large or small, operate at the same frequency and with their sinusoidal outputs matched to other generators in the grid.

In the old days, synchronous operation was something for the power-systems engineers and system operators to worry about. They did their job well. Managing the synchronous operation was predictable and well understood, made easier because the generators used in coal, natural gas and hydropower systems are well-behaved, synchronous machines.

Fast forward to the era of solar and wind generators and it is not so easy. Solar generators are DC and must be connected to the AC electricity grid through electronic inverters. Wind generators are inherently AC, but they work moment to moment at a frequency determined by the wind, so they, too, must be connected to the AC electricity grid through electronic inverters. As the penetration of solar and wind increases, it becomes more difficult to maintain synchronous operation. If it is lost, the grid will collapse. A variety of technologies is used to match the solar and wind generators to the electricity grid frequency and phase.

Chief among the tools used to date are synchronous condensers, which are rotating masses with coils, passively spinning in lock step with the grid frequency. Because of their rotational inertia, they help to smooth out any disturbances in the alternating current or voltage. Synchronous condensers can be dedicated devices weighing hundreds of tonnes and specially installed, or they can be existing gas and hydropower generators disconnected from their input energy source and acting like a synchronous condenser.

A more modern option is the grid-forming inverter, made from sophisticated high-voltage electronics. When implemented at large scale, grid-forming inverters help solar and wind maintain the grid frequency in much the same way as traditional synchronous generators work. Short-duration batteries that are relatively cheap can be fitted with grid-forming inverter technology and placed at key points in the electricity grid. Of course, long-duration, more expensive batteries can do this too. This capability represents an important role for batteries beyond their more obvious storage role.

Demand response

Demand-response management is the other side of supply management. It is an important, minute-by-minute system optimisation that helps to ensure system reliability. It is defined by the Australian Energy Market Commission as a consumer choice to turn down or turn off their electricity use in response to a signal to do so. Consumers might be small householders or giant aluminium smelters, and in general there is a price reward offered by the retailer.

Because the significance of demand-response management is sometimes over-interpreted, it is important to say what it isn't. It is not a process to reduce the total energy consumed over intervals of days or weeks. It is a means of ensuring system reliability. Indirectly, it could be claimed that it contributes to lower emissions in the long term because it enables greater uptake of solar and wind electricity, but it does not directly reduce emissions.

As an example, a householder, in exchange for an incentive payment, might agree to postpone using the dishwasher and washing machine, but eventually the machines have to be turned on so that those dishes and clothes are washed. Ultimately, the energy is consumed, but at a more convenient time. At a larger scale, a hydrogen production plant supplying vehicle refuelling stations necessarily has a lot of local hydrogen storage, and thus it can postpone production if requested and catch up a few hours later.

Another form of demand response is called 'peak shaving'. One form of peak shaving is based on installing a battery at the point of use specifically to minimise the peak power drawn by the user. For example, the owner of a commercial building in the central business district could install a battery on the roof or in the basement to charge at night and contribute to the supply during the day, thereby minimising the peak current drawn from the grid during working hours. Doing so helps the customer because commercial customers pay for the size of their connection to the electricity grid, and it helps the distributor because it reduces the need to upgrade the distribution cables and transformers.

The supply-chain aspect of demand response is reflected in keeping the electricity system running optimally in times of stress so that essential electricity can be supplied to the industries that are making the products that ultimately assist with the clean energy transition.

Sector coupling

One of the buzz phrases in the renewable electricity industry is 'sector coupling'. It refers to the integration of the major energy-consuming sectors – transport, heat and industry – with the electricity supply sector. Like demand-response management, it does not change the overall emissions, but if implemented well helps to minimise costs and maximise flexibility in the system. It is happening already, whether it is called by the term or not.

Transport is being coupled to the electricity sector through the shift to batteries and hydrogen displacing petrol and diesel for transport. We can in principle control the time of charging vehicles and producing hydrogen to match the availability of electricity supply.

Building heating is already coupled to the electricity sector through radiative and heat-pump space heating, and this will increase. In addition, a shift to heat-pump hot-water heating is underway, displacing natural gas. These uses of electricity increase the opportunities for demand-response management because it is possible to advance or postpone building and hot-water heating for a few hours to match the availability of the electricity supply.

In industry, process heat and steam production are being increasingly coupled to the electricity supply sector as coal, oil and gas are phased out in favour of electricity to directly power machines, produce steam and provide intermediate-level heat. For very high temperatures such as is required in brick-making kilns, electricity can be used to produce hydrogen that can then be used instead of natural gas to provide high-temperature direct-flame heating.

Digitalisation

When my colleagues and I went to Dublin in 2017 to learn from the Irish systems operator EirGrid, we were impressed.

Their electrical grid spans the whole island, despite the political division into the Republic of Ireland and Northern Ireland. EirGrid was dealing with very high amounts of wind generation installed in response to government incentives. This was making real-time management of the system difficult, not just because of the variability, but because wind-generated electricity does not play by the traditional rules and at high penetration levels reduces the stability of the AC electricity system. Countries such as Denmark that have an even higher level of wind electricity penetration rely on their strong interconnection to the surrounding countries to strengthen their system, but that is not the case for the island system managed by EirGrid.

Through careful and progressive deployment, EirGrid found that they could maintain system stability with up to 50% wind electricity. However, they were determined to push past that limit because it meant curtailing about 25% of the installed wind capacity and as a result the island would fall short of its renewable electricity targets.

They anticipated that with careful system management, they would be able to support up to 75% wind electricity before curtailing the generators. Some of the system-management improvements were basic things such as setting the right connection standards for the wind turbines and better wind forecasting, but the rest of the system-management improvements relied on advanced control-room software and digital measurement and control. In the control room they were implementing exotic-sounding procedures such as a wind security assessment tool to analyse the anticipated stability based on snapshots of the power flows minute by minute across the system, inertia monitoring and rate of change of frequency monitoring. They were working on implementing a future suite of equally exotic-sounding tools such as synchronous generators, power-ramp rate services, voltage-trajectory control and wind security assessment look-ahead.

Fast forward to 2022 in Australia and the system operator, AEMO, is planning for a system that by 2025 will be able to operate stably at 100% instantaneous renewable electricity using similar tools and the fast-frequency control services provided by batteries and their electronic interface systems.[28] This AEMO roadmap is unprecedented elsewhere in the world.

A key theme in this improved ability to manage high-penetration levels of wind and solar is digitalisation. To deliver maximum value, buildings, industrial loads and solar rooftops should have internal digital management systems that can communicate directly with the systems operator or indirectly through an intermediary known as an aggregator. The advantage of an aggregator is that it manages thousands of buildings and industrial loads and enables local power sharing, then communicates status and takes instruction from the system operator. The system operator therefore only has to deal simultaneously with thousands of aggregators and large generators and users, rather than many millions of individual customers.

Other new developments that will be key to the digitalisation of the electricity system include artificial intelligence, analytics, big data, blockchain, the 'internet of things' and 5G communications.

The upside of digitalisation is a cost-effective and reliable zero-emissions electricity system. The downside is that it raises new cyber security and customer privacy risks.[29] The main supply-chain concern around digitalisation is the availability of skilled workforces. A secondary concern is the availability of electronic components for sensors, communications and control rooms.

Efficiency

Of course, the best way to reduce emissions is to reduce the need for electricity in the first place. That is, there is nothing more effective than properly insulating our buildings and using high-efficiency appliances and machinery. Another superb way to reduce the need for electricity is to use solar thermal hot-water systems for domestic and low temperature industrial hot water.

Everybody benefits from efficient use of energy. Individual homeowners pay less on their energy bills if their home's thermal efficiency reduces the need for heating and cooling and if their lighting and appliances are modern, highly efficient versions. Likewise, commercial and industrial building operators pay less if their buildings are well insulated, councils pay less if street lighting uses light-emitting diodes, and data-centre operators can do more computing for less energy using the latest microprocessors.

Transmission and distribution network owners will avoid the need to invest in expensive new poles and wires if consumers meet their needs more efficiently.

The planet will be better off if industrial processes are more efficient, because there will be fewer greenhouse gas emissions from the energy consumed and from the industrial processes themselves.

And, of course, in a more efficient world the supply chain will be under less pressure because there will be less need for solar panels, wind turbines and utility-scale batteries if the energy consumption per economic output unit is minimised. A gigawatt not used is a gigawatt not generated.

In short, every government, every business and every householder should invest in improving energy efficiency, although with awareness that there will be a point of diminishing returns.

Germany provides a good case study. The German government has had an enduring commitment to optimising energy efficiency, predating the short-term measures introduced in response to the energy shortages caused by Russia's war against Ukraine. In Germany's *Energy Efficiency Strategy 2050*, published in 2020, the first

Figure 8: Energy efficiency in Germany has improved annually from 2000 to 2018, with the largest improvement being 2.2% per year for households and the lowest being 0.77% per year for industry. Index 100% in year 2000. Note that the Y axis is not zero-based. (Source: odyssee-mure.eu)

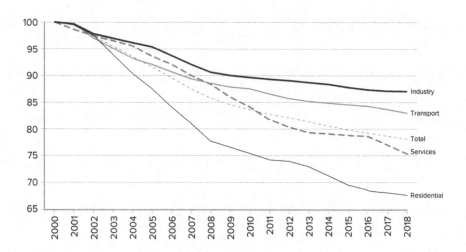

sentence makes a key point: 'How sustainable an economy really is depends to a large extent on how efficiently it uses energy.'[30] That statement may seem self-evident, but it is not often pursued. This logic underpins Germany's ambition to be the most energy-efficient country in the world. Its strategy addresses all relevant sectors: building, industry, commerce and transport. The consistent benefits since the year 2000 are shown in Figure 8.

•   •   •

Without a well-functioning electricity system, the manufacturing plants that produce solar panels, wind turbines, batteries, electric cars and other essential components of the clean-energy supply chain will either grind to a halt or make their products using high-emissions coal-fired and gas-fired electricity. It is clear that firming solar and wind electricity is key to successfully deploying these two zero-emissions energy sources at large scale.

Of course, countries that are not blessed with substantial wind or solar resources do not have the same firming challenges. Their problem is bigger, though, as they try to wean themselves off fossil fuels. Some will turn to hydropower, some will invest in nuclear power, but many will have to import their clean energy. The next chapter looks at how that might be achieved.

6.
Shipping Sunshine: Green Hydrogen

Hydrogen is the backstop of energy and chemistry. Where batteries are inadequate for high-density storage – enter hydrogen. Where we need a chemical to make fertiliser – enter hydrogen. Where we need a chemical to reduce iron oxide to iron to make steel – enter hydrogen. Where we need a chemical to synthesise jet fuel for long-distance aviation – enter hydrogen.

Just as some countries have an abundance of fossil-fuel energy, there are countries blessed with an abundance of renewable energy and others that will not be able to meet their requirements. Thus, in future, there needs to be a system for international trade of renewable energy, most likely carried by ships. The benefit of trading by ships rather than cables or pipelines is that ships can be diverted to respond to shortages and changing priorities, and thousands of ships cannot be arbitrarily shut down in the way that a pipeline can be, as we have seen with the gas pipelines from Russia to Europe.

The most practical way to transport electricity by ship between the continents is to convert it into hydrogen or a chemical derivative such as ammonia to be used as an energy carrier, or to embed hydrogen in finished products such as steel and fertilisers. Assuming the hydrogen is made from solar, wind or large-scale hydropower, I call this process shipping sunshine.

Same movie, or a sequel?

A sceptic recently said to me, 'Alan, don't you realise that this is an old movie being played again? There was strong interest in hydrogen as a fuel in the 1940s, the 1970s and again in the early 2000s. Each time, it fizzled out!'

I used to be a sceptic myself, back in 2010 when I was working for an electric car-charging company, Better Place. The reason for my scepticism was because all we looked at then was the energy efficiency of a battery-electric car compared with a hydrogen-electric car. On that basis, the battery system wins hands down, being more than twice as efficient. Since then, I have learned that energy efficiency for transport is not the only thing that counts. There is also economic efficiency, specialised transport needs, and the many other uses of hydrogen both as a chemical and as a high-temperature heating source. Gradually, I converted from sceptic to agnostic to believer.

The hydrogen movie this time around has an extended plot, new props and new starring actors. Instead of a rerun we are watching a sequel, with what looks like being a far happier ending.

The first significant reason things are different this time is that the motivation is stronger than ever before. After the Paris Agreement, the global pressure to decarbonise ratcheted up and all scalable low-emissions technologies are being called upon, hydrogen included.

Japan made commitments under the Paris Agreement, but the challenge for Japan is particularly acute because it does not have a simple alternative to the oil, coal and gas it imports to meet more than 90% of its energy needs. Importing hydrogen as liquid hydrogen, or hydrogen chemically carried in ammonia or a liquid organic hydrogen carrier, is the simplest alternative for Japan, although admittedly price is a hurdle.

Cognisant of its own special needs, Japan was the first country in the world to publish a national hydrogen strategy, in December 2017. The second was Korea, with its Korean Hydrogen Economy Roadmap, published in January 2019. Australia was third, with the

Australian National Hydrogen Strategy published in November 2019. By now, about 40 countries plus the European Union have published hydrogen strategies, roadmaps or preliminary guidelines.[1]

The second big reason things are different this time is that the cost to produce green hydrogen has dropped dramatically, thanks to the extraordinary decrease in the price of solar and wind electricity. It is anticipated that the price of electrolysers will also drop in coming years.

The third big difference is improved technology for using hydrogen. In 2021, for the first time, the technology for using hydrogen as a chemical to reduce iron ore into elemental iron was implemented at pilot scale. Fuel cells for hydrogen-electric vehicles today are smaller, cheaper and have much longer mean times between failure than in previous screenings of the movie. And the unsung hero is the carbon-fibre reinforced fuel tank that can hold hydrogen at over 700 atmospheres of pressure, giving passenger hydrogen electric cars a range of about 600 kilometres. This is an extraordinarily high pressure, about three times what is achieved in a scuba tank for underwater diving.[2] It is the pressure you would feel on your lungs and eardrums if you went freediving seven kilometres deep in a Pacific Ocean trench. Not recommended. These hydrogen tanks first went into commercially available vehicles in 2013 in the Hyundai Tucson ix35 and in 2014 in the Toyota Mirai.

Hydrogen production

There are three key supply-chain challenges for clean hydrogen: production, storage and shipping.

While so-called blue hydrogen can be made from fossil fuels with carbon dioxide by-products minimised, captured and stored, most of the international focus is on green hydrogen made by electrolysis of water using renewable electricity.

The generally accepted long-term goal is to get the price of producing green hydrogen down to US$1 per kilogram of hydrogen.

Comparing this price to natural gas is not easy because natural gas is priced in dollars per cubic metre, in dollars per thousand cubic feet, in dollars per million British thermal units (BTU), in dollars per tonne, in dollars per kilowatt-hour and in dollars per gigajoule. The last one, dollars per gigajoule, is what we use in Australia, and it is the only one that is a scientific unit, so we'll use dollars per gigajoule.

Another complication is that when comparing kilograms of hydrogen to an energy equivalent such as gigajoules of natural gas, there are two different energy conversion factors for hydrogen. One is called the higher heating value (HHV), equal to 140 megajoules per kilogram of hydrogen. The other is called the lower heating value (LHV), equal to 120 megajoules per kilogram. In practice, the higher heating value of hydrogen can rarely be utilised, so all discussions in this book use the lower heating value without further qualification.

At 120 megajoules per kilogram, it takes just over 8 kilograms of hydrogen to provide 1 gigajoule of energy, thus at US$1 per kilogram the energy price of hydrogen is approximately US$8 per gigajoule. In the United States market, US$8 per gigajoule of hydrogen would be considered high, because natural gas is normally very cheap. During the years 2010–2019, the so-called 'Henry Hub' price, the benchmark price for domestic natural gas in the United States, was just over US$3 per gigajoule.[3] In Australia, the price in southeast Queensland in 2018 and 2019 averaged just over US$5 per gigajoule.[4] But in many countries, considerably higher prices are common. For example, in Germany the price of imported natural gas during the years 2010–2019 was approximately US$8 per gigajoule.[5] In Japan, the price of imported liquefied natural gas during the same period was approximately US$12 per gigajoule.[6] In 2022, natural gas prices spiked around the world because Russia withheld supply from its European customers. Prices more than doubled in the United States to about US$8 per gigajoule and were over US$20 per gigajoule in Japan and over US$50 per gigajoule in Germany.[7]

All up, if hydrogen can be produced and used at about US$1 per kilogram (US$8 per gigajoule), that puts it in the ballpark.

The three main contributions to the production cost of green hydrogen are the cost of electricity, the capital cost of the electrolyser including the balance of plant needed to make it operational, and the capacity factor of the renewable electricity source.

To start, let's develop a rule of thumb for the relationship between the price of electricity and the price of the hydrogen produced. We can begin by calibrating against the prices we are familiar with. In many developed countries, the price of electricity for householders is in the vicinity of 20 US cents per kilowatt-hour. In the bigger energy units used in the wholesale market that converts to US$200 per megawatt-hour. Industrial users might pay US$100 per megawatt-hour, while the wholesale market for electricity generated in most developed countries has historically been about US$40 per megawatt-hour.

A typical large-scale electrolyser, including its balance of plant, would use about 0.06 megawatt-hours to produce one kilogram of hydrogen. This gives us our rule of thumb: add 60 cents to the price per kilogram for each $10 per megawatt-hour in the electricity price.

This rule of thumb is a guide; it is not a law of nature. The relationship between the price of electricity and the price of the hydrogen produced depends on the efficiency of the electrolyser. It is 60 cents added to the price per kilogram for each $10 per megawatt-hour for a conventional electrolyser, falling as low as 43 cents for the kind of high-efficiency electrolyser produced by the Australian start-up Hysata.

Using 60 cents as our rule of thumb, at a wholesale price of $40 per megawatt-hour the electricity contribution to the final price of the hydrogen would be US$2.40 per kilogram; at an industrial price of US$100 per megawatt-hour, the electricity contribution would be US$6 per kilogram. Clearly, the historical wholesale and industrial electricity prices are not compatible with the target of US$1 per kilogram of hydrogen. An electricity price of about US$10 per megawatt-hour will be required.

So, the question becomes, is US$10 per megawatt-hour feasible? Certainly not by using conventional coal and natural gas generation. Certainly not by using electricity supplied over the national electricity grid, because of the cost of using transmission lines.

In the Gulf countries of the Middle East and in India, this incredible low electricity price target is in sight. Contracts to supply solar electricity at less than US$20 per megawatt-hour are now routine, and one contract has been written at US$13.50 per megawatt-hour.[8] In other countries the price is higher but continually falling. The global financial advisory firm Lazard estimates that globally the cost of electricity produced from solar is between US$30 and US$41 per megawatt-hour. The cost produced from onshore wind is between US$26 and US$50 per megawatt-hour.[9] These prices do not include battery firming, but if the electricity is being used onsite to produce hydrogen that might not be required.

To achieve US$1 per kilogram of hydrogen, the solar, wind and hydropower will have to be co-located with the electrolysers to avoid the added cost of transmission. In addition, the facility that uses the hydrogen will consume a lot of renewable electricity for process heat and power. By locating the solar, wind, water pre-treatment, electrolysers and facility on one site, the cost of electricity transmission and hydrogen pipelining can be avoided.

The second main contribution to the cost of hydrogen production is the price of the electrolysers. They are usually rated by their electrical input, even though the hydrogen output depends on their efficiency. In 2020, the fully installed cost of electrolysers was estimated by the US Department of Energy at about US$1.5 million per megawatt capacity.[10] At that price, the amortised contribution of the capital cost of the electrolyser over the life of the project is approximately US$2.20 per kilogram of hydrogen produced. The price of electrolysers will have to fall more than 80%, to less than

US$300,000 per megawatt, for their amortised contribution to get down to about 40 cents per kilogram of hydrogen produced.

Add that to the 60 cents of electricity noted above and the facility is on track to produce hydrogen for US$1 per kilogram. Of course, there are many other project-specific costs, but this exercise shows that the target is feasible.

The prospects for electrolyser prices falling are good because of the rapid ramp-up in manufacturing capacity. The International Energy Agency estimated that the worldwide installed capacity of electrolysers by the end of 2021 was only 513 megawatts but predicts that it will reach up to 17,000 megawatts by the end of 2026.[11] This will be achieved by a number of manufacturers building electrolyser gigafactories in the coming years.

The third main contribution to the cost of hydrogen production is the capacity factor of the renewable electricity. The capacity factor is the percentage of time over the course of a year that the electricity is available. Traditional generators such as coal, gas or nuclear power can in principle operate for more than 90% of the hours in a year. But solar electricity operates much less than that, with a capacity factor of just over 10% in northern Europe and up to 30% or thereabouts in optimally placed solar farms in sunny climates. Wind electricity can have capacity factors ranging from 30% to 50% depending on siting.

If the sole input to the electrolyser is solar electricity with a capacity factor of 25%, the electrolyser will be significantly underutilised and its amortised cost contribution will be high. If solar and wind are combined, as in the US Department of Energy's price calculations, so that the hybrid capacity factor is above 50%, the amortised cost contribution will be medium. If the renewable electricity capacity factor is above 90%, the amortised cost contribution will be low and the target of $1 per kilogram could be achieved even if the electrolyser cost is well above the US$300,000 target. A capacity factor above 90% can be achieved by combining wind electricity with hydropower.

To achieve a better capacity factor at hydrogen production facilities that happen to be connected to an electricity grid, producers can sign contracts with remote solar or wind generators to produce and supply the required amount of electricity. The electrons consumed at the production facility will be drawn from a mix of nearby generators, but the contract guarantees that the exact same number of electrons will be generated by the solar and wind generators over the course of a day, week or month, and not sold twice. This is practical, fair and reasonable.

But not for the European Union. The European Union in February 2023 published a Delegated Act that requires hydrogen production to be supplied by additional renewable electricity generation on a monthly basis until 2030 and on an hourly basis thereafter.[12] Markus Krebber, CEO of the German energy company RWE AG, which is rapidly transforming into a renewable energy leader, complains that these requirements risk strangling the development of the hydrogen economy.[13] This kind of requirement is not imposed on other sectors of the economy, such as electric vehicle charging or cryptocurrency mining. The Delegated Act appears to be a classic case of the pursuit of perfection being the enemy of the good.

Blue hydrogen

We have accepted as a fundamental premise that in future, fossil fuels will be replaced by electrifying everything and, where electricity is not directly suitable, using hydrogen and its chemical derivatives. The International Renewable Energy Agency World Energy Transitions Outlook 2022 report estimates that 12% of final energy delivery will be as hydrogen, used as an energy carrier or as a chemical.[14]

The trouble is, when we produce 'green' hydrogen by cracking water using renewable electricity, much of the electrical energy is lost in producing and using the hydrogen. Let's assume that across a variety of production and use cases half the electrical energy is lost.

In that case, in a future energy system where 12% of the final energy delivery is green hydrogen, to include the electricity for hydrogen production the actual electricity generation would be 112% of what would be needed if all of the final energy delivery were electricity. That means more energy transition materials, more mining and more strain on the supply chain.

An alternative is to produce the hydrogen from natural gas or other fossil fuels. This is called 'blue' hydrogen, and would use negligible quantities of energy transition materials compared with green hydrogen production. However, unless something is done to prevent it, large quantities of carbon dioxide would be released into the atmosphere as a by-product. For hydrogen made this way to be acceptable, the upstream and processing systems would have to be emissions-free, and the emissions from the chemical reaction to make the hydrogen would have to be captured and buried, essentially forever, in a process called carbon capture and storage (CCS). Success will depend on economics, which in turn will be dependent on the price of natural gas, the price of constructing new facilities and the availability of government support such as the substantial tax credits available in the United States for each tonne of carbon dioxide permanently stored.

The blue hydrogen must be subject to a certification process to verify the emissions intensity during production. Achieving low levels will require considerable financial investment to reduce upstream methane leakage from the natural gas wells and pipelines, the construction of new processing plants that use renewable electricity for their process heat and pressure, and CCS at the 90% capture level or better. These investments will substantially increase the cost of blue hydrogen. Green hydrogen produced by electrolysis will be subject to the same certification process, but the cost of ensuring and proving low-emissions intensity for green hydrogen will be low.

There is widespread criticism of blue hydrogen, for two reasons. First, some people object to it because it is likely to be developed by a global fossil-fuel industry that for too long has promoted impractical technologies as an excuse for delay. Top of the list of delaying technologies in Australia was the so-called high efficiency, low emissions (HELE) coal-fired plants that were promoted as clean when in fact they were only incrementally better than the incumbent coal-fired plants. They could more accurately have been called high *emissions*, low *efficiency* (HELE) coal-fired plants.

Globally, the delaying tactic was CCS applied to coal-fired plants, an approach that has comprehensively failed to deliver cost-effective solutions despite decades of trying. The point of failure is the capture step in CCS, not the storage step. Capturing the carbon dioxide from the chimney-flue gases is expensive and inefficient, and is the main reason that CCS applied to coal-fired power plants has been a financial failure wherever it has been tried. In contrast, when hydrogen is produced from natural gas, the flue gas is almost pure carbon dioxide, thus the capture step is virtually free.

The second reason for the criticism of blue hydrogen is that some developers of green hydrogen criticise it to undermine it as a competitor.

In both cases, instead of criticism, it would be more effective to support a robust hydrogen emissions intensity certification scheme that guarantees the clean credentials of the hydrogen irrespective of its origin or 'colour'. Such a scheme will inevitably favour green hydrogen because it will be costly for blue hydrogen producers to achieve an acceptably low emissions intensity.

Guarantee of origin

With hydrogen and hydrogen-derived products, there is not a forensic laboratory anywhere in the world that can work out what the carbon dioxide by-product emissions were during production of the hydrogen. Instead, rigorous certification schemes will be central to ensuring transparency in international hydrogen markets.

Australia has been at the forefront of global certification efforts to date. Internationally, we have been working as a member of the International Partnership for Hydrogen and Fuel Cells in the Economy (IPHE) to develop globally consistent carbon measurement methodologies for the clean hydrogen supply chain, including derivative chemical products that will be used to transport clean hydrogen, such as ammonia. In Australia, the Clean Energy Regulator is trialling the IPHE's methods with industry and developing a Guarantee of Origin certification scheme based on the IPHE's work.

The Guarantee of Origin scheme will not decree to countries or companies the acceptable value of emissions. Instead, each country will retain responsibility for deciding its own acceptability threshold. The important things are that the certification scheme encourages producers to go the extra mile, and that the measured emissions intensity is robust and gives decision makers confidence that it was accurately tabulated and tracked. Similar certification schemes will be required for other commodities such as green ammonia, steel and aluminium.

Market transparency helps to build an efficient global supply chain. In addition to emissions, it declares the technology and country of origin and protects against unacceptable practices such as human rights abuses.

Hydrogen storage

A serious supply-chain limitation to widespread hydrogen use is storage. Traditional fuels are easy to store: coal in a pile; natural gas in tanks, caverns or distribution pipes; oil in tanks or caverns. But hydrogen is trickier.

The main challenge arises because hydrogen has a very low density on a volume basis, despite having a very high density on a mass basis. The volumetric energy density of hydrogen stored at 700 atmospheres is only one-sixth the volumetric energy density of petrol. The volumetric energy density of hydrogen stored as a cryogenic liquid is a quarter of the volumetric energy density of petrol. This means that a tank of compressed hydrogen will be at least six times bigger than a tank of petrol, and a tank of liquid hydrogen will be at least four times bigger. In practice, the hydrogen tanks will be even bigger because the tank walls will be thicker to contain the pressure or preserve the cold, respectively.

On the other hand, the mass energy density of hydrogen is more than twice the mass energy density of petrol. Although this may look like a handy advantage for hydrogen, in practice it is not. In most cases, such as powering an aeroplane or storing hydrogen onsite at a chemical factory, volume is more important than mass.

• • •

To be stored as a gas, hydrogen must be stored either in high-pressure tanks between about 200 and 700 atmospheres, or at low pressure in huge underground caverns. The high-pressure tanks are expensive and impractical for the large volumes that would be required for industrial processes, utility-scale backup or international shipping.

Underground caverns can be salt caverns, porous rocks below sealing layers, or depleted oil and gas fields. Such caverns have been used widely for storage of natural gas and oil, and occasionally for storage of hydrogen. For example, oil-giant Chevron and its partners have stored hydrogen since the 1980s in a salt cavern not far from Galveston, Texas, near the Gulf of Mexico. The cavern is a cylinder 50 metres in diameter and 300 metres tall, with its roof 850 metres below ground.[15] It stores 2,500 tonnes of hydrogen. Wonderful as that is, the trouble with this method of storage is that suitable geological formations are not widely available.

To be stored as a liquid, hydrogen has to be cooled to −253°C. That is much colder and more difficult to achieve than the −161°C temperature of liquified natural gas (LNG). Perhaps it does not sound that much colder; after all, based solely on the numbers it looks to be about 60% colder, not even twice as cold. But the numbers in the Celsius temperature scale are not the numbers to which the laws of physics respond. The temperature should be measured on the absolute temperature scale, called degrees Kelvin (K). Zero on the Kelvin scale is so cold that atoms stop vibrating. There is no lower temperature. Zero degrees on the Kelvin scale happens to be –273 degrees on the Celsius scale. On the Kelvin scale, hydrogen liquefies at 20°K and natural gas liquefies at 112°K. From these numbers, you can see that the temperature of liquefied hydrogen is less than a fifth of the temperature of liquefied natural gas. Liquefied hydrogen is very, very cold.

Getting down to this low temperature takes a lot of sophisticated refrigeration machinery and uses approximately 30% as much electrical energy as the chemical energy in the hydrogen being liquefied.[16] This is not as serious a problem as it might appear, because in an export situation the energy for the liquefaction process would be supplied by inexpensive renewable electricity in the exporting country rather than expensive electricity in the importing country. The amount of energy required to unload the liquefied hydrogen cargo at the importing country is negligible.

All up, shipping hydrogen between continents as liquid hydrogen is expensive. For starters, it requires custom-built ships to carry the cryogenic liquid. There is only one such ship in existence today, an intermediate-sized prototype capable of carrying about 80 tonnes of liquefied hydrogen, built in Japan by Kawasaki Heavy Industries. It is called the *Suiso Frontier*, honouring the Japanese word *suiso*, meaning hydrogen. I was a guest at the ship's launch at the port of Kobe in December 2020. It struck me as representing the beginning of a new era, in which humans will send renewable energy between the continents. Although I have no idea the cost of this sophisticated ship, it is without doubt much more expensive than a coal-carrying cargo ship, which is basically a floating tank with an engine and propeller. The full-scale version of the *Suiso Frontier* planned by Kawasaki has been designed to carry about 10,000 tonnes of liquefied hydrogen.[17] Kawasaki's aim is for the ship to be in service by the end of the decade. It will be a very sophisticated and very expensive ship.

A cheaper alternative is to chemically convert the hydrogen into ammonia. This has the benefit that there are already ships that routinely transport ammonia. If ammonia made from green hydrogen is widely adopted in future, there will be a need for trading hubs, large-scale ammonia storage facilities and many more ammonia cargo ships. The volumetric storage density after chemical conversion is quite a bit higher than for liquid hydrogen.[18] For example, the volumetric energy density of pure ammonia is 50% greater than liquid hydrogen. If the hydrogen is combined with carbon dioxide to make methanol, the volumetric energy density of the methanol is 85% greater than liquid hydrogen.

The process of releasing hydrogen from chemical storage is called dehydrogenation. This is usually quite difficult, requiring catalysts, energy and purification steps. Much simpler is to use the derivative as it is. Ammonia can be burned as a fuel, so if it is practical to do so it makes sense to burn it rather than take steps to release and burn the hydrogen.

In that light, ammonia is being tested in Japan as a co-firing fuel to replace up to 30% of the coal in coal-fired electricity plants.[19] To materially reduce emissions, the replacement rate will have to be much higher, ultimately 100%. At this time, there are too many fuel-supply and combustion challenges to know when that might be achieved. Ammonia has also been proposed as a replacement for bunker fuel in big ships. Like everything, it isn't as simple as it sounds, because ammonia is particularly dangerous to handle, and when it burns there are nitrogen-oxide by-products. Considerable work is being done on furnace and engine designs to minimise these by-products.

Yet another means of chemical storage is to bind the hydrogen into a class of compounds called liquid-organic hydrogen carriers. Prominent among them is methylcyclohexane, or MCH. The process begins with toluene, a petroleum product with many industrial uses including as a paint thinner and an ink solvent. Hydrogen is added to the toluene to chemically convert it into MCH. When hydrogen is needed, heat and catalysts are used to release the hydrogen, leaving behind the original toluene for shipment back to the producer country to start the cycle again.

There are many other carriers for storage, including metal organic frameworks, metal hydrides and potassium borate. All of these are being investigated in academic and corporate labs. The challenges relate to energy density, the amount of conversion energy required and the hydrogenation and dehydrogenation speed.

Domestic distribution logistics

Where hydrogen is to be used remotely, there will be the usual problem of rights of way to build pipelines to send hydrogen from where it is produced to where it is needed. There have been several studies on the re-use of existing long-distance pipelines to carry hydrogen, but the opportunities to do so will be minimal for two reasons. First, the green hydrogen production facility is unlikely to be located near a natural gas field, and so the existing pipelines from the natural gas field to a distribution centre will not traverse the required route. Second, on the principle of building the new before shutting down the old, the hydrogen will need to be transported before the demand for natural gas disappears, and the natural gas pipelines will therefore in many cases not be available for repurposing.

An exception to this logic is playing out in the Netherlands, backed by strong European Union policy support. There, five major industrial clusters – Zeeland, Rotterdam, Amsterdam, Groningen and Limburg – are already connected to each other by a natural gas pipeline loop. Significantly, most of that loop consists of two parallel pipelines, one of which can be repurposed now that gas usage has declined. According to Gasunie, the company responsible for gas transport and storage in the Netherlands and the northern part of Germany, about 85% of the hydrogen pipeline network under construction will use repurposed natural gas pipelines.[20] Adding icing to the cake, Gasunie is also committed to connecting the hydrogen pipeline loop to large underground hydrogen storage caverns currently being developed in the north, in the province of Groningen.[21]

The main challenge for hydrogen distribution is what is referred to as 'final mile' logistics. Where there is an intention to introduce hydrogen as a zero-emissions substitute for natural gas in the metropolitan gas distribution system, the immediate concern is that the pipes will leak hydrogen. Old pipes, made of cast iron, can in principle carry hydrogen at the low pressures used for metropolitan distribution, but because of their age they are not all in good condition. Fortunately, in most cities the old distribution pipes have been upgraded to polyethylene or nylon. Both these materials handle hydrogen very well. The bigger problem is the piping and appliances inside houses and commercial buildings. If hydrogen is blended with natural gas at about 15% or less by volume, many studies have shown that there is no problem. However, if the natural gas were to be replaced by 100% hydrogen, every single building would have to be inspected and the internal piping and appliances upgraded. This would be expensive.

In the absence of using the existing gas distribution systems, there needs to be a solution for distributing sizeable quantities of hydrogen to commercial sites for specific uses. For example, if large commercial buildings and hospitals replace their diesel backup systems with hydrogen backup systems, hydrogen will have to be supplied.

Similarly, hydrogen must be supplied to vehicle refuelling stations. In the early days, hydrogen for vehicles is being produced at the refuelling station sites. But this will not be practical as the number of refuelling stations grows, because the electrolysers used for onsite hydrogen production are complex machines that need maintenance and take up a lot of space. Instead, the electrolysers should be remotely located. The hydrogen could be distributed using swap-and-go containers, like for barbecues, although much bigger, probably in the form of 20-foot and 40-foot shipping containers. The same swap-and-go distribution system would be used to supply backup systems in commercial buildings and hospitals. Hydrogen can also be distributed efficiently as liquid hydrogen. The goal should be for the hydrogen delivery logistics to be as efficient as the existing truck-based system for distributing petrol and diesel fuels.

Myth busting

Building the global hydrogen industry we dream about will be hard enough, so it is important not to get distracted. As we set about doing so, there will be critics and pessimists who will see fatal flaws. These seeds of doubt are sincerely sewn, but not necessarily good predictors of future outcomes.

I am reminded of the famous Lord Kelvin, who formulated the first and second laws of thermodynamics and after whom the absolute temperature scale is named, but who didn't get everything right. In 1895 he thundered, 'Heavier-than-air flying machines are impossible!' Awkwardly for him, just eight years later, Orville and Wilbur Wright successfully launched their heavier-than-air aeroplane from the sandy dunes of Kitty Hawk.

Let's look at a couple of oversimplifications that are myths undermining important low-emissions technologies.

The first concerns hydropower. I recall half a dozen years ago reading reports claiming that because of methane emissions from anaerobic decay of submerged plant matter, the emissions from hydropower reservoirs per megawatt-hour of electricity produced were worse than those from coal and gas power plants. But that was a gross simplification.

In a careful review prepared as a background paper for the 2004 United Nations Symposium on Hydropower and Sustainable Development, scientists from Hydro-Québec and the University of Quebec concluded that although emissions from hydropower reservoirs are real, hydropower in temperate and high-latitude climates is as good as solar electricity.[22]

In tropical climates, emissions from hydropower reservoirs are more complicated. A 2019 study by scientists from Cornell University concluded that the median carbon intensity of proposed Amazon upland reservoirs was just 39 kilograms of carbon-dioxide equivalent per megawatt-hour of electricity produced, while for proposed lowland reservoirs the median carbon intensity was 133 kilograms.[23] A small number of the proposed lowland reservoirs were very bad, with emissions potentially exceeding that of the 900 kilograms from a coal-fired plant. The logical conclusion must be that rather than condemning the hydropower industry as a whole, critics should focus on the emissions from individual proposed reservoirs, especially in tropical climates.

The second myth started with two papers published in 2022 on a UK government website. One, by academics from the National Centre for Atmospheric Science, the University of Cambridge and the University of Reading, described a credible new approach to calculating the 100-year global warming potential of hydrogen, yielding a value of 11, double the previous estimates.[24] Interestingly, hydrogen itself is not a greenhouse gas. Instead, it has an indirect effect, reacting with methane and ozone in the troposphere to increase their global warming potential, and similarly with stratospheric water vapour and ozone.

The other paper was quite alarmist. It was a report by Frazer-Nash Consultancy.[25] This report suggested that possible high rates of leakage during electrolysis, compression and shipping, combined with the high global warming potential of hydrogen, meant that green hydrogen production and use might be as emissions intensive as fossil fuels.

But the leakage rates used for this analysis were so substantial that they lacked credibility. The hydrogen losses would be costly, dangerous and inconsistent with modern production technology. First of all, hydrogen is expensive, so producers do not want substantial amounts going to waste. Second, hydrogen is dangerous, so producers cannot allow it to leak. Finally, facilities will mostly be new and will be designed to maximise production.

In early 2022, I had the opportunity to put to rest one of the claims, which is that hydrogen leakage to the atmosphere would be very high during shipment of liquefied hydrogen. I visited the *Suiso Frontier* after it made a test voyage from Kobe, Japan, to the Port of Hastings near Melbourne, Victoria, with its insulated tank filled with liquefied hydrogen.

The losses on a liquid hydrogen carrier ship are known as boil-off. The captain kept meticulous records. The boil-off rate was remarkably low. During their 30-day voyage, it was about 0.15% per day. More importantly, instead of venting the hydrogen to the atmosphere they burned it first. End result? The only gas vented to the atmosphere was water vapour. That is, instead of large amounts of hydrogen leakage as postulated in the consultant's report, the amount of hydrogen vented was zero. Despite hydrogen having a global warming potential of 11, the simple arithmetic is that zero times eleven is zero.

In summary, assuming usual best practices, there is no reason for concern that a future hydrogen industry will contribute to global warming.

The moral is to always interrogate underlying assumptions and analyses, so you know where they got it right and where they got it wrong.

Use it where you make it

When I led the development of Australia's National Hydrogen Strategy in 2018 and 2019, much of the focus was on shipping sunshine, consistent with the way natural gas is produced and consumed. That is, the site of use is far from the wellhead, with the gas delivered long distances by pipeline or up to halfway round the world by ship.

But my thinking has developed since then. Large quantities of renewable electricity and hydrogen are required to produce green iron, green fertiliser, green methanol and synthetic jet fuel, so why not produce these decarbonised products where the electricity and hydrogen are immediately available? The benefit arises from avoiding the handling and transportation costs of the low-density raw materials.

Let's look at the numbers. As we have already noted, the generally accepted target for the unsubsidised cost to produce hydrogen from electrolysis is US$2 per kilogram by the end of 2030, falling to US$1 per kilogram in the longer term.

The trouble is that the rapid drop in production costs is not likely to be matched by a drop in handling and transportation costs, with the perverse result being that these could exceed the cost of the hydrogen itself. A joint Australian and German study called HySupply found that international shipping of one kilogram of hydrogen in liquefied form will add US$2.80 for the pipelining to the liquefaction facility, storage, liquefaction, shipping and transfer to storage at the receiving port. The same study found that handling, conversions and shipping of one kilogram of hydrogen chemically bound up in ammonia adds about US$2.30.[26]

Compared to the targeted US$1 per kilogram, the handling and transportation costs of hydrogen are very significant. In contrast, shipping high-density end products such as green iron, green fertiliser and synthetic fuels is cheap.

The inevitable conclusion is that instead of shipping hydrogen and raw materials separately over long distances, a more efficient approach is to build integrated facilities that combine renewable electricity and hydrogen production and specific manufacturing plants to produce 'X', where X could be hot-briquetted iron, steel, alumina, fertiliser, synthetic aviation fuel or ammonia.

In many cases, using hydrogen where it is made would also apply to the immediate opportunity to use green hydrogen to replace existing uses of grey hydrogen, where the term 'grey hydrogen' is used to describe the production of hydrogen from fossil fuels without any attempt to eliminate by-product carbon dioxide emissions during production.

In summary, to avoid the expense of shipping hydrogen, implement an integrated usage model, following the mantra *use it where you make it*. Some important examples follow.

Green iron

It is not much of an exaggeration to refer to iron ore as rust. As soon as deposits of iron consolidated during the formation of the Earth's crust, the iron started to oxidise and turned into fields of rust. Hence, the red colour of iron-ore mine sites.

In traditional steel making, the first step is to reverse the millions of years of rusting by stripping off the oxygen to leave behind elemental iron. That is done in a blast furnace. There are many refinements that can be made to blast furnaces to incrementally cut their emissions, but in a world where customer interest is in zero-emissions products and where the sense of urgency to decarbonise is increasing, the only technologies we will discuss here are those that aim to eliminate emissions. Further, because global steel demand is forecast to increase more than 50% by 2050, driven by economic development in Asia and Africa, there is ample opportunity for steelmakers to invest in new plants that aim for zero, rather than invest in incrementally reducing the emissions intensity of their existing plants.[27]

There are two main ingredients that go into the blast furnace: metallurgical coal and iron ore. The metallurgical coal is about 90% carbon. The iron ore is about 60% iron oxide; the rest is a mix of worthless earthy substances known as gangue. The metallurgical coal has two roles. The first is to be the fuel that heats the iron-ore mixture in the blast furnace to 1,600°C and higher. As the coal burns, carbon dioxide is produced.

The second role is to be a chemical that will reverse the natural rusting process and turn the iron oxide into pure iron. In chemistry, this chemical reaction is called 'reduction'. In the blast furnace, the unburned carbon directly reacts with oxygen in the hot air introduced into the furnace and produces carbon monoxide. The carbon monoxide molecules chemically interact with the iron oxide to remove the oxygen atoms from the iron. The outputs of this chemical reduction process are carbon dioxide and molten iron.

In both roles, huge amounts of carbon dioxide are produced. Globally, the steel industry is responsible for about 8% of carbon dioxide emissions.

The alternative, low-emissions approach gaining much attention uses hydrogen as the reducing agent. The use of coal is entirely eliminated. The new process is called hydrogen direct reduction (HDR) of iron ore.

To start, renewable electricity is used to produce green hydrogen. Separately, additional renewable electricity pre-heats iron-ore pellets. The iron-ore pellets are dropped down a vertical reduction shaft, where they mix with hydrogen pre-heated to 800°C rising from the bottom.[28] The hydrogen removes oxygen atoms from the iron and bonds with them to form water vapour, which is harmlessly released to the atmosphere, leaving behind elemental iron. The pellets remain solid throughout; that is, they do not reach melting temperature. The iron emerges at the bottom of the shaft as solid but porous pellets known as sponge iron, which from a distance look somewhat like truffles.

The sponge iron can be immediately fed to an electric arc furnace where it is alloyed with other elements to make the desired grade of steel. Alternatively it can be compacted and turned into hot briquetted iron (HBI) to be shipped to other sites at home or abroad for the specialised production of steel and fabricated steel products. It makes economic sense for steel to continue be made by traditional steelmakers close to where it is used, because there are so many varieties of steel produced to meet customer needs. Steel is made from iron to which different amounts of carbon, manganese, chromium, nickel, molybdenum, titanium, cobalt and vanadium are added to produce the alloys that optimise cost, strength and durability for applications as varied as automobile panels, high-rise buildings and all-weather balustrades and marine bollards. And in addition to a plethora of alloy compositions, the steel is fabricated into a variety of shapes. In contrast, green iron is green iron.

Separating the iron making from the steel making is poised to be a revolutionary change to the global steel supply chain. In countries like Australia, today we ship the iron ore very cheaply in big ships that can carry more than 200,000 tonnes and cost about US$100 million each. The metallurgical coal is transported in similar giant ships that cost a similar amount. Because shipping is so efficient and inexpensive, there is no economic reason for traditional blast furnace production of iron to take place in Australia, other than for our own domestic needs.

For an importing country such as Japan or Korea to continue to undertake both the iron making and the steel making in future HDR processing, they would have to import hydrogen, at great expense. They would also need to be able to supply renewable electricity for the HDR process despite that being in short supply in their country. It makes more sense in future for the iron-making step to take place in Australia.

The theoretical quantity of hydrogen for reducing hematite to pure iron is 54 kilograms of hydrogen per tonne of iron.[29] The actual amount required in practice is very close to this value, with 58 kilograms of hydrogen per tonne of iron being reported by the Energy and Resources Institute in New Delhi.[30] Producing a tonne of new steel typically requires about 0.77 tonnes of metallurgical coal.[31]

Looking at the costs, the forecast price of metallurgical coal out to 2024 is approximately US$150 per tonne.[32] At this price, the cost of 0.77 tonnes of coal would be US$115. The commonly expressed target price for green hydrogen by the end of this decade is US$2 per kilogram. At this price, the cost of 58 kilograms of hydrogen would be US$116, competitive with coal. The very ambitious target price from the United States Department of Energy for green hydrogen is US$1 per kilogram by the end of the decade. At this price, the cost of 58 kilograms of hydrogen would be US$58, cheaper than coal.

Of course, it is not as simple as this because of capital costs and other plant operating costs, but this basic comparison shows that the hydrogen pathway for green steel can ultimately be cost-competitive with coal. The biggest difference is that with HDR, most of the costs are upfront capital costs, whereas for conventional blast-furnace technology with metallurgical coal, operational expenses make up a much bigger portion of the total cost.

The most commonly used iron ores for making iron and steel today are hematite (Fe_2O_3) and magnetite (Fe_3O_4). The HDR iron process ideally requires iron ore with an iron content of 67% or more.[33] The majority of iron ore mined today is lower-grade than this, but magnetite can be more easily beneficiated, or concentrated, in part because magnetite is magnetic, making it easier to separate from gangue.

For this reason, many new iron-ore mine projects are focussed on magnetite, potentially shifting the supply chain focus away from hematite. This is of concern to the existing miners of hematite, who are investigating means to ensure its ongoing suitability.

The potential for direct-reduced iron has inspired a major new project in Sweden, near the Arctic Circle. A start-up named H2 Green Steel has raised €260 million (A$320 million) in equity and €3.5 billion (A$5.6 billion) in debt financing for the establishment of a steel-making facility expected to produce 2.5 million tonnes of green steel per year.[34] Green hydrogen will be produced onsite from locally sourced hydropower and wind electricity, a combination that will allow constant supply 24 hours per day.

Interest has been strong, and H2 Green Steel has advance contracts for 1.5 million tonnes per year from car makers BMW and Mercedes-Benz, and appliance makers Electrolux and Miele. These manufacturers are responding to the preference of their customers for green products.[35] Commentators are excited, seeing this as marking the rebirth of heavy industry in Europe in the post-fossil fuel era. Adair Turner of the Energy Transitions Commission said that decarbonising European industry has turned from mission impossible to 'mission possible'.

As the effort to use hydrogen instead of coal in the reduction of iron ore to elemental iron gathers pace, another horse has entered the race: molten oxide electrolysis (MOE), being the direct electrolysis of iron oxide (iron ore) to elemental iron, akin to the direct electrolysis of aluminium oxide (alumina) to elemental aluminium in an aluminium smelter. Pioneered by a United States start-up, Boston Metal, the process begins by adding iron oxide to a molten electrolyte in a containment vessel. A powerful electric current heats the iron oxide and electrolyte to 1,600°C, at which point the electrons in the current split the bonds in the iron oxide. Pure liquid iron sinks to the bottom of the containment vessel and oxygen bubbles out the top.[36]

A potentially important advantage of molten oxide electrolysis claimed by Boston Metal is that it works with all grades of iron ore. Boston Metal was founded in 2013. It hopes to have its first commercial plants in operation in the mid 2020s.

In the commercialisation race, HDR of iron is several lengths ahead of molten oxide electrolysis, but with two horses in the race the additional competition is likely to drive more ingenuity and better outcomes.

Green ammonia

The world uses lots of ammonia, 235 million tonnes in 2021.[37] About 70% is used in the production of fertiliser, a little is used to make domestic cleaning products, some is used in hairdressing salons in hair colouring, and the rest is used in industrial applications such as plastics, synthetic fibres and mining-industry explosives.[38] New uses for green ammonia include its potential use as a transport fuel for large ships and to replace coal in existing thermal power stations.

In addition to having a higher energy density per litre than liquid hydrogen, another advantage of ammonia over liquid hydrogen to power ships is that it is much easier to handle. Ammonia kept at 17 atmospheres of pressure is a liquid at temperatures up to 45°C. While 17 atmospheres of pressure might sound like a lot, it is routinely managed in many industries, including the existing global ammonia industry. Significantly, it is far, far lower than the 700 atmospheres at which gaseous hydrogen is stored in a fuel-cell electric vehicle. Equally important, transporting and operating at ambient temperature is obviously much easier than operating at the −253°C temperature of liquid hydrogen.

Simply put, green ammonia made from green hydrogen and a zero-emissions synthesis process could potentially scale up as an easy to handle, easy to store and easy to use zero-emissions fuel. It would underpin a future supply chain not that much more difficult than the oil-based supply chain so widely used at present.

Of course, nothing is ever so simple. There are two disadvantages of ammonia. The first is that it is toxic and corrosive to human tissue on contact. Yet ammonia is one of the most widely used chemicals in the world. Like for electricity and other fuels, strict safety regulations and proper handling procedures must be followed.

If ammonia is to be used as a clean fuel for the maritime fleet, it is unlikely to be used for passenger ships or inland waterway ships, but would be suitable for ocean-going cargo ships.[39] Of the 70,000 or so large ships in regular use, fewer than 10% are passenger ships.[40] Thus, if green ammonia were used on large cargo ships but not passenger ships, the potential to reduce emissions in the international maritime fleet would be substantial.

The second disadvantage of ammonia is that when it burns in an internal combustion engine or turbine, the combustion is never complete and nitrogen oxides (NOx) are emitted. These contribute to acid rain and can also cause respiratory diseases such as emphysema and bronchitis. So, if by burning ammonia the level of nitrogen oxides pollution were to rise significantly, that would simply be trading one problem for another. Manufacturers of marine reciprocating engines and turbines are working hard to design fuel-injection systems and catalytic converters to minimise the nitrogen oxide emissions to the levels allowed by international standards.

An alternative approach is to use ammonia as the fuel in high-temperature fuel cells such as solid oxide fuel cells (SOFCs).[41] For most applications, SOFCs are not suitable because of their long start-up times and poor response times. But they would work well if paired with batteries for long voyages at sea.[42] They operate at high efficiency levels of 60% or more to produce electricity to drive electric motors. Best of all, with careful design they operate without any nitrogen emissions.[43] The only emissions are water vapour and nitrogen.

Production of ammonia (NH_3) requires that one atom of nitrogen be combined with three atoms of hydrogen. Traditionally, the hydrogen is produced from natural gas in a process that emits large quantities of carbon dioxide. For green ammonia, the hydrogen must be sourced from renewable electrolysis.

Nitrogen is abundant in the Earth's crust but importantly, it is 78% of the atmosphere. The easiest way to obtain pure nitrogen is to remove it from the atmosphere by refrigerating the air to approximately −200°C, at which point both the oxygen and the nitrogen liquefy and can be separated in a distillation column. The nitrogen and hydrogen are combined at high heat and high pressure using the Haber-Bosch process. This process is energy-intensive, typically powered by natural gas. Ammonia production using the conventional Haber-Bosch process accounts for 3% of global carbon dioxide emissions.

The ammonia of the future must be produced without by-product emissions. The refrigeration process to extract nitrogen from the air and the electrolysis process to split water to produce hydrogen lend themselves directly to running on renewable electricity. The Haber-Bosch process can continue to be used if it is powered by zero-emissions electricity. In general, that will require either a major overhaul of existing plants or building them from scratch.

Green fertiliser

While increasingly the word 'green' is used to describe renewable energy and emissions-free industrial production, it is worth considering for a moment the earlier use of the word, going back to the 1960s, to describe the agricultural revolution pioneered by Norman Borlaug.

Crop yields in Asia were not keeping up with population growth. Borlaug realised that one of the reasons was that the tall wheat varieties prevalent at the time were investing too much of their energy into the stalks and not enough into the grains in the spike at the top of the stalk. He bred a variety of dwarf wheat that had much heavier spikes and doubled the yield per hectare. At the same time, through Borlaug's and other scientists' work, rice and wheat cropping intensity increased from once per year to two or three crops per year, increasing the annual yield even further.

That was step one. Step two was to encourage the use of inorganic fertiliser made from ammonia and its derivatives, urea and ammonium nitrate. Both techniques were applied to other crops, and over the decades in the United States, corn yields increased fivefold and rice yields increased more than threefold.[44] While some environmentalists are critical of the use of high-yield crops and inorganic fertiliser, the stark reality is that without them we would need three times the world's current agricultural land to produce the amount of food consumed today.[45]

The fertiliser that is part of the green revolution is most often made from ammonia. By replacing the high-emissions ammonia used today with ammonia made from hydrogen in a modified Haber-Bosch process powered by renewable electricity, both meanings of the word 'green' will be applicable to the green revolution.

Integrated plants in which solar and wind electricity and perhaps hydropower are used to produce hydrogen from water, extract nitrogen from the atmosphere, then combine the two to make ammonia could reduce global emissions by 3%. There are many locations around the world suitable for such plants, and so there is every reason to expect that there will be country diversity in the supply chain.

Renewable diesel

For a variety of reasons, growth in biofuels over the last 30 years has been slow. Innovation to produce higher-quality varieties might be the shot in the arm the sector needs.

Conventional biodiesel is made from plant oils through a chemical reaction called transesterification. About 1 kilogram of an alcohol such as methanol in the presence of a catalyst such as sodium hydroxide is mixed with 10 kilograms of plant oil to yield 10 kilograms of biodiesel and 1 kilogram of glycerine as a by-product.[46] No hydrogen required. The feedstock can be recycled vegetable oil, or more likely oils freshly extracted from crops such as palm, rapeseed, canola and soybean.

The main technical limitation of conventional biodiesel is that it tends to gel at low temperatures. The gel temperature depends on the feedstock, ranging from +16°C for biodiesel from palm oil to – 10°C for biodiesel from canola oil. For use in winter, biodiesel must be selected for the climate and blended with fossil diesel.

To overcome these limitations, interest is growing in a modern alternative called renewable diesel, also known as green diesel or hydrogen-treated vegetable oil. It starts with the same plant-oil feedstock but is made by using hydrogen to break large molecules into smaller ones, or by adding hydrogen to existing molecules.

Renewable diesel is a much higher-quality product than biodiesel. It has very similar characteristics to fossil diesel, including a very low gel temperature. It is potentially a drop-in substitute for use in diesel vehicles. The Finnish company Neste, which is the largest producer of renewable diesel, estimates that the reduction of greenhouse gas emissions over the fuel's lifecycle is up to 90% compared with fossil diesel, depending on the source. Neste's 2022 global production is predicted to reach 3.8 billion litres.[47]

The US Department of Energy predicts that renewable diesel production in the United States will increase from 2.2 billion litres per year to 7.6 billion litres per year by the end of this decade.[48] This compares to consumption of 177 billion litres per year of conventional diesel fuel in the United States.[49] Some analysts predict that farmers in the United States will not be able to increase their acreage of soybeans to provide the feedstock for forecast quantities of renewable diesel.[50]

There is also a broader debate about using food crops for fuel, both in terms of the environmental impact of broad-acre farming, and ethical concerns while people continue to be malnourished in less developed parts of the world.

Sustainable aviation fuel from biomass

Sustainable aviation fuel (SAF) may be made from a wide variety of biomass feedstocks, including harvest waste, forestry residues, plant oils and municipal waste. It is a drop-in alternative to jet fuel refined from crude oil. Jet fuel is used in aircraft that have turbine engines, such as jet aeroplanes, turboprop aeroplanes and most helicopters.

One of the most significant sources of harvest waste is bagasse, the dry, pulpy residue after the juice is squeezed from sugarcane. Bagasse is particularly suitable because it is available in bulk at the sugar refinery, thereby minimising collection costs. It would otherwise mainly be used to generate electricity and heat, which is a good but not particularly high-value use of the material and contributes to particulate pollution.

Another high-volume harvest waste is the rice straw that remains in the drained fields at the end of the rice harvest. The term 'straw' refers to the stalks left over after the rice grains have been harvested. In the past the straw was left to decompose and contribute to the nutrients in the soil, but with the intensification of agriculture most rice is grown in two or three crops per year, leaving insufficient time between crops for the straw to decompose. As a result, the trend is to burn the straw, which is not only a waste of the nutrient and calorific value but also adds to atmospheric particulate pollution, which is a significant problem in the north of India.[51] In short, rice straw is an ideal source of biomass. The problem is that globally, rice straw is spread over more than 160 million hectares. The cost of collecting it would add significantly to the cost of producing SAF. The same is true of other grassy crops, including wheat, oat and barley.

Another potential material is the biogas that is emitted from landfill, waste organics and wastewater treatment. Largely consisting of a mixture of methane and carbon dioxide, it can be processed directly into SAF, while the addition of green hydrogen will increase the yield and reduce process carbon dioxide emissions as more of it is combined with the hydrogen to produce liquid fuel.[52] In Nevada, Fulcrum BioEnergy has produced its first crude oil from municipal solid waste that otherwise would have gone to landfill, with the synthesised oil to be refined alongside fossil crude.

Feedstock from forestry and plant oils depends on implementing sustainable farming practices that do not compete with food agriculture needs or result in further land clearing or loss of biodiversity. The US Department of Energy estimates that theoretically, enough deliberately grown feedstock and waste streams exist in the United States to supply the projected fuel demands of the country's aviation industry.[53] However there are also competing uses for these feedstocks including diesel-powered road vehicles and electricity generation.

Finally, there is increasing interest in SAF made from ethanol, known as alcohol-to-jet-fuel. Several different processing pathways are in development, with a big attraction being that ethanol from sugarcane or corn grain is already a large global industry, particularly in Brazil and the United States.

In the long term, demand for SAF is likely to outstrip demand for renewable diesel, since most road and rail vehicles will be electrified. In the meantime, many feedstocks and production pathways can produce either SAF or renewable diesel, or both. The most common production pathway is the hydrotreated esters and fatty acids (HEFA) process, which converts fats, oils and greases into liquid fuel.[54] Most demonstration flights and early contracts for commercial quantities of SAF are based on HEFA.

However, because the aviation industry, for good reason, is very conservative, no SAF is yet allowed to be used as a drop-in replacement. Instead, it can be blended at up to 50% with fossil jet fuel, yielding a product that is so similar to fossil jet fuel that it creates no operational restrictions. By the end of the current decade, it is expected that most SAFs will be allowed as a drop-in replacement, although in practice, for reasons of availability and cost, they will likely continue to be blended.

Neste is aiming to produce 1.9 billion litres of SAF fuel in 2023. This would be a massive increase in supply, which worldwide was just 0.125 billion litres in 2021, but it is nevertheless small compared with global consumption of fossil jet fuel, which was 360 billion litres in 2019.[55] There is no consensus that there will be enough biogenic feedstock for SAF to replace fossil jet fuel in the long term, but a coalition of aviation experts known as the Air Transport Action Group estimates that there will be enough feedstock if there is a global commitment to scaling up supply, with US$1.5 trillion investment required out to 2050.

Significantly, the Action Group makes the point that it will be essential to channel feedstocks towards aviation rather than electricity generation and other transport sectors such as trucking, where alternative energy sources are already available.[56] They also note that batteries and hydrogen in short-haul and medium-haul aircraft, respectively, will to some extent reduce the need for SAF.

Solar kerosene

Fossil jet fuel is a complex mixture of hydrocarbons distilled from crude oil. The actual mix depends on the source of the oil and the refinery processes. Reduced to its basics, jet fuel is kerosene, with small amounts of additives. Each molecule of kerosene is like a string of pearls, where the carbon atoms are the pearls and the hydrogen atoms decorate them. There are two hydrogen atoms attached to each carbon atom in the string, except the two carbon atoms at the end of the string, which each have three hydrogen atoms. The shortest string is usually 12 carbon atoms long and the longest string 15 carbons long.

Albeit at high cost, kerosene can be synthesised from its two elemental ingredients – hydrogen and carbon. No other elements required. The carbon can come from carbon dioxide captured from the air, as will be described in the next section. The hydrogen can come from water electrolysis. Renewable electricity can be used to drive both processes and the synthesis that combines the carbon and hydrogen.

That is, the three ingredients to produce synthetic kerosene are renewable electricity, air and water. In a paper by researchers from ETH Zurich and published in *Nature*, the authors described a pilot-scale solar refinery that demonstrated the feasibility of the entire process for converting solar electricity, air and water into synthetic fuels. In a moment of marketing brilliance, they referred to this high-end product as 'solar kerosene'.[57] To avoid confusion, we will use the more common terminology, synthetic jet fuel.

In fundamental terms, synthetic jet fuel is a circular process with no waste and the only input being renewable energy. It is truly carbon neutral; the same quantity of carbon dioxide that is expelled from the jet engine when the fuel is burned is used as an input to the synthesis process to make the replacement fuel for subsequent flights. The problem is that the amount of input energy required is large, making synthetic jet fuel very expensive, at least for now.

One way to synthesise jet fuel from the carbon dioxide and hydrogen ingredients, used by the oil giant Shell in a pilot project, is to combine the hydrogen and carbon dioxide using the Fischer-Tropsch process.[58] Small quantities of synthetic jet fuel made this way were blended with regular jet fuel and used in February 2021 for a flight from Amsterdam to Madrid, which was the first in the world to use synthetic jet fuel.

This is very much a case of innovation building on innovation. The Fischer-Tropsch process was developed in the 1920s by German scientists to use its abundant reserves of coal to produce petrol and diesel that it desperately needed.

This kind of innovation could ultimately lead to an unlimited source of aviation fuel, able to be made in any country that has abundant renewable electricity.

Direct air capture of carbon dioxide

We saw in the previous section that to make carbon-neutral synthetic jet fuel, the carbon dioxide ingredient must be captured from the air. It sounds implausibly difficult, but companies and academic researchers are making good progress. Today, synthetic jet fuel made this way would be much too expensive, but engineers and developers are optimistic, having seen the prices of solar electricity, wind electricity and batteries drop at previously inconceivable rates.

They are motivated not just by the opportunity to produce a solution for the aviation industry but also by the opportunity to reduce the atmospheric concentration of carbon dioxide. The phrase constantly in the media and on everybody's lips is 'net zero emissions by 2050'. Nobody talks about achieving 'zero emissions by 2050'. For good reason. There are many sources of emissions from agriculture, waste decomposition and industrial processes that are too costly, too difficult, or verging on impossible to avoid. Thus, we cannot hope to get to zero emissions. But if we can remove carbon dioxide from the air and permanently sequester it, and if we can do that at the scale of the residual emissions after we have done as much as we can to reduce emissions, then we can achieve net zero.

The International Energy Agency's *Net Zero by 2050* report modelled the need for 7.6 billion tonnes of carbon dioxide to be removed annually from the atmosphere by 2050 to get to net zero. The United Nations IPCC scenarios on average require twice that, 15 billion tonnes, to be removed annually.[59] This is a huge task, between 15% and 30% of the approximately 50 billion tonnes of greenhouse gas emissions emitted annually today. The world has barely begun this journey.

One way to remove carbon dioxide from the atmosphere is through nature-based solutions, such as growing and preserving forests. Another is to use technology to directly capture carbon dioxide from the air. In brief, fans are used to direct air towards a medium that captures carbon dioxide. Once the capture medium has become saturated, it is heated or chemically treated so that the carbon dioxide is released and sent off for permanent storage by burying it underground or reacting it with rock formations.

The first cost challenge in capturing carbon dioxide is that considerable electrical energy is required to heat the capture medium. Minimising this energy requirement is an area for continuing research.

The second cost challenge is that because the concentration of carbon dioxide in the atmosphere is very low, most of the electricity to drive the fans is wasted drawing in nitrogen, oxygen, argon and water vapour. The concentration of carbon dioxide in the atmosphere is a little over 0.04%. That is just 1 carbon dioxide molecule for every 2,500 air molecules. The hard-working fans have to move 2,499 freeloaders for every carbon dioxide molecule presented to the capture medium.

This is very inefficient. Part of the solution is to turn the fans slowly. The energy required to move a given mass of air depends on the speed squared. That is, if the fan's air-flow velocity is doubled, it takes four times as much electrical energy to move a kilogram of air to the capture medium. Conversely, if the fan's air-flow velocity is halved, it takes only a quarter as much electrical energy to move a kilogram of air to the capture medium.

If the captured carbon is permanently sequestered, the process is known as direct air capture and storage (DACS). The sequestration step is the same as the storage step in carbon capture and storage (CCS). Each tonne of carbon dioxide stored can be sold as a carbon offset. Today, the price of removing and storing a tonne of carbon dioxide is too high, more than US$1,000 per tonne, compared with prices in various carbon trading markets that range from a few dollars up to a hundred dollars or so. The price is expected to drop to below US$300 by the end of the decade, with some technology optimists hoping for US$100 or thereabouts.[60] To help DACS companies get through the costly start-up phase, visionary companies such as Microsoft and the payments company Stripe have been willing to pay premium prices. In one instance, Stripe agreed to pay over US$2,000 per tonne for 250 tonnes of carbon removal.[61]

Two companies that have been prominent in this area are Climeworks and Carbon Engineering, both founded in 2009. In 2021, Climeworks commenced operations at what they billed as the world's largest direct air capture plant, called Orca, in Iceland, to capture and store 4,000 tonnes per year, and in 2022 they started construction of a 36,000 tonne per year facility named Mammoth.[62] Carbon Engineering and its partners Occidental and 1PointFive started site works in 2022 for a 500,000 tonne per year facility in Texas.[63]

These companies do all their processing for a given project at a centralised facility that draws electricity from transmission lines. An Australian company, Southern Green Gas, has opted for a very different approach. They build standalone modules about the size of a two-person tent. Each module has solar panels on the outside surface of its sloping walls. Inside the tent are tiny fans, the capture medium and a battery to support 24-hours-a-day operation. When the capture medium is full, the fans stop and electricity is used to heat it, thereby driving off the carbon dioxide, which enters a pipe, combines with the carbon dioxide from the other modules and goes to a central location for use or storage. Each module can capture up to two tonnes of carbon dioxide per year. The economic logic here is to drive the price down through high-volume manufacturing, much like the way solar farms are cost-effective because each of the millions of solar panels is manufactured at low cost.

All up, these pilot-scale projects are removing a tiny quantity of carbon dioxide from the atmosphere compared with the billions of tonnes that need to be removed annually, but they are the first tentative steps in a critically important direction. It is very early days, but with innovation, generous early funding and markets designed for sustained operation, DACS might be the technology that closes the gap for net zero. It is unlikely that voluntary offset purchases will be sufficient to achieve this goal, so the ultimate success may depend on a mandated high price on carbon emissions in all major markets.

Green cement

Green cement production does not use hydrogen, but it is described in this chapter on the basis that it is a decarbonised product, and an important one indeed because it is the key ingredient in concrete. Huge quantities of concrete are used in wind farms and hydropower reservoirs. The concrete is made by mixing cement, aggregate, sand and water. Making the concrete does not produce significant greenhouse gas emissions, but producing the cement does.

To produce cement, limestone and some clay-like substances are heated in a kiln to 1,400°C. Limestone is calcium carbonate, with the chemical formula $CaCO_3$. The high heat drives a chemical change in which the calcium carbonate is converted to calcium oxide (CaO), also known as lime, by the release of a carbon dioxide molecule (CO_2). The cooled material that comes out of the kiln is ground to form a lumpy substance called clinker, which is then combined with gypsum to form cement. It is important to note that the carbon dioxide emissions described here are from the chemical conversion of limestone into lime. Traditionally, the kiln is heated by burning coal, oil or gas, which is a separate source of carbon dioxide emissions.

Cement manufacturing worldwide in 2021 was responsible for the emission of 2.6 billion tonnes of carbon dioxide, which is more than 7% of the global emissions of 36 billion tonnes.[64] Of that, about half was from burning fossil fuels to heat the kilns and operate the processing plant, and about half was the by-product of the chemical conversion of limestone into lime.[65]

The half from burning fossil fuels can be eliminated by shifting to renewables. However, there is no scalable alternative to the use of limestone to make lime for the cement. For decades, researchers and innovators have replaced some or all of the lime with other cementitious materials, including the slag that is the waste product from blast furnaces, fly ash that is the waste product from coal-fired power stations, and a naturally occurring clay called metakaolin. However, none of these have been adopted in volume, in part because the test and validation requirements for concrete in construction are extensive and difficult, and in part because the sheer volume of concrete used worldwide makes it unlikely that substitutes to limestone will ever be available at the volume required. Concrete is the most extensively used manufactured product in the world, with 30 billion tonnes used every year, nearly 4 tonnes for every human being on the planet.[66]

The most likely way forward is to capture the chemically produced carbon dioxide. In traditional cement making, the flue gas is a mixture of nitrogen, oxygen and carbon dioxide. Separating out the carbon dioxide is difficult and expensive.[67] The difficulty and expense can be overcome in innovative new systems in which the flue gas is a pure stream of carbon dioxide, ready to be taken away and used or buried. For example, Australian company Calix Limited has developed a process in which limestone in a cylinder is indirectly heated and the only gas that emerges is carbon dioxide. This technology is part of a trial in Belgium in which over 7,000 tonnes of chemically produced carbon dioxide will be captured each year.

If the decision is made to permanently sequester the carbon dioxide it is an example of CCS. An alternative is to use the captured carbon in products such as building materials, or even synthetic jet fuel. The benefit of using carbon dioxide captured from cement making to produce a consumable product like jet fuel is that emissions are reduced to 50% of what they would have been if the carbon dioxide vented into the atmosphere and the jet fuel was fossil based. However, good as this is, it is not nearly as good as the alternative of permanently sequestering the carbon dioxide emissions.

Naysayers

Returning to the movie metaphor with which we started the chapter, a constant theme in both the original and the sequel is the presence of naysayers who try to spoil the story.

There are minor roles for marksmen quick to point out that using electricity to make hydrogen to make electricity is not efficient, and that it is more energy efficient to drive a battery electric car than a hydrogen electric car and to use a heat pump to warm a house instead of a hydrogen gas burner. These statements are all true. The laws of thermodynamics are immutable and dictate that there will be inevitable energy losses when using hydrogen instead of electricity, which translates into increased use of resources and higher costs.

This is well known. The intention is not to use hydrogen for hydrogen's sake. Instead, the intention is to use it for those applications where it is more practical than using electricity directly, such as the ones we have discussed, including shipping sunshine as hydrogen or ammonia, in green iron, green fertiliser, renewable diesel, sustainable aviation fuel and synthetic jet fuel, and as a concentrated energy source for long-distance, heavy-haul trucks and forklifts that operate virtually non-stop day after day. There are circumstances, too, where a hydrogen passenger car might be the preferred choice, such as for owners who do not have off-street parking. In some cities, hydrogen might be the most cost-effective solution for heating because of weather and infrastructure.

Other characters make cameo appearances to cry 'Danger!' It is true, hydrogen is dangerous, but so are all fuels, including petrol, diesel, natural gas, propane and electricity. That is the nature of a fuel; their job is to create heat and transfer energy. It is the job of industry, regulators and users to make sure that safety is maximised at all times. Hydrogen has been used extensively for industrial purposes for 100 years with a good safety record. As its use broadens, regulators and industry must ensure that standards are appropriately refined to cover new applications. This is nothing unusual; it is how regulations evolve and standards improve. We already manage the daily use of many dangerous products. Strong medicines have side effects. We manage them by training doctors. Batteries in electric cars catch fire. We minimise the consequences by ensuring firefighters are trained in the specific techniques for fighting battery fires. Cars, bicycles, scooters, trains, trucks, helicopters and aeroplanes are all extremely dangerous, but they have important benefits, so instead of banning them or shunning them we minimise the risks.

Take electricity. We cannot be without it, but it is very dangerous. Deaths and injuries are widespread despite more than a century of constant improvements in testing, certification, work practices, wiring and appliances. In the United States in 2015, electricity caused nearly 5% of deaths in the workplace, four people died on average every week from electrocution at home, and faulty electrical appliances and equipment caused about 140,000 home and workplace fires that claimed an additional 400 lives.[68]

The goal is to minimise emissions reliably, affordably and safely. We need to use all the tools that we can to achieve that goal. Hydrogen is an essential tool in the mix, and for that reason we should not jump at shadows. Instead, we should be aware of its risks and limitations and include them in project planning and regulation design.

Progress

The biggest risk to the hydrogen industry is that it develops too slowly. But is it unusually slow? You could take the start of the modern hydrogen industry as 2017, when Japan published its national strategy, or 2014, when Toyota started commercial sales of the Toyota Mirai, or 2013, when Hyundai began production of the ix35 fuel-cell electric car. It would be reasonable to say that the modern industry is about ten years old. Wind and solar electricity generation started in the mid-1970s, so on that basis those industries are much more mature, approaching 50 years old.

Recently we have started to see some big wins for hydrogen. In 2022, under its first contract to supply hydrogen trains, French train manufacturer Alstom started delivering 14 hydrogen-powered passenger trains to completely replace diesel-powered trains in Bremervörde, Germany.[69] These emissions-free trains have a range of more than 1,000 kilometres and can carry 300 passengers. Alstom has contracts to supply 27 trains for the Frankfurt metropolitan area, six in Lombardy, Italy, and 12 to be used in four different regions in France.[70]

In August 2022, global e-commerce company Amazon announced that it had signed a contract to purchase over 10,000 tonnes per year of green hydrogen from hydrogen mobility company Plug Power. Amazon says this will be enough to operate 30,000 forklifts or 800 heavy-duty trucks used in long-haul transportation. The company already uses more than 15,000 fuel-cell forklifts.[71]

These tangible signs of progress are encouraging, indicating that the hydrogen industry has some runs on the board and is accelerating. Many of the forty countries that have published their hydrogen strategies are providing substantial government incentives to stimulate the industry. Private-sector investment is being attracted by government incentive funding, in particular in the United States, Europe, China and India. It is likely that hydrogen for decarbonised products, specialised transport and synthesised fuels will be well established by the end of the decade.

The combination of policy certainty, significant funding and technology advances provide an exciting script for this movie sequel. It gives me cause to be optimistic that hydrogen will win the 2030 Oscar for best supporting clean technology – with electricity winning the Oscar for best overall.

7.
Getting the Policy Settings Right

The shift from a biomass-based economy to one powered by coal, oil and gas was driven by industrialists, homeowners, shopkeepers, generals, farmers and transportation mavericks. These energy sources were easy to use and the economic and social benefits were transformational.

In contrast, the clean energy transition underway right now is driven by the externality of carbon dioxide emissions, brought to our attention by scientists. There is no way that the transition would be happening if it had been left to ordinary market economics or immediate end-user benefits. Solar panels would be relegated to powering orbiting satellites, and wind turbines would be spinning hard to provide power to lighthouses.

Government interventions are essential to realising this unnatural transition. While many countries should be admired for what they have achieved, globally there is too little action. Despite the catchcry of the Paris Agreement, the likelihood of keeping the temperature rise to 1.5°C was slim at the time. The higher levels of emissions every year since then, with the exception of 2020, are the death knell of this target. Clinging to the catchcry risks prolonging the mistake of taking comfort from targets unaccompanied by well-planned and well-executed transition pathways.

When evaluating the importance of government policy, the poster child is Denmark. At the time of the oil crisis in 1973, when Arab-state members of the Organisation of Petroleum Exporting Countries (OPEC) deliberately restricted oil production, Denmark was importing 90% of its energy supply.[1] The Danish government responded to the crisis by encouraging the development of oil and gas reserves in the North Sea, while at the same time turning to bioenergy and wind. The government used tax policies and mandates to drive the shift towards wood pellets, solar power and wind power. These included grants to support the adoption of wind turbines on private properties and taxes on electricity consumption to fund investment in renewables. These subsidies were accompanied by a legislated focus on efficiency, such as requiring power companies to build new natural gas power plants within the city limits and capture the waste heat from their generators to heat buildings and water. Subsidies for wind power were so successful that by 2022 they were no longer required for offshore wind farms to be profitable. Almost without precedent in other countries, the five decades of progress since 1973 have enjoyed cross-parliamentary support.

In dollar terms, Germany's commitment was much greater. Feed-in tariffs for solar electricity were legislated in 1991 and helped pay for the boom in wind and solar power. In later years, the financial support shifted to reverse auctions for solar and wind farms. Decades of subsidising investments in renewables have added up to more than US$580 billion through to 2025, including more than US$210 billion in the eight years from 2013 to 2020.[2] Germany is rightly credited with having helped to establish the modern era of solar electricity for the world.

Following the Global Financial Crisis, in 2009 the Chinese government launched an economic stimulus package, of which more than US$30 billion was for solar power and other clean power deployments.[3] This was followed by US$43 billion for solar-panel production in 2010.[4] By 2016, the annual cost of subsidies for renewables in China was US$9 billion per year.[5] These and other industrial policies in China have resulted in China deploying far more solar and wind electricity across the nation than any other country. Other subsidies and mandates have led to China building and selling more electric vehicles than the rest of the world combined.

The United States, Australia and many other countries have provided incentives and implemented mandates and renewable energy schemes for solar, wind and other zero-emissions technologies. In Australia, these policies, over more than a decade, led to the highest solar capacity per person in the world. In the United States, in 2022, Congress passed the most significant climate legislation in its history, an enormous package of hundreds of billions of dollars of direct incentives.

Carbon-pricing instruments such as carbon taxes and emissions trading schemes to encourage the shift to low-emissions practices have been adopted by Europe, the United Kingdom, Canada, Norway and 64 other national and sub-national jurisdictions. The World Bank reported that in 2021, 36 carbon-tax schemes and 32 emissions trading schemes covering 23% of global emissions provided revenue to governments of US$84 billion. However, fewer than 4% of global emissions were at a carbon price of US$50 or more, regarded as the price needed to meet the Paris Agreement goals.[6]

Despite the enormous success these public investments have stimulated, much more needs to be done to drive the rapid electrification required for net zero.

Carrots vs sticks

Most economists argue that an economy-wide price on carbon dioxide emissions – a carbon tax or an emissions trading scheme – is the most efficient and cost-effective way to stimulate the shift to net zero emissions. The principle is that with an explicit price on emissions, the market will find the most economical paths forward, and financial markets will be mobilised globally at the enormous scale required.

A fundamentally different alternative to carbon pricing is the use of subsidies funded from the public purse. Examples include feed-in tariffs, renewable energy certificates, reverse auctions, grants, loans, production tax credits and capital expenditure tax credits. The rationale for using government spending is the urgency of deploying zero-emissions alternatives.

One way to compare carbon pricing with the use of subsidies is to consider the 'green premium', a term made prominent by Bill Gates in his 2020 book *How to Avoid a Climate Disaster*. The green premium is the difference in price between an incumbent carbon-intensive product and a zero-emissions alternative. If the green premium shrinks to zero, a rational purchaser will buy the zero-emissions alternative.

There are two ways to eliminate the green premium. The first is the imposition of carbon prices to make the incumbent more expensive. The second is the use of subsidies to drive down the price of the zero-emissions alternative.

In the vernacular, subsidies are the carrots, while carbon prices and capital constraints are the sticks.

Sticks

Carbon pricing

The idea for an emissions trading scheme took root at the Kyoto Protocol meeting in 1997. The following year, economists Richard Cooper of Harvard University and William Nordhaus of Yale University proposed carbon taxes as, in their view, a more efficient alternative.[7] Emissions trading schemes, also known as cap-and-trade schemes, create a market out of a product – a tonne of carbon dioxide – that would not otherwise be valued. Taxes impose a specified cost on that same product and generate revenue.

In an emissions trading scheme, the government authority determines the total acceptable emissions for the year, which are then divided into tradeable units called carbon credits and allocated to scheme participants. Participants who emit above their allocated units must purchase credits from others who have surpluses. The European emissions trading scheme is by far the largest by revenue in the world. It has been in place since 2005.

The price of the one-tonne 'allowances' under this scheme has risen fivefold over the last five years, trading at €88 (A$140) at the close of 2022.[8] The scheme covers carbon dioxide and nitrous oxide emissions, but notably does not include methane emissions. About 40% of the European Union's greenhouse gas emissions are covered.[9]

The desirable outcome, in which companies take steps to reduce their emissions, is not guaranteed, because some companies will choose to pass on their costs to consumers, or purchase credits, or pay penalties rather than invest in expensive low-emissions technologies or efficiency measures. Although purchasing credits is consistent with the economy-wide goal of reducing emissions for that year, it postpones the kind of investment by the company that would provide long-term emissions reductions. Prices are volatile, so to manage risks companies turn to secondary markets and brokers, paying fees that impose non-productive costs on the sector.

Carbon taxes, by contrast, are predictable and cannot be avoided by purchasing credits, but they require governments to have a high degree of insight into the appropriate dollar value to be levied.

Ideally, the revenue raised by carbon taxes or by government sales of allocations in emissions trading schemes is used for a combination of support for economically less well-off segments of the population who are disproportionally affected by higher prices of basics like energy and food, and direct support for clean technologies through research, development and deployment.[10]

In the two years from 2012 to 2014 that Australia had a carbon tax, the government did exactly that. Revenue was returned to households indirectly as increases in the tax-free threshold and social security payments.[11]

Not all governments provide such compensation. The 'Yellow Vests' protests that started in France in 2018 were sparked by anger at the government's planned increase to fuel taxes, a policy intended to discourage consumption. The fuel tax was a carbon tax that inadvertently put financial pressure on consumers who were unable to change their fuel consumption, such as farmers, truck drivers and rural residents who did not have access to the same mass transportation options as urban residents.

Carbon consumption tax

Ideally, carbon-pricing schemes (taxes or trading schemes) would be implemented across the economy, and in all countries. However, they have been compromised in their implementation and have not driven investments as efficiently as hoped. The compromises have been to limit carbon-pricing schemes to certain sectors of the economy and to apply them to production within the host economy. These production-linked carbon-pricing schemes put domestic manufacturers at a disadvantage compared with foreign manufacturers, contributing to de-industrialisation in the host economy and domestic emissions being offshored to other countries. The planet is no better off. To avoid this, numerous exemptions are allowed, often gamed by the domestic manufacturers.

Because not all countries have or are likely to implement carbon-pricing schemes, and because even if they did, they would probably not agree to the same rate per tonne, a better alternative to carbon-production pricing would be a carbon consumption tax. Such a tax would be applied to all goods, whether produced domestically or imported. Carbon consumption taxes avoid the need to protect trade-exposed industries, avoid the offshoring of manufacturing, and allow countries to do what is right without fear of being disadvantaged.

In his 2012 book *The Carbon Crunch*, Oxford University economist Dieter Helm argued for a carbon consumption tax with two parts: a domestic tax on carbon and a tax on carbon imports. Finally, ten years later, the European Union committed to implementing the second part of Helm's proposal, the carbon border adjustment mechanism (CBAM), to tax the carbon content of some imports. The CBAM will commence in January 2026 and apply to imported aluminium, cement, electricity, hydrogen, fertilisers, iron and steel. Importers will pay the difference between the European carbon price and any carbon price that may have been paid in the country of origin.[12] With the addition of the CBAM, the European emissions trading scheme will no longer put trade-exposed European companies at a competitive disadvantage that might lead to them transferring production to other countries. The CBAM will be more efficient than the current compensation, which provides free allowances to selected companies, and it will eventually lead to those allowances being phased out.[13]

The headwinds today are blowing in the direction of government subsidies, but efficient carbon pricing such as the carbon consumption tax would encourage innovative solutions in sectors of the economy not specifically covered by subsidies.

Capital constraints and shareholder pressure

A variation on carbon pricing is the imposition of capital constraints through investors withholding funds. The intention is that the threat or reality of reduced access to funding will discourage further investment in fossil-fuel assets.

Other measures exist that are also intended to force behavioural change. One well-known such measure, driven by shareholder activists and environmental, social and governance (ESG) investment, is to pressure companies to divest their fossil-fuel assets. The desire is laudable – put pressure on companies that extract and refine fossil fuels so that they get out of the fossil-fuel business. But the pressure to divest is subject to the saying from Aesop's Fables, 'Be careful what you wish for.'

Shareholder pressure and capital constraints have led many high-profile companies, such as ExxonMobil, Royal Dutch Shell and BP, to start selling what is likely to be US$100 billion worth of oil and gas fields.[14] However, for every seller, there is a buyer, and this is the problem. Before divestment, the oil and gas fields are in the hands of publicly traded, highly accountable companies. The buyers are typically private or state-owned companies that are not accountable to the public and in many cases run the oil and gas fields less carefully, with the result that the planet is worse off. An example was the sale by Royal Dutch Shell of its share of the Umuechem oil field in Nigeria in 2021. Immediately afterwards, operating procedures changed and the new operators started to burn excess gas at such a significant rate that it was detected from space.

An alternative to pushing companies to divest their oil and gas assets would be for investors to encourage them to spend a substantial share of their net revenue from those assets on developing and deploying low-emissions alternatives, which would then become a new revenue stream while lowering the demand for oil and gas, eventually leading to those oil and gas assets becoming obsolete and closing down.

The ambition should be *investment, not divestment*. Investment in the clean technologies for a sustainable future rather than selling high-emissions assets to less-accountable operators.

An example of a company pivoting to *investment, not divestment* was the closure of the Hazelwood power station in Victoria in 2017. The owner-operator was French multinational utility company ENGIE. Its mission statement is 'to act to accelerate the transition towards a carbon-neutral economy'.[15] Consistent with that philosophy, and faced with substantial maintenance costs, ENGIE judged that alternative suppliers in the electricity market could fill the gap and closed the power station. There was an electricity price spike as a result, but then a return to normal. ENGIE chose to invest in clean technology solutions and to close its thermal coal asset rather than divest. Today, ENGIE has 2,000 megawatts of wind, solar and utility-scale battery projects under development in Australia.[16] It was far from a painless exercise, however, because ENGIE failed to give adequate notice to the government and local communities, leaving workers and their families distressed and with no plan for the future.

The *investment, not divestment* approach has been successful time and time again. An example of investing in superior alternatives is what happened with the displacement of fixed-line telephones by mobile phones. It is what happened with the replacement of incandescent light globes by light-emitting diodes. In both cases, government had a role early on but once the new contender was perceived by consumers as being superior, the market blossomed, and the rest is history.

Carrots

Increasingly, governments are turning to subsidies to drive the transition to low-emissions solutions across their economies.

The advantage of taxpayer-funded subsidies is that they can be specifically directed to drive the adoption of initiatives that would otherwise be unaffordable before reaching scale. These initiatives include scaling up zero-emissions technologies, permanently reducing demand through efficiency measures, and ensuring that important elements of the supply chain are available from a variety of source countries and suppliers.

Such measures provide lasting benefits in the host country and ultimately in other countries by driving down costs for future adoption. They can also be used to thwart unacceptable practices in the supply chain, such as forced labour and child labour. In some cases, they are also used to achieve economic benefits such as the creation of regional jobs, and foreign policy benefits such as avoiding supply-chain dependencies on Russia and other countries of concern.

Made in America (the United States Inflation Reduction Act)

On 16 August 2022, President Biden signed into law the awkwardly named *Inflation Reduction Act* (the Act). The centrepiece of the Act is a series of investment and production tax credits estimated by the Congressional Budget Office to amount to US$391 billion over ten years. That's big, but because many of the measures are open-ended, the amount may end up being considerably higher. Global investment bank Credit Suisse estimates that the likely spending will be in the vicinity of US$800 billion.[17] Given these tax credits will attract several investor dollars for every dollar in tax credits, the total investment driven by the Act into clean energy technologies will be in the trillions. The hope is that this big step in spending will enable the United States to cut its emissions by 42% below 2005 levels by 2030.[18]

The Act is all carrot. That is, it is silent on carbon taxes and silent on emissions trading schemes, either by deliberate choice by the administration or in tacit acknowledgment that carbon pricing would never have been agreed to by a divided Congress. The Act offers tax credits, loans and grants for investments in specific technologies, including solar farms and solar rooftops, wind farms, electric vehicles, batteries, hydrogen, carbon capture and storage and sustainable aviation fuels. Other areas funded are lifetime extensions of existing nuclear power plants, home energy-efficiency upgrades, advanced manufacturing, so-called climate-smart agriculture and other assorted community-oriented expenditures.

Some of the production subsidies are quite extraordinary. Let's look at three examples.

To start, renewable generation projects such as wind, biomass, geothermal, hydropower, municipal solid waste, and wave and tidal electricity are eligible for a production tax credit that could be as high as US$33 per megawatt-hour.[19] In its March 2022 update, the US Department of Energy estimated that the unsubsidised cost of wind electricity will be US$37 per megawatt-hour for new wind generation entering service in 2027.[20] Thus, the fully subsidised price would be an astonishingly low US$4 per megawatt-hour.

Next up is carbon capture and storage (CCS). Eligible CCS projects will qualify for a US$85 production tax credit for each tonne of carbon dioxide captured and sequestered. Given the costs for CCS depend greatly on the process from which the carbon dioxide is captured and the distance to the storage site, the costs range between US$20 and US$140 per tonne. The level of production tax credit offered by the Act could eliminate the cost overhead of capturing and permanently storing carbon dioxide emissions in many industrial processes, especially those that produce a highly concentrated stream of carbon dioxide that is easily captured and is in proximity to cost-effective storage sites such as depleted oil and gas wells.[21]

An even higher production tax credit applies to CCS where the carbon dioxide is drawn from the atmosphere via direct air capture. In this case, the rate can be as high as US$180 per tonne of carbon dioxide sequestered.[22] This incentive has the potential to massively accelerate the rate of adoption of this important but expensive approach to closing the final gap between emissions and net zero.

The third example is the production tax credit for hydrogen, which can be as much as US$3 per kilogram if all the wage, apprenticeship and emissions intensity requirements are met. Notably, the Act does not care whether the hydrogen is green hydrogen made using renewable electricity, purple hydrogen made using nuclear electricity, or blue hydrogen made using natural gas with CCS.

The emissions-intensity requirement is very stringent. To earn the maximum production tax credit, the lifecycle emissions to produce the hydrogen must be less than 0.45 kilograms per kilogram of hydrogen produced.[23] This is a very tough but laudable goal. There are consolation prizes for facilities that do not meet this goal, because the production tax credit is provided on a sliding scale. If the lifecycle emissions are more than 4 kilograms per kilogram of hydrogen produced, there is no production tax credit at all. This is appropriate, because at that level the emissions are not much lower than burning natural gas.

The current trading price for grey hydrogen in the United States is between US$1.50 and US$2 per kilogram, whereas green hydrogen is trading for between US$4 and US$8 per kilogram. The US$3 per kilogram subsidy for eligible green hydrogen would make it immediately cheaper than grey hydrogen in some cases. If the production price for green hydrogen falls to the US Department of Energy stretch goal of US$1 per kilogram, eligible facilities will be able to give away their hydrogen for free and still make a handsome profit, limited only by the fact that the production tax credit is restricted to the first ten years of the facility operation. All up, this tax credit is likely to spur a boom in green hydrogen production and the electrolysers to make it.

On the estimates calculated by the Congressional Budget Office, the *Inflation Reduction Act* raises more revenue than it spends. The estimated savings will come mostly from reducing expenditure on prescription drugs. The revenue comes mainly from introducing a 15% corporate minimum tax, tax-collection enforcement, new taxes on stock buybacks and other measures. The spending is mostly on energy transition and climate-change mitigation, plus US$108 billion to extend Obamacare and to subsidise vaccines and insulin. The net deficit reduction estimated by the Congressional Budget Office is US$238 billion over ten years.[24]

While the estimates may be wobbly because the tax credits are uncapped, the Act itself is not, at least not for the next two years. It was legislated as a reconciliation bill, which means that the spending is fully appropriated and authorised. The only way it could be reduced would be by passage of new legislation through both houses of Congress, and even then President Biden could veto the legislation. So, the Act is safe at least until the 2024 election.

It is important to note that the *Inflation Reduction Act* is not simply an economic bill, focused on revenues and expenditure. It also includes many political and social provisions. President Biden has proudly referred to it as pro-worker and pro-union.[25] He points out that it will lower the cost of prescription drugs, healthcare and energy, and that no one earning less than US$400,000 will pay a dollar more in personal taxes. To earn the full tax credits, businesses will have to pay prevailing wages and hire apprentices. Tax credits will be further increased if clean energy projects are established in communities that were previously reliant on coal, oil or natural gas industries.

Very significantly, the Act is replete with 'made in America' provisions. If we did the same in Australia, our own economists would cry foul and we would expect to be chased through the courthouses of the World Trade Organization (WTO).

Under the *Inflation Reduction Act*, businesses will be incentivised to manufacture on American shores.[26] Tax credits will be higher if American steel is used in wind turbines. Other local-content provisions ensure that buyers of electric vehicles will only qualify for subsidies if the minerals used in their batteries were mined and processed in America, Canada, Mexico or countries such as Australia and Chile, with which the United States has a free trade agreement (FTA).

These provisions hurt producers in the European Union because the European Union does not have an FTA with the United States and thus buyers of European cars will not qualify for the purchase subsidy. European automakers are angry, and their concerns are being examined by a taskforce of officials from the European Union and the United States, created two months after the Act was signed into law.[27] President Emmanuel Macron of France suggested that the European Union should consider a 'Buy European' Act to protect European car makers. His frustration was clear: 'You have China that is protecting its industry, the US that is protecting its industry and Europe that is an open house.'[28]

One can only hope that officials on both sides will find a way forward to preserve the benefits of globalisation and avert a subsidies-driven trade war. The declared position of the United States is that Europe should copy the American subsidy model for its own industries.[29] The fear in Europe and the UK is that in the long run, the *Inflation Reduction Act*, together with tensions with China, will threaten the competitiveness of the European Union and the UK.

Within days of the passage of the Act, the South Korean industry minister declared that his country would consider whether to file a complaint with the WTO on the basis that the Act may violate WTO rules and the bilateral trade agreement between the United States and Korea. In December 2022, the Chinese Ministry of Commerce told a meeting of the WTO's Council for Trade in Goods that they suspect the Act violates WTO principles and will seriously damage global trade and investment.[30]

The general risk for most countries is that the *Inflation Reduction Act* will act like a magnet, prompting companies to set up new factories in the United States because of the massive financial incentives. America will increasingly attract global investment and skilled workers. At the end of August, shortly after the Act was passed by Congress, battery manufacturer Panasonic Holdings announced its intention to build a US$4 billion battery plant in the United States.[31] Not to be outdone, Japanese car company Honda announced that it will retool its existing facilities in Ohio to produce electric cars. In a joint venture, Honda and Korean battery company LG Energy Solution announced a US$3.5 billion battery plant in Ohio to supply Honda's car-production facilities.[32] All up, by the end of February 2022, just six months after the *Inflation Reduction Act* was legislated, US$90 billion of investment had been committed to clean energy projects, including solar panel, electric vehicle and battery factories.[33]

Even though it might disrupt global trade, the Act will ultimately benefit the world by reducing the future cost of green technologies, just as subsidies in Germany reduced the cost of solar electricity in the early days. The massive investment in research and innovation and the scaling up of manufacturing will, like the leading riders in a bicycle peloton, cut through the cost barriers and reduce the difficulty of decarbonisation in developing countries.

There is another important provision in the Act that does not get as much coverage as the tax credits. This provision authorised the Department of Energy to issue up to US$250 billion in low-interest loans for projects to transform existing energy infrastructure.[34] In plain terms, the loans are for renovating and repurposing existing infrastructure for new clean-energy projects. For example, placing utility-scale batteries at closed coal-fired power plants in order to use the existing land, transformers and transmission lines. Loans could also be provided to help nuclear plants to stay open longer, or for the repurposing of oil refineries to produce modern biofuels.

The *Inflation Reduction Act* was the capstone following two other important pieces of legislation. One week earlier, in August 2022, the US$253 billion *CHIPS and Science Act* was signed into law. The CHIPS part provides US$79 billion for subsidies to build semiconductor chip-fabrication plants in the United States and for semiconductor research and development. The Science part provides more than US$170 billion over five years for science and technology education, research and innovation.[35] None of this is specific to energy or climate, but there will be indirect benefits from strengthening technological innovation and workforce skills.

Nine months earlier, in November 2021, the *Infrastructure Investment and Jobs Act*, more commonly known as the Bipartisan Infrastructure Law, was signed into law. Of the US$1.2 trillion spending provision, US$550 billion was for new spending.[36] Some of this was for clean energy and power programs, including US$9.5 billion for clean hydrogen hubs and electrolyser manufacturing, US$7.5 billion to contribute to a national electric vehicle charging network, US$5 billion for electric school buses and US$73 billion for transmission lines.

The Bipartisan Infrastructure Law also allocated US$3.5 billion to support four large-scale direct air capture hubs and US$4.9 billion for three carbon capture and storage projects.[37] Together, these funding allocations are likely to massively accelerate the adoption of direct air capture for negative emissions.

Fields of orange

The *Inflation Reduction Act* does more than dispassionately invest in the clean energy transition. It has a strong focus on jobs creation. But not just any jobs. It favours jobs that are well paid, skilled, and located in rural and regional areas, especially areas at risk of losing traditional jobs. For example, there will be dedicated grants and tax credit multipliers to support jobs and investment in the traditional car-building regions.

If you took a flight east to west, north to south across America, you would see fields of orange in all directions, being the tinge from the carrots that are bringing economic stimuli to all regions.

All up, Republican-governed (red) states benefit as much as Democratic-governed (blue) states. Indeed, the top three states for wind generation are red – Texas, Iowa and Oklahoma.[38] In October 2022, a series of grants totalling nearly US$3 billion for batteries and critical mineral production went to companies in eight red states and four blue states.[39] At the end of August 2022, First Solar, the largest solar- panel manufacturer in the United States, announced major expansion plans. It committed to upgrading the capacity of its existing facilities in Ohio, another red state, and to building a major new manufacturing facility that it subsequently declared will be in Alabama, another red state.[40] In announcing the decision, the company specifically stated that its decision was in response to the passing of the *Inflation Reduction Act*.

Investments like these mean that even if the US election in November 2024 returns the presidency to the Republican Party, it is unlikely that Republican representatives in a future national Congress would want to reverse legislation that is driving investment in their states. Weaning governors and business from the financial teat would be difficult.

The US federal government support for the clean energy transition is not unique. Let's look at some of the responses.

Europe

In March 2023, the European Commission, the executive arm of the EU, released new rules that will allow member countries to match subsidies provided by other nations where there is a risk that investments in batteries, solar panels, wind turbines and heat pumps will be diverted away from Europe.[41] This relaxation of the state aid guidelines is a direct response to the subsidy race started by the US *Inflation Reduction Act*.

At around the same time, the European Union also announced their *Critical Raw Materials Act* to ensure that the EU will have access to the energy transition materials needed for its electric vehicle, wind and solar industries. Under the *Critical Raw Materials Act*, the European Union will aim for 10% of its raw energy transition materials to be mined onshore and 40% to be refined onshore.[42] While it was not decided at the time of writing, there was discussion about enhancing the provisions for energy and raw materials in existing free trade agreements with supplier countries.

California, Canada, Germany and Japan

In legislation passed in late August 2022, a few weeks after the *Inflation Reduction Act*, California committed to reaching net zero by 2045. Specifically, California intends to cut greenhouse gas emissions at least 85% by then, and to offset its remaining emissions by planting trees and using direct air capture and storage.[43] Following nearly a decade of reliance on an emissions trading scheme, California approved a budget that will directly spend US$54 billion over five years on climate programs, including electric vehicles, public transport and the electricity grid. The funding also extends the operation of the Diablo Canyon nuclear power plant by five years, from its previously scheduled closure in 2025 to 2030. Weeks earlier, the California government announced that by 2035, all new cars and small trucks sold in California must be zero emissions.[44] To hasten the uptake of large zero-emissions trucks, California committed to providing an incentive of up to US$288,000 per truck.[45]

In Canada, all ten provinces have been required since 2018 to have either a carbon tax or an emissions trading scheme in place. In March 2022, the Canadian government announced a 2030

Emissions Reduction Plan to help it achieve its target to cut emissions by 40% in 2030 compared with its 2005 baseline. This includes direct investment in electric vehicle charging infrastructure and a mandate for all new passenger vehicles to be zero-emissions by 2035. The plan covers building efficiency, industry decarbonisation, CCS, wind power, solar power, reducing upstream emissions in oil and natural gas projects, and nature-based carbon dioxide sequestration. There was also a C$3.8 billion (A$4.2 billion) commitment to supporting the development of Canada's critical minerals industry.

In November 2022, taking a leaf out of the *Inflation Reduction Act*, the Canadian government proposed a 30% tax credit for investment in solar, wind, nuclear power and water-based electricity generation (small hydro, run-of-river, wave and tidal), electricity storage, clean hydrogen, heat pumps, solar heating, and hydrogen and battery electric heavy-duty vehicles used in mining and construction.

Recently, among other endeavours, Germany committed to investing €9 billion (A$14 billion) to support green hydrogen projects.[46] In July 2022, Germany committed a further €178 billion (A$280 billion) over four years to accelerate its shift to clean energy. The funding will be used to improve the energy efficiency of older buildings, to further develop the hydrogen sector and to incentivise the uptake of electric vehicles among lower-income and middle-income earners. In another clean energy transition commitment, in 2022 Germany announced a target to install 500,000 electric heat pumps annually from 2024 onwards, to permanently cut reliance on fossil-fuel heating. This will be achieved by banning new oil and gas heating and yet-to-be-specified government support for ramping up production.[47] Adding to the funding pool but not directly in support of the clean energy transition, in October 2022 Germany announced €200 billion (A$320 billion) to fund energy price caps and subsidies for German industry and consumers over the following two years.[48]

Japan, in December 2022, announced details of its green transformation roadmap, known as the GX Roadmap.[49] The roadmap calls for the government to spend ¥20 trillion (A$220 billion) this decade to stimulate much greater private investment. The government spending will be financed by the issue of GX transition bonds that themselves will be repaid by a carbon pricing scheme. The ambition is to transform not just the energy industry but society, too. It is a comprehensive package of measures that includes regulations, subsidies, carbon pricing, disclosures and financing. The carbon pricing is planned to commence in 2026 with the introduction of emissions trading for power companies that have high emissions, and then to expand to other industrial sectors by 2028. The roadmap will promote the use of hydrogen and ammonia and the construction of new transmission lines. In a major step, the roadmap declares the Japanese government's intention to extend the life of existing nuclear power plants and to consider replacing decommissioned nuclear power plants with new ones.

Australia

Australia has been moderately successful in its solar and wind uptake. Following record levels of investment, solar and wind's share of electricity generation across the nation jumped from 9% in 2017 to 27% in 2022.[50] As a consequence, coal-fired electricity's share fell from 71% to 56% and natural-gas-fired electricity fell from 13% to 9%. By the end of 2021, the installed solar generation capacity was 990 watts per person in Australia, the highest in the world, followed by 760 watts per person in the Netherlands and 710 watts per person in Germany.[51]

The more ambitious targets and policies brought in by the change of government in May 2022 will build on this base, with a target of 82% renewables by 2030 (inclusive of an estimated 6% hydropower). The passage of legislation by the previous government in 2021 to enable offshore wind farms in Australia will open up new opportunities for the 2030s.[52]

The federal government policies that have been effective in Australia are the grants from the Australian Renewable Energy Agency

(ARENA), debt and equity financing from the Clean Energy Finance Corporation (CEFC), the Renewable Energy Target, Export Finance Australia (EFA) and the Northern Australia Infrastructure Facility (NAIF). The Renewable Energy Target was particularly effective, and Ross Garnaut has advocated for its extension beyond 2030. The Low Emissions Technology Roadmap in 2020 and 2021 provided funding for hydrogen, supported a ten-year funding allocation for ARENA, international partnerships in low-emissions technology demonstration programs and high-efficiency, low-cost solar.

The Albanese government has committed A$20 billion to a loan program for transmission lines and a further A$3.5 billion for grant funding and allocations to support the transition to net zero.[53] In addition, the government has announced A$3 billion to support Australian industry to produce green iron and green aluminium, and clean-energy components such as wind-turbine blades and electrolysers.[54]

There are no carbon taxes or emissions trading schemes in Australia. However, the government is in the process of activating an existing scheme called the Safeguard Mechanism that will require Australia's largest greenhouse gas emitters to keep their net emissions below a baseline allowance. The baseline will be progressively reduced each year through to 2050. Companies that emit less than their baseline will receive credits they can sell. Companies that emit more than their baseline will be required to purchase safeguard mechanism credits.[55] It is a version of emissions trading known as a baseline-and-credit scheme.[56]

As with such schemes in other countries, there is a concern that export-oriented companies will suffer a competitive disadvantage, and thus the government has expressed its intention to provide 'tailored treatment' for trade-exposed businesses.[57] This might take the form of financial assistance and differentiated baseline decline rates, or perhaps the allocation of safeguard-mechanism credits.[58] An additional suggestion from the Australian Industry Group, an industry organisation, is for the early introduction of an Australian

Carbon Border Adjustment Mechanism similar to the mechanism announced by the European Union.[59]

The stronger policy efforts of the Albanese government are well supported by increasingly ambitious state governments, which for some years now have provided revenue support for investors through contracts for difference and reverse auctions to stimulate investment in renewables.

The NSW Electricity Infrastructure Roadmap is an ambitious plan to build solar and wind generation, storage and transmission infrastructure sooner rather than later, to fill the gap that would otherwise occur when four out of five of the state's coal-fired power plants retire in the coming decade.[60] In December 2022, the NSW government committed to 70% emissions reduction across the state's economy by 2035.[61]

The Queensland government has committed to 70% renewables by 2032, extensive new transmission lines and two new pumped-hydro storage facilities with a combined 7 gigawatts of storage of 24 hours' duration.[62]

The most recent announcement at the time of writing was from the Victorian government, which committed to introduce legislation to reach 95% renewable electricity by 2035 and net zero emissions by 2045.[63]

The focus on the clean energy transformation is strong, across the nation.

India

India's population is big and growing. In 2023 it is expected to overtake the population of China, with each exceeding 1.4 billion.[64]

India's economy is big and growing. In the last quarter of 2021, the Indian economy overtook that of the UK and became the fifth-largest in the world.[65]

India's energy consumption is big and growing. Driven by rapid industrialisation and urbanisation and a rising standard of living and population growth, energy consumption in India doubled from 2000 to 2022, and India became the third-largest energy consumer in the world after China and the US.[66]

The vast majority of India's energy mix is currently met by three sources: coal, oil and traditional biomass. Rapid economic development saw demand for coal nearly triple between 2000 and 2019, while oil demand more than doubled.

Meanwhile, the share of solar and wind electricity more than doubled from 2014 to nearly 10% of India's total electricity generation in 2021.[67] In 2022, the Indian government declared its target is to increase renewable energy generation, mostly solar and wind, to 500 gigawatts in 2030 from the current installed capacity of about 120 gigawatts.[68] To support this, it has introduced incentives for local production and imposed customs duties of 25% on imported solar photovoltaic cells and 40% on assembled solar modules.[69] The Indian government has also declared its intention to produce at least five million tonnes of green hydrogen a year by 2030.[70] Financial incentives will be provided to boost competitiveness and domestic manufacturing of green hydrogen.

Large Indian companies are eyeing the opportunity to become significant participants in the global supply chain. Reliance Industries, the largest private-sector corporation in India, in 2022 commenced an initial three-year investment of US$10 billion in facilities to manufacture solar panels, wind turbines, batteries and electrolysers.[71] It has also agreed to invest over US$75 billion in the state of Gujarat to establish solar and wind electricity generation capability and green hydrogen production.[72]

China

And then there is China.

Yes, China burns a lot of coal, and it is building new plants at a rapid rate. Of the 176 gigawatts of coal-fired electricity capacity under construction in 2021, 52% was in China. This investment contributes to meeting the inexorably growing demand for electricity from its citizens as they increasingly aspire to advanced-economy living standards. It also provides heat and electricity to power the industries that make the products the rest of the world purchases in vast quantities.

At the same time, however, China is strongly investing in the clean energy future. In 2021, China deployed 48 gigawatts of wind power; the United States deployed 13 gigawatts, the European Union 11 gigawatts and no other country came close. In solar, China deployed 53 gigawatts; the European Union deployed 25 gigawatts, the United States 20 gigawatts and no other country came close. In hydropower, China deployed 21 gigawatts; the United States went backwards by 4 gigawatts and the rest of the world deployed 8 giga-watts.[73] Of 56 nuclear power stations under construction in 2022, 21 are in China.[74] When it comes to zero-emissions electricity, China leads the world, by a long margin.

So, too, in electric vehicles. We have already seen that produc-tion and sales in China were almost 60% of the world total in 2022. Remarkably, during the same year, Chinese car maker BYD (Build Your Dreams) raced past Tesla to become the world's largest manufacturer of electric vehicles.[75] In electric vehicle batteries, the Contemporary Amperex Technology (CATL) company took gold, with 166 gigawatt-hours of battery cells installed from Jan-uary to November 2022, representing a 33% share of the global market. BYD took silver, with 61 gigawatt-hours installed, taking a 14% share of the global market.[76] Between them, these two com-panies produced nearly half the world's supply of electric vehicle batteries.

This success in electric vehicles and battery production is very much to the credit of Chinese manufacturers and their initiative, but government played an important role too. I recall visiting Shenzhen in 2019, where all 17,000 of its buses and all 22,000 of its taxis were already battery electric.[77] To get a sense of the size of those fleets, consider that London has approximately 9,000 buses and New York City has approximately 14,000 taxis.[78] In Shenzhen, 80% of those electric buses and taxis were built by the local company, BYD. The wholesale changeover to electric vehicles was driven by a government mandate supported by generous national and local government subsidies. This combination of mandate and assistance helped to propel BYD to be a world-class manufacturer of battery and plug-in hybrid electric vehicles.[79] I visited the two-storey BYD battery gigafactory and was overwhelmed by the size, the automation, and the fact that there were ten times more research and design engineers in the top-floor offices than production workers on the ground floor.

Similar leadership is shown by China in heat pumps, transmission lines and green hydrogen. As energy analyst Tim Buckley says, 'China literally leads the world in every zero-emissions technology.'[80]

Part of China's success results from its investment in research and innovation. In March 2023, the Australian Strategic Policy Institute published an analysis of more than 2 million research publications in 44 important technological domains such as energy, robotics, batteries, synthetic biology, environment, 5G and 6G networks, defence and artificial intelligence. They found that, stunningly, China was the global leader in 37 of the 44 domains.[81]

All up, energy transition investments in China in 2022 were US$546 billion, almost half of the US$1.1 trillion invested worldwide.[82] This extraordinary level of investment in China, coupled with the substantial investments in the United States, the European Union and many other countries, is good for the planet. However, the parochial nature of much of the investment will continue to challenge the global free-trade mechanisms that have underpinned economic growth since the end of World War II.

Deglobalisation

When I say that we are undertaking the most difficult energy and economic transition since the start of agriculture, I am referring to the enormous technological challenge to build the reliable, affordable, zero-emissions energy system of the future and the huge amount of financing that will be required. Technologically, we are already in the early stages of an exciting transition that will usher in the Electric Age and bring climate change to a halt. In the Electric Age, we will have sufficient clean energy for all our economic needs without the anthropogenic emissions that have created global warming.

What I didn't anticipate is that the transition to clean energy might contribute to a growing global policy concern that has been referred to as deglobalisation. Deglobalisation is described by Markus Kornprobst from the Vienna School of International Studies and Jon Wallace from the independent policy institute Chatham House as 'a movement towards a less connected world, characterized by powerful nation states, local solutions, and border controls rather than global institutions, treaties, and free movement.'[83] The director-general of the WTO, Ngozi Okonjo-Iweala, has referred to present circumstances as a 'polycrisis'.[84]

Whether deglobalisation in the present era is real or not will be judged by history. The most prominent example from the past was the decade leading up to World War II, characterised by isolationism and nationalist foreign policies.[85] The precursors were World War I, the Spanish flu and the 1929 financial crash. In response to these events, countries implemented economic nationalism through import tariffs, localised trading blocs and rejection of international bodies.

In the present era, we have had the Covid-19 pandemic, the Russian war in Ukraine, supply-chain disruptions, the global energy crisis, inflation and debt distress. We have the political turmoil following Brexit and Make America Great Again. There is a growing trend towards bigger government, securing supply chains and focusing economic stimuli on protecting the domestic market. The potential disruptions include lower earnings multiples, reduced investment in productivity, higher costs of capital, higher prices, widening growth rates between countries and lower corporate returns.

We are far from a 1930s world. The concern is the early hints, with much of it centred on the trade pushback by the United States against China's growing global dominance of decarbonised industries of the future. The hope is that we will all benefit from the global technology race to net zero.

Well-functioning markets

Fossil-fuel markets worked. They worked because they brought tremendous convenience to consumers.

We need clean energy markets to work. A supply chain has two ends, as captured in the phrase 'the law of supply and demand'.

When it comes to supplying zero-emissions energy, the market demand is already there. The trick is to ensure the reliability of the new energy sources and to produce policies that help them reach price parity, so that they push out the fossil-fuel incumbents. There is no doubt that solar and wind electricity are already the cheapest forms of new electricity generation, but there is equally no doubt that they force extra costs into the system because of the need to provide firming services through transmission lines, storage, over-building and systems operations.

But these extra costs should not be compared with the *zero* cost of doing nothing. They should be compared with the counterfactual that most developed countries have ageing electricity grids and generation systems that will have to be replaced in any event. With modern requirements for safety and environmental performance, those replacements will be expensive.

Governments can stimulate demand for clean energy through subsidies, mandates, procurement, direct investment and carbon prices. Systematically building demand will attract investors. It provides signals to mining companies and the manufacturers of solar panels, wind turbines and electrolysers that enable them to invest early, thereby minimising supply-chain disruptions.

For example, demand for battery and hydrogen electric vehicles can be greatly stimulated by acknowledging the importance of electric vehicles and providing rebates, tax relief, regulatory design, co-funded charging and refuelling stations, and procurement policies for government fleets. The supply chain will respond: mining companies, battery manufacturers, hydrogen producers and car manufacturers will plan and invest for the future.

Consistent government policies, as in Denmark, where the government and the opposition agree on the fundamental goal and only bicker on the details, provide confidence to investors. This is particularly important for investors in inevitably protracted projects such as transmission lines or copper mines.

Ultimately, the scale of required investment is much greater than what can be achieved by government alone. Well-functioning markets are the answer. Governments can nurture the growth of these markets through sensible regulatory regimes and disclosure rules to ensure transparency in products and transactions.

The moral dilemma of coal exports

The ethics of exports are vexed, and context makes a difference. Back in 2015, then prime minister of Australia, Malcolm Turnbull, said that ceasing Australian coal exports 'would make not the blindest bit of difference to global emissions' because importing countries would turn to other suppliers. He further noted the ongoing role of coal-fired electricity in alleviating hunger and promoting prosperity.

In 2021, Turnbull's successor as prime minister, Scott Morrison, resisted calls to phase out coal exports, saying that the mines had 10, 20 or 30 years of operations ahead of them.

Most recently, Australia's current prime minister, Anthony Albanese, despite his government's strong commitment to rapidly reducing domestic emissions, when asked about stopping fossil-fuel exports, said, 'What you would see is a replacement with coal from other countries that's likely to produce higher emissions.'

This repeated argument is sad but true. This kind of position is sometimes dismissed as the drug dealer's argument: if I don't supply it, others will. But to be fair, there is no moral equivalence. In the case of illicit drugs, there are no worthy outcomes to balance the extreme harm. In the case of coal supplied to countries in need, the worthy outcome is that governments can ensure the provision of electricity to their citizens and heat for their industries. The undesirable outcome, of course, is the compounding damage to our climate.

For Australia to continue to supply coal without investing in both decarbonising our own society and building our export capability to supply energy transition materials to assist the rest of the world would be inexcusable. Increasingly, Australia is making those forward-leaning investments. As Australia and other early-adopter countries invest in clean energy alternatives, the volumes increase, the prices decrease and the clean energy technologies become attractive in their own right for the late adopters and the less economically developed countries.

Developed countries – especially those that are fossil-fuel exporters – should help developing countries build renewable energy microgrids and attract developed-world finance into large-scale renewable projects. Just as we expect companies to do, as nations we should be investing in building alternatives that will eliminate the demand for thermal coal and eventually other fossil fuels.

The developing-world dilemma

The Paris Agreement has failed to deliver on the principle of 'common but differentiated contributions', which acknowledges that the developed world contributed the vast majority of historical carbon emissions, and so should help the developing world to adopt zero-emissions energy systems going forward.

Given that much of the growth in the demand for energy will come from the developing world, net zero globally will not be achieved without the developed world helping the developing world. Decarbonisation is particularly challenging for developing countries given that capital constraints are a key limitation for them. Zero-emissions projects are capital-heavy at construction but have minimal operating costs once built.

The developed world can assist by commercialising and scaling up zero-emissions technologies as has been described, and by providing finance and technological assistance to help developing countries adopt clean energy technologies. At the United Nations climate change conference in Sharm el-Sheikh in 2022, one of the few significant commitments was agreement to provide 'loss and damage' funding for vulnerable countries hit hard by climate disasters. Like many of the other commitments from this series of meetings, the design and operationalisation of this fund was kicked ahead to the next meeting, in Dubai, in December 2023. The dilemma for developing-world countries is the risk to which they are exposed and their inability to attract funding to help them contribute to reducing the risk.

Interest rates

Throughout the world, interest rates rose in 2022 and continued at relatively high levels in 2023 as the central banks fought inflation. The inflation has been driven by the Russian invasion of Ukraine, lingering Covid-related supply-chain pressures, and rising food prices caused by wars, floods and fires.

This is an emerging risk for many clean energy industries, including solar, wind and transmission lines, because most of their costs are capital expenditures rather than operating expenditures. New projects will be hit hard. The majority of the solar and wind assets operating today were built between 2009 and 2021, when interest rates were unusually low.

High interest rates tend to disproportionately affect developing nations. At the COP27 meeting in Sharm el-Sheikh, Prime Minister Shehbaz Sharif of Pakistan referred to the 'debt trap' that is making it difficult for Pakistan and other developing nations to fund projects that would help them with adaptation and decarbonisation. The cost of remedying flood damage in Pakistan in the summer of 2022 was estimated at about US\$32 billion.[86]

At the same conference, the United Nations estimated that more than 50 countries are likely to default in the next few years as a result of high interest rates, high energy prices and high food prices.[87] These problems will inevitably reduce or eliminate their expenditure on climate action. A solution would be 'climate finance', by which rich nations would require public multilateral development banks and export credit agencies to ensure a sustained increase in access to capital at lower interest rates for climate projects in developing countries.[88]

One measure that governments can implement is loan guarantees to help projects obtain the best rates. Other measures, such as reverse auctions and contracts for differences, meet the needs of the electricity system while giving some certainty to projects, thereby helping developers to borrow at best rates. All of this helps, but nothing will help more than getting inflation under control and interest rates down.

Offshoring

Closing down high-emissions industries rather than transitioning them to low-emissions equivalents does not help the planet. For example, in the UK, for complex economic reasons, there has been a gradual decline in heavy industry and manufacturing over many decades, in a phenomenon often referred to as 'offshoring'. The goods that would otherwise have been made in the UK still had to be made somewhere for UK consumers. In practice, industrial output and emissions shifted to China, Thailand and other countries. Back in the UK, emissions attributable to total consumption in 2019 were 41% higher than domestic emissions alone. In China, it was the other way round, with emissions based on consumption being 14% lower than domestic emissions.

Offshoring of industries has been driven more by economics and lifestyle than by deliberate intention, although the latter does happen. For example, to reduce its nitrogen emissions, the Netherlands is proposing to halve its dairy cattle headcount by 2030. Farmers are outraged and have been blocking food distribution centres with their tractors, dumping manure on the roads to create traffic jams and throwing burning bales of hay onto roadside verges. At the cost of devastating the country's dairy industry, these government-dictated measures will indeed reduce nitrogen emissions from the sector – in the Netherlands. The reduced output of milk and cheese will be picked up by farmers in other countries, and the planet will be no better off.[89]

For the common good, it is proper for economically developed countries to lead by example and bear the early-adopter cost of low-emissions alternatives while scaling up their deployment. By doing so, developed countries will eliminate the green premium, thereby making low-emissions technologies more accessible to poor countries.

Closure of coal-fired electricity plants

Even as we celebrate the progressive closure of coal-fired electricity generators, we should give the coal industry credit for having enabled the Industrial Revolution. The steam from coal furnaces and the electricity from coal-fired generators underpinned extraordinary advances in health and wealth for approximately two centuries. Unfortunately, the benefits of coal come with side effects: particulate pollution, which is manageable through technological advances, and carbon dioxide emissions, which are not.

In advanced economies like Australia, coal-fired electricity generators are closing because they can no longer economically compete with solar and wind generation. It is time for them to go, and to applaud the fact that policy settings have created the circumstances where they are being driven out by market economics rather than arbitrarily banned by legislation. This is an example of planned obsolescence providing value to our society.

The clean energy transition will cause pain in some communities, particularly coal-industry communities. Governments are obliged to ensure that workers and communities are well supported. In general, this requires that there be three years' notice of closure – preferably more – to communities to adjust. A well respected example is Germany's Just Transition Fund, which ensures everyone benefits from the clean transition, including coal-industry workers and communities.

ESG: environmental, social and governance standards

Spiderman, in the 2015 Hollywood movie, received astute advice from his Uncle Ben: 'With great power comes great responsibility.'

Similarly, the great power of finance comes with great responsibility. Consideration of environmental, social and governance (ESG) criteria is an attempt to ensure these responsibilities are incorporated into the decisions of corporations and of private, banking, institutional and government investors.

Worthy as the ESG intention is, there is a growing chorus of concern directed against its implementation. In July 2022, an article in *The Economist* argued that 'the environmental, social and governance approach to investment is broken'. [90] Two months earlier, in response to claims that Deutsche Bank had misled investors about the use of ESG criteria in its investment portfolio, German authorities raided the bank's offices in Frankfurt, looking for evidence of greenwashing. Shortly afterwards, the US government opened an investigation into the ESG funds offered by global investment bank Goldman Sachs, citing concerns that the company's disclosures to clients did not accurately describe its investment practices. [91]

One of the problems with ESG is that by grouping environmental, social and governance standards into a single rating, it is difficult to know what a high ESG rating means. Most casual observers tend to focus on the *E*, tacitly assuming that a company's ESG rating reflects its environmental credentials. Even more specifically, they tend to assume that environmental credentials are almost solely about greenhouse gas emissions.

A case in point is Tesla Motors. In May 2022, Tesla was dumped from the S&P 500 ESG Index, a widely followed rating produced by S&P Dow Jones Indices. Tesla CEO Elon Musk responded by tweeting 'ESG is a scam!' Personally, I was shocked, because it is hard to think of a company that has done more to reduce global emissions through the widespread introduction of its zero-emissions vehicles and by stimulating every automaker in the world to start electrifying its fleet. Tesla didn't fail because of the *E*, however: the company failed on the *S* and the *G*. Tesla was removed from the index because of claims of racial discrimination and poor working conditions at some of its factories, and because of crashes linked to the autopilot on its vehicles.[92]

An argument could be made for separating the evaluation into *E*, *S* and *G*, and indeed some indices do provide this breakdown to their subscribers. Even then, however, it is important to be clear what *E* means. Many investors would think it means the company is doing good things for the planet. That may be, but in some cases it means the company is engaging in 'greenwashing' – cleansing its balance sheet, often at the expense of harm to the planet.

For example, although Tesla Motors was dumped from the S&P 500 ESG Index, ExxonMobil was retained. The oil company is on the list partly because the *E* in ESG is a measure of the risk faced by the company, not the risk to the planet. ExxonMobil has managed its risk of being abandoned by financiers or undermined by activist shareholders by selling off some of its oil and gas assets, even though, as we have seen, such sales can produce worse environmental outcomes.

Global mining giant BHP was returned to the Australian S&P/ASX 200 ESG Index in April 2021 after it sold part of its thermal coal business the year before. Explaining why BHP had been excluded and was now being returned, S&P Dow Jones Indices stated, 'the exclusion of BHP Group Ltd prior to the April 2021 rebalance was solely due to its revenue exposure to thermal coal, which was above the threshold of 5% at the time of the previous rebalance.'[93] That is, BHP was excluded because of its exposure to the financial risks associated with having thermal coal assets, rather than because of the impact of those coal assets on the environment. Instead of punishing the company for selling off its thermal coal business, the ratings agency rewarded it.

Putting it in the affirmative tense, the E should reward companies for reducing the emissions intensity of the products they produce, not for offloading products. The E should reward companies for investing in low-emissions substitutes for their high-emissions product lines. An E factor based on these affirmative interpretations would set the stage for transition finance to support sustained emissions reductions within the company's portfolio and at the planetary level.

There are shortcomings in the S and G, too. Investigations by two NGOs, Inclusive Development International and ALTSEAN-Burma, found that in March 2022, more than a year after the military junta took power in Myanmar, 33 companies that were actively providing weapons and communications technology to the junta retained their ESG ratings.[94] In November, Thomas Andrews, the United Nations special rapporteur on human rights in Myanmar, urged companies to make sure that their operations do not directly benefit the junta.[95]

Despite the current pitfalls, it should be acknowledged that responsible investing can help direct finance to mining projects that respect the environment, local communities and their workforces, and to companies that are currently high-emitting but are actively reducing their emissions by investing in new technologies rather than selling off their problems.

Responsible investing would bring more money into the supply chain and the clean energy transition, so tackling the shortcomings in ESG investment portfolios would be better than abandoning the approach. Governments are aware of the problem and taking action, although it is not clear that they are addressing the fundamental problem resulting from ESG funds focusing on risk to the company without simultaneously addressing risk to the natural and societal environment.

In March 2022, the US Securities and Exchange Commission announced new climate-related disclosure requirements for companies. The new requirements unfortunately formalise the focus on risks to the company rather than to the planet, but on the plus side they require all companies to itemise their Scope 1 emissions (that is, emissions caused directly by company-controlled resources) and Scope 2 emissions (indirect emissions from energy purchased by the company). Companies that set an emissions reduction target that includes Scope 3 emissions, or for which Scope 3 emissions are significant, will also have to disclose Scope 3 emissions.[96]

Scope 3 emissions are emissions from sources not owned or controlled by the company. They include transportation of purchased goods, commercial airline flights for company business, and consumption of the company's products by its customers. Requiring companies to disclose these emissions is an awareness-building exercise, as Scope 3 emissions are fundamentally the responsibility of other companies and are already counted in the emissions of those other companies.

In Europe, in June 2022, the European Council and European Parliament announced plans to update the Corporate Sustainability Reporting Directive to ensure that European consumers will 'be better informed about the impact of business on human rights and the environment'.[97] The details are being finalised, with the new requirements to be rolled out in three stages, starting in 2024 and being fully implemented in 2026.

In Australia, ESG or other sustainability reporting is not yet a mandatory requirement, but the corporate regulator has put companies operating in Australia on notice that it is coming.[98]

Globally, the International Sustainability Standards Board (ISSB) and the Global Sustainability Standards Board (GSSB) are working together to coordinate their programs and standards.[99] The intention is to produce a single set of standards that will act as a global baseline for sustainability-related disclosures. However, as with ESG in general, the prime focus is on the sustainability-related risk to companies rather than the net benefit to the planet.[100]

Encouragingly, another approach to driving investment in low-emissions technologies across the economy is the Financing the Transition to a Net-Zero Future (FTT) initiative of the World Economic Forum, launched in 2020.[101] The FTT has developed financing blueprints for the aviation, steel and shipping sectors with a clear focus on the *E*, and on benefit to the planet rather than to companies.

To add to the complexity, a new set of rules, the European Sustainable Finance Disclosure Regulation (SFDR), came into effect in 2021. It imposes mandatory ESG disclosure obligations on asset managers and financial advisors. It operates alongside the European Taxonomy Regulation, which attempts to minimise 'greenwashing' by setting out criteria for determining if an activity is environmentally sustainable.[102] Together, the Taxonomy Regulation and the SFDR strive to ensure transparency in the consideration of sustainability risks and adverse sustainability impacts. Between them, the FTT initiative and the SFDR might drive a welcome shift in focus towards companies' material impact on the environment and society alongside their financial performance.[103] The European Union created the term 'double materiality' in 2019 to describe this approach.

As yet, most of the worldwide US$40 trillion ESG funds are 'single materiality'. That is, they have a singular focus on risks to the company. A shift to double materiality would encourage investment in activities that provide long-term benefit to the environment, such as the clean energy transition.

Carbon credits and offsets

Carbon credits and offsets are actions that compensate for atmospheric emissions of greenhouse gases through a remotely located process unrelated to the organisation's core business. They are controversial for two reasons. First, because of concerns about integrity and scalability. Second, because they are often used by companies as an expedient alternative to permanently eliminating emissions from their routine activities. It would be far better for those companies to switch to low-emissions technologies, improve the energy efficiency of their practices, adopt renewable energy supplies and increase recycling. That is, carbon offsets should be used as a last resort.

If projects are properly documented using agreed methods, they can produce carbon credits or offsets that can be sold and traded. Formally, a carbon credit represents emissions avoided and a carbon offset represents emissions removed from the atmosphere. In both cases, the unit of trade is one tonne of carbon dioxide. Another distinction between carbon credits and carbon offsets is that carbon credits are generally transacted in a government regulated compliance market such as the European emissions trading scheme, while carbon offsets are generally transacted in voluntary carbon markets.[104] It is common, though, for these two terms to used interchangeably.

Carbon dioxide removal activities can be subdivided into nature-based and technology-based solutions.

The most common nature-based removal projects grow forests on land that had been previously cleared (reforestation) or on land that hasn't recently had any tree cover (afforestation). As the forests grow, the trees absorb carbon dioxide. The permanence of the removal is linked to contracts for preserving the mature forests. The amount of carbon stored is estimated from parameters such as tree diameter, height and wood density, with uncertainty of up to 20%.[105] Less developed and more difficult to quantify removal projects include changing agricultural practices to increase the amount of carbon stored in soil and restoration of coastal wetlands. Ancillary benefits such as improved productivity, cleaner ground water and biodiversity are often claimed, but they are incidental and difficult to substantiate.

A possible problem with nature-based removal projects is that carbon storage in trees or in the soil is not truly permanent. The carbon could be returned to the atmosphere because of the election of a reactionary government that cancels preservation contracts, or it could be destroyed by an act of god – bushfires, floods or crop disease.

Technology-based removal projects are still in their early stages of development but show substantial potential. The most promising approach is direct air capture with storage, as discussed earlier. The main advantage of this removal activity is that if the carbon dioxide is stored underground using the same techniques that have been developed for carbon capture and storage (CCS), the removal is permanent. A secondary advantage is that the quantity removed from the atmosphere can be accurately measured. The disadvantage is the high cost.

Note, we see here for direct air capture and storage, and previously for cement production, that CCS has a crucial role to play. This is a point that has been made consistently by the International Energy Agency and the United Nations. Critics of CCS should give consideration to the difference between CCS applied to fossil-fuel activities and CCS applied to non-fossil-fuel activities, the most prominent of which are cement production and direct air capture and storage.

The attraction of carbon dioxide avoidance activities is that there is nothing better than not generating emissions in the first place. Examples include installing energy-efficient lighting, cooking, heating and cooling systems, and the displacement of high-emissions energy sources such as coal, oil and gas with low-emissions energy. If methane from landfill is captured and used to generate electricity, that is electricity that does not otherwise have to be generated from fossil fuels. Further, the combustion converts the landfill methane into carbon dioxide, which has much lower global warming potential than the methane that would otherwise have vented into the atmosphere.

However, these kinds of avoided emissions provide direct economic benefit to the owner and there is no obvious reason for the owners to be paid for doing what they would otherwise do.

Another type of avoided emissions is the retention of native forests that would otherwise have been cleared. Proving that there was a pre-existing intention to clear the forest is difficult and requires that strict methods be followed.

Credibility is variable

To be credible, nature-based solutions need to use agreed methods and be verified by a recognised third party.

For carbon credits traded in Australia, that role is the responsibility of the government agency known as the Clean Energy Regulator. Each tonne of emissions avoided or carbon dioxide removed is identified by an Australian Carbon Credit Unit (ACCU) that is tradeable. The integrity of the ACCUs was reviewed in 2022 by a panel led by former Australian Chief Scientist Ian Chubb. In its report released in January 2023, the review found that the methods allowed by the Clean Energy Regulator are sound, regularly reviewed and continuously improved.[106]

Equally dependable are credits traded in Europe. Certification is achieved under the rules of the European Union emissions trading scheme. Similarly, for credits traded in California, certification is achieved under the rules of the California Carbon Market.

On the other hand, the reputation of internationally traded carbon offsets is woeful. The original trading took place after the introduction of the Clean Development Mechanism (CDM) defined in the 1997 Kyoto Protocol. Trading was run by the United Nations, but from its inception the CDM was subject to fraud, corruption and racketeering. In fact, there were claims that the operations were so badly managed that the CDM handed out billions of dollars to chemical, oil and coal companies to invest in projects that increased net greenhouse gas emissions, and which the companies would have built anyway.[107] It doesn't get much worse than that.

Eighteen years later, under Article 6 of the Paris Agreement, the right for countries to trade carbon offsets with each other to meet their climate targets was formalised. However, the rules were not agreed. There was some progress but not finalisation at the COP26 meeting in Glasgow six years later. The completion of the rules was postponed to the COP27 meeting in Sharm el-Sheikh – where a final agreement was tossed forward again. It is now 26 years since the first introduction of international trading in carbon offsets and the rules have still not been agreed.

In the absence of international regulation, numerous voluntary self-regulated carbon offset markets have emerged, and trading is growing rapidly. In 2021, nearly 350 million carbon offsets were issued internationally, up 220% on the prior year.[108] However, the entities that verify these voluntary carbon offsets are not subject to regulatory scrutiny, and there is growing scepticism about their credibility. A 2022 analysis by financial data company Bloomberg found that about 40% of voluntary market offsets consisted of avoided emissions from projects that would have been built anyway.[109] That is, there was little or no additionality. Take, for example, the 1.8 million tonnes of emissions from constructing seven stadiums, new roads and dozens of hotels for the 2022 FIFA World Cup in Qatar that were fully offset by purchasing carbon offsets. The credibility of this effort was called into question because most of the offsets were for renewable energy projects in India, Turkey and Serbia that experts say would have been constructed even without the offset payments.[110]

There is no absolute way to judge the quality of carbon offsets and credits, but price is a clue. In November 2022, prices in the long-established and well-regulated compliance markets in the European Union, New Zealand, Australia and California ranged between US$30 and US$100. In three voluntary markets – Aviation Industry Offset, Nature Based Offset and Tech Based Offset – prices were between US$1 and US$3.[111] These very low prices should raise a big red flag.

In January 2023, *the Guardian* newspaper published findings that 90% of international forest carbon offsets covered by the world's largest voluntary markets program – the Verified Carbon Standard Program, administered by the Verra non-profit organisation – were 'phantom credits' that were 'worthless' and could even make global warming worse.[112] Given Verra has brokered more than 1 billion carbon offsets, far more than any other organisation, this is serious cause for concern.

Verra responded that the article in *the Guardian* had miscalculated the impact of its offset programs, but *the Guardian* stood by its reporting.[113] The one certainty is that uncertainty abounds in the international voluntary carbon markets. In January 2023, reflecting their poor reputation, nature-based carbon offsets from the Verra registry were hovering around the very low price of US$3.[114]

The importance of carbon offsets to the supply chain is that the goal is to get to net zero. This necessarily requires substantial carbon removal and storage and therefore government support through incentives, mandates and markets to drive efficient trade. As always, efficient markets depend on transparency and integrity, which in turn depend on governments to provide regulatory rigour.

Individual consumer behaviour

Beyond voting, the strongest impact individuals can have is through their purchasing decisions. Paying a premium to purchase a dishwasher that is made from zero-emissions steel and aluminium sends a message to the appliance manufacturer, who in turn sends the message to its steel and aluminium suppliers. Companies produce what customers want, thus consumer purchasing decisions are disproportionately powerful.

If they own their own home, and if their budget allows, consumers can take successively higher-impact actions. To start, they can change their gas stovetops to induction electric stovetops. Then they can replace their gas hot-water heaters or conventional electric hot-water services with electric heat-pump hot-water services. They can change their gas heating systems to electric heat-pump systems. They can improve their home insulation and install double-glazed windows. They can purchase 'green' electricity. For those who have off-street parking and can afford it, they can make their next car an electric car. Although the sticker price might be higher than an equivalent petrol car, the total cost of ownership might be lower because of the cheaper service and fuel costs.

Consumers should also keep an eye out for ethical stamps, and purchase from brands that can verify they use ethically mined products and do not use child labour or forced labour in their factories.

Cumulatively, these purchasing decisions send signals all the way up the supply chain, making it easier for miners and refiners to plan their investments and ensuring that their approach is ethical and community minded.

Energy equity

The clean energy transition is an opportunity to improve energy equity. In developing economies, the term is taken to mean the provision of energy at reasonable cost, without local pollution, so that all members of society can meet their basic needs for cooking, heating and transportation.

The World Health Organization reports that indoor fires burning charcoal, sticks, dry manure and agricultural waste are used by 2.4 billion people around the world, and that indoor smoke is linked to the premature deaths of 3.2 million people annually.[115] The deadly diseases resulting from exposure to household air pollution include stroke, ischaemic heart disease, chronic obstructive pulmonary disease (COPD) and lung cancer.

Designs for stoves that will burn more cleanly abound, but they are far from perfect and are not always deemed acceptable by the women expected to use them. Bottled-gas stoves and alcohol-fuel stoves would also solve the indoor pollution problem, but distribution is difficult in impoverished communities.

Replacing indoor fires with electric appliances for cooking and heating would eliminate indoor pollution. This would be equally true any time in the last 100 years, even if the source of the electricity was a high-emissions, coal-fired electricity plant far away.

In China, 100% of the population has access to electricity, and in India access has increased rapidly in the last two decades to 99%, but in many poor countries the transmission and distribution lines have not been built and so cooking on indoor fires continues. The breakthrough opportunity with renewables is to install solar panels on rooftops or in local community facilities, thereby avoiding the need to build transmission and distribution lines while providing a clean, potentially low-cost solution for all.

Once installed, solar thermal hot-water heaters, rooftop solar, community solar and community batteries do not depend on distribution logistics or fuel costs. However, there are still numerous supply chain challenges: financing the installations, training the workforce to install them, lowering costs, and standardising designs for small micro grids that are efficient, easy to deliver and easy to install. Seeking to address some of these issues in India, the German development bank KfW is working with the State Bank of India to meet the specialist lending requirements for small-scale financing of distributed energy systems.[116]

Within advanced economies, poorer communities tend to be burdened with disproportionate energy costs, and by lack of access to the benefits of home solar, batteries, energy-efficient housing and energy-efficient transportation. An equitable energy system ensures that the economic, health and social benefits of affordable energy extend to all levels of society.

Re-skilling

Workforces will need to be trained to support all aspects of the clean energy supply chain, from operating new mining vehicles through to extensive manufacturing opportunities in batteries, electrolysers and solar panels. We should be deeply optimistic about the opportunities inherent in the clean energy transition. The International Energy Agency estimated that 5 million jobs will be lost, but 30 million direct and indirect jobs will be created, right across the supply chain.

Regulatory reform

To provide the raw materials for the clean energy transition, new mines and mine expansions will be required. However, regulatory hurdles will slow that down. Take Australia as an example. We have some of the highest standards in the world for environmental protection. That's a plus, but many of the regulations are duplicative, complex, prescriptive, subject to multiple challenges and slow to issue. One of the biggest problems is inconsistency and overlap between jurisdictions, in particular at the state and federal level, but also between different government departments. This morass of vertically and horizontally intersecting legislation can take years for proponents of new projects to navigate. The problem plagues transmission lines, hydropower reservoirs, solar farms, wind farms, mine expansions and new mines. Furthermore, policies to protect the local environment often trump policies to protect the global environment.

Australia's regulatory complexity and slowness are typical. Indeed, the regulatory thicket in developed countries is often the rate-limiting step for expanding and opening new mines. Investors are wary of the uncertainty created by confusing regulatory requirements. Although there are statutory timeframes within which decisions about new projects must be made, legislated and common-law rights often entitle objectors to seek further information, which can delay the approval process.

Good regulation should fulfill two purposes. The first is to protect: protect the public, the workforce, the environment, and the rights of Traditional Owners and other landholders. The second is to facilitate: facilitate commerce and production. Over the years, in their efforts to quell public unease, around the world governments have increasingly applied regulations rather than leadership, with the result that regulations have become suboptimal. The operative intent must be to protect *and* facilitate, rather than protect *or* facilitate. Regulations should not be viewed as a zero-sum game between protecting and facilitating, but as an opportunity to optimise both. As far as possible, regulations should be performance-based rather than prescriptive.

All sides and all interests must be respected, but if the clean energy transition is to proceed at pace, the regulatory processes must be quicker and easier to navigate. Denying or approving a development application rapidly is much fairer to developers, investors and local communities alike.

There is no simple solution. The only way to reduce the regulatory thicket is for state and national governments to commit to reform.

A Canadian think tank, the Fraser Institute, publishes an annual survey of the attractiveness of jurisdictions to investors in the mining industry. Even within one country, the differences between jurisdictions can be significant. For example, in Canada in 2021, Saskatchewan province was ranked second out of 84 worldwide jurisdictions, while Nova Scotia province was ranked 71st. In Australia, Western Australia was ranked first in the world, while Victoria was ranked 39th. There is no reason to think that Western Australia or Saskatchewan have compromised their regulatory frameworks. Instead, they have optimised them.

That should be the mantra of all regulators: *Optimise, don't compromise.*

•   •   •

No one point of view will ever, realistically, determine political and practical outcomes. The Covid-19 pandemic provides an example. We saw in Australia that health and scientific advice was taken into account to an unprecedented degree by the prime minister, premiers, health ministers and public. But if decisions had been based solely on the health advice, we would have faced an economic disaster. Instead, the politicians also listened to the advice of state, territory and federal treasuries and other economic experts. The combined health and economic outcomes in Australia were among the best in the world.

Similarly, when it comes to responding to the threat of climate change, we must listen to the scientists. But we also need to listen to the engineers who operate our energy networks and the economists who are experts on the financial markets. We need to reduce emissions as rapidly as possible while ensuring ongoing economic prosperity. To choose one over the other would be irresponsible.

So, when scientists make the argument that we must shut down coal-fired generation immediately because the science says so, this ambition needs be reconciled with the reality that in Australia nearly 60% of our electricity generation still comes from coal. Shutting it down immediately is not an option. Instead, we must make coal-fired electricity obsolete by rapidly replacing it with clean, firm, cheap and abundant alternatives.

Globally, the clean energy transition will happen more quickly if we use all the tools at our disposal. These include solar, wind, batteries, transmission lines, digitalisation, management of distributed resources, large-scale hydropower, nuclear power, green hydrogen, blue hydrogen, carbon capture and storage, modern biofuels, synthetic fuels and natural gas generation for firming. No country, however, will have the social licence or capacity to use them all. Instead, each country must identify the right technology mix to suit its unique circumstances. The more technologies that are brought to bear on the task, the easier it will be. We should only reject possible options after giving them balanced consideration.

Difficult as the clean energy transition is, for forward-looking countries, companies and individuals, it is full of opportunity. The next chapter will focus on the special opportunities for Australia.

8.
Opportunities for Australia

When Donald Horne coined the term 'the lucky country', he meant it as a rebuke, criticising his fellow Australians for lack of enterprise and for relying for our prosperity on abundant resources and immigration instead of technology and innovation. It is true, we are lucky. However, I am a believer in the principle that you make your luck. As golf legend Gary Player once wrote, 'The harder I practice the luckier I get'. So, too, Australian mining mavericks and companies have made their luck, by taking risks and implementing innovative mining practices.

However, anybody who believes that, by luck, what has worked in the past will work in the future is living in a parallel reality. Although we are blessed with mineral and fossil-fuel resources that are in international demand, the nature of that international demand has already started to change and will be almost unrecognisable three decades from now.

In the fiscal year ending 30 June 2022, Australia's top 12 resource and energy exports were:[1]

Fossil fuels	
LNG	A$70 billion
Metallurgical coal	A$66 billion
Thermal coal	A$46 billion
Crude oil	A$14 billion
Total	*A$196 billion*

Non-energy related metals	
Iron ore	A$134 billion
Gold	A$23 billion
Zinc	A$5 billion
Total	*A$162 billion*

Energy transition materials	
Copper	A$12 billion
Alumina	A$9 billion
Aluminium	A$6 billion
Lithium	A$5 billion
Nickel	A$4 billion
Total	*A$36 billion*

By 2050, thermal coal, metallurgical coal, crude oil and natural-gas exports will be gone or significantly diminished. Lithium, nickel, cobalt, manganese, graphite, copper and rare earth elements will be the new oil. Energy carriers such as hydrogen and ammonia will partially replace the fossil-fuel exports, and there will be new exports of decarbonised products such as green iron, green fertiliser and synthetic fuels that are not in the top 12 today.

With the right policy settings, Australia can be one of the future electrostates where the clean energy supply chains begin. The opportunities for Australia to supply the world with zero-carbon goods have been well articulated by Ross Garnaut in his books *Superpower* (2019) and *The Superpower Transformation* (2022).

In addition to decarbonising the domestic economy and providing regional assistance, some significant areas of opportunity for Australia in the clean energy transition are:

- *Energy transition materials*: mining and refining of ores such as nickel, lithium, cobalt, copper and rare earth elements.
- *Shipping sunshine*: exporting energy carriers such as hydrogen and ammonia, and synthetic fuels.
- *Decarbonised products*: green iron, green aluminium and green fertiliser.
- *Exportable carbon offsets*: such as direct air capture and storage (DACS).
- *Advanced manufacturing*: focused on services and specialised clean energy products, such as electrolysers and DACS devices.

These opportunities all have a common, indispensable enabling factor – clean, green, renewable electricity supplied 24 hours a day, 7 days a week.

In Australia, we have so much going for us that if we do not succeed in building new opportunities, the failure to do so should be classed as an own-goal. As Kobad Bhavnagri from BloombergNEF has said, 'The world's problem is Australia's opportunity.'

Mining and refining

Australia has troves of most of the energy transition materials required to decarbonise the supply chain and reach net zero. We are also well positioned to build on our existing status as a world-leading supplier of traditional minerals such as copper and aluminium, while substantially expanding our role as an exporter of refined lithium, cobalt, nickel, manganese, graphite, copper and rare earths.

Table 3: Data from the US Geological Survey, in tonnes of contained metal, except rare earths are in tonnes of oxide. Graphite and platinum group metals production and reserves are the year 2020 from Australia's Identified Mineral Resources 2021 publication by Geoscience Australia, an agency of the Australian government. (Source: https://pubs.usgs.gov/periodicals/mcs2022/mcs2022.pdf; www.ga.gov.au/digital-publication/aimr2021)

Material	Australian production 2021, tonnes (% of world)	Global production 2021, tonnes	Australian reserves, tonnes (% of world)	World reserves tonnes
Copper	900,000 (4.3%)	21,000,000	93,000,000 (11%)	880,000,000
Bauxite	110,000,000 (28.2%)	390,000,000	5,300,000,000 (17%)	32,000,000,000
Graphite (natural)	none	1,000,000	8,000,000 (2%)	332,000,000
Lithium	55,000 (55.0%)	100,000	5,700,000 (26%)	22,000,000
Manganese ore	3,330 (16.7%)	20,000	270,000 (18%)	1,500,000
Nickel	160,000 (5.9%)	2,700,000	21,000,000 (22%)	95,000,000
Cobalt	5,600 (3.3%)	170,000	1,400,000 (18%)	7,600,000
Rare earth element oxides	22,000 (7.9%)	280,000	4,000,000 (3%)	120,000,000
Silver	1,300 (5.4%)	24,000	90,000 (17%)	530,000
Platinum group	0.52 (0.3%)	180	110 (0.2%)	70,000

Table 3 shows Australia's production and reserves of key energy transition materials compared with global levels.

It is likely that as Europe and the United States seek to diversify their supply chains and ensure that the materials they purchase have been ethically mined, they will turn to Australia as a reliable source – not only as a supplier of the raw materials out of the ground, but as a location where those minerals can be refined using renewable electricity for use in batteries, electric vehicles and wind turbines.

Under the US *Inflation Reduction Act*, Australia is well positioned because our free trade agreement (FTA) with the US gives us preferential treatment as a supplier of battery materials and rare earth elements. The European *Critical Raw Materials Act* is likely to have similar preferential treatment for FTA countries.[2] Australia is actively negotiating an FTA with the European Union, with the potential benefits now being even higher.

Australia is particularly well positioned to become a preferred cobalt supplier given its strong environmental protection and land rights laws and the fact that we have the world's second-largest known reserves, after the Congo.

Australia is already the world's largest exporter of lithium, in the form of spodumene. Until last year, exports consisted of rocks sent straight from the quarry to the ship. However, in 2022, three processing plants were under construction in Western Australia to refine the spodumene into lithium hydroxide ready to be used in batteries. In addition, supported by government financing, Lynas Rare Earths and Iluka Resources are implementing first-stage rare-element processing facilities in Australia, refining ores such as monazite and xenotime into pure elements such as lanthanum and cerium.[3] And BHP is starting to refine its nickel sulphide and laterite ore into nickel sulphate, ready to be used in battery manufacturing.[4]

Change is in the air, and it has a fresh smell.

Shipping sunshine

As the rest of the world weans itself off fossil fuels, Australia is well positioned to replace a substantial fraction of our coal and natural gas exports with hydrogen made using our abundant solar and wind electricity to split water molecules.

However, the growth of the hydrogen export market is difficult to predict. Through the *Inflation Reduction Act* and the *Bipartisan Infrastructure Law*, the United States has committed tens of billions of dollars to domestic clean hydrogen production, as has the European Union. Both these jurisdictions are likely to meet much of their domestic needs. China is already investing heavily in green hydrogen production and the indications are that it will meet many if not all of its needs. Japan, on the other hand, and South Korea to some extent, will not be able to produce all the clean hydrogen they require and will need to import hydrogen or derived energy carriers such as ammonia.

If international demand is strong, Australia is poised to be a world-leading renewable energy exporter in the form of hydrogen, ammonia, methanol and other liquid fuels. We will do so by taking advantage of our abundant solar and wind electricity, landmass and industry knowhow, demonstrated by our strength in building large-volume, high-quality export industries such as iron ore, coal, LNG and lithium.

Much of the future use of hydrogen will be through a *use it where you make it* approach to producing decarbonised versions of existing commodities. When the Australian National Hydrogen Strategy was developed in 2019, the commitment to hydrogen production in the United States incentivised by the *Inflation Reduction Act* was not envisioned, nor was the development of cost-effective international hydrogen transport expected to be as slow as it has been, hence the *use it where you make it* approach was not baked into the strategy. For this reason, the strategy needs to be refreshed. In February 2023, the federal and state energy ministers committed to doing so. For Australian industry to move fast and in the light of the incentives offered in other countries, substantial funding will need to be attached to the strategy.

A simple analysis of the renewable energy required to replace our coal and LNG exports reveals some mind-boggling figures. However, it is important to keep in mind that this kind of analysis is not a prediction of future demand; instead it is a 'what if' consideration of the potential.

To keep it simple, let's invent a new energy unit, the 'ozziewatt-hour', which equates to the entire 265 terawatt-hour annual production of electricity in Australia.[5]

Expressed in this enormous unit, our existing solar and wind generation contributes slightly over a quarter of an ozziewatt-hour. Thus, to complete the transformation of our existing electricity grid, Australia will need four times as much solar and wind generation as we have today. The bigger challenge is that our economy also uses roughly two ozziewatt-hours of energy outside the electricity system, through the direct combustion of oil, natural gas and a small amount of coal, for industrial heat, for steam and hot water, for transport and for building heating. Thus, to replace our use of fossil fuels with renewables, Australia's domestic electricity system of tomorrow will need 12 times as much solar and wind generation to annually generate three ozziewatt-hours, almost entirely from solar and wind.

Now consider the quantities of LNG that we currently export. Measured by energy equivalent, we would need to export 34 million tonnes of hydrogen to be the energy equivalent of the 81 million tonnes of LNG exported in 2021.[6] To make this quantity of hydrogen by electrolysis, we would need 8 ozziewatt-hours of solar and wind electricity.

If we expand the exercise to export as hydrogen the energy equivalent of our coal exports, that's another 14 ozziewatt-hours.

Eight plus fourteen: that's a whopping 22 ozziewatt-hours. Add in the three ozziewatt-hours we'll be generating for domestic use, and you've got an eye-watering grand total of 25 ozziewatt-hours.

That's more than the annual electricity generation of the entire United States, which sits at about 16 ozziewatt-hours.

If, instead of shipping these vast quantities of sunshine, we use the hydrogen to produce decarbonised export products such as green iron, the volumes of hydrogen consumed will still require this order of magnitude of electricity generation.

This scale will not overwhelm Australia's domestic electricity grid because most of the export-oriented hydrogen production facilities will be remotely located. Nevertheless, achieving this level of direct and embedded hydrogen exports will require planning, financing and massive investments in infrastructure like ports, roads, rail, pipelines, liquefaction plants and hydrogen storage.

Electrolyser manufacturing

According to the Advanced Manufacturing Growth Centre, which regards manufacturing not as a specific sector but as the capacity to make things, nearly 1.3 million people are employed in various aspects of manufacturing in Australia, contributing over A$110 billion per year to the economy in fields as diverse as medical products, food and beverage, and defence.[7]

Given the potentially enormous onshore demand for hydrogen production, the clean energy transition could be an excellent opportunity to expand into the manufacturing of large-scale, complex products such as electrolysers.

As we have discussed, production of green hydrogen for the energy equivalent of Australia's LNG exports would use 8 ozziewatt-hours of solar and wind electricity. This would require more than 500,000 megawatts of electrolysis.[8] That is a huge amount, given that by the end of 2021 the cumulative installed capacity of electrolysis worldwide was only 513 megawatts.[9] Even if our hydrogen needs were a quarter of this ambitious requirement, it would still be a lot. Many Australians will remember that our long foray into domestic automobile assembly came to a sorry end, partly because we are a very small car market compared with the rest of the world. However, in the case of electrolysers, the market in Australia could be one of the biggest in the world, thereby bolstering the argument for domestic manufacturing.

The time-critical opportunity for Australia is that unlike other products for the clean energy transition, electrolysers are in the earliest stages of their global adoption. Thus, it is possible for Australia to get in early. In contrast, the manufacture of other clean energy products such as solar panels, wind turbines and batteries is globally mature and closer to commodity pricing.

An electrolyser is like a factory, with power-conditioning electronics, electrolyser stack, cooling systems, water deionising systems, pumps, hydrogen dewatering systems, safety systems, pipes and compressors. Like any factory, large electrolyser systems will be complex to configure and require ongoing repairs and preventative maintenance. Manufacturing in Australia would confer many benefits, including that it would ensure a workforce with the skills to install and maintain these sophisticated machines. If, instead, Australia were to import large quantities of electrolysers, we would also have to attract large numbers of foreign experts for the initial installations and the ongoing maintenance.

Other manufacturing opportunities

Southern Green Gas is looking to mass-produce modular direct air-capture systems. Their long-term success will be driven by the significance of their innovative approaches and large-scale deployment opportunities in Australia. Direct air capture is at an even earlier stage of global adoption than electrolysis, which means that Australian manufacturers of direct air-capture systems should be competing on a level global playing field. In practice, however, there is a big bump in the playing field, because the US *Inflation Reduction Act* offers direct air-capture companies a US$180 per tonne subsidy for sequestering carbon dioxide.

Australia's competitive advantage is abundant sunshine. If each Southern Green Gas capture module captures two tonnes of carbon dioxide per year, 500,000 modules will be needed to capture one million tonnes of carbon dioxide. Assuming each unit occupies about 20 square metres, including allowance for space between units, the total land coverage would be 1,000 hectares. In Australia there are many locations with the necessary land area and sunshine that would also be near to an onshore sequestration site.[10] Non-modular approaches to direct air capture will need ultra-low-cost electricity supplied by an integrated solar farm, so again Australia, with its sunshine and vast land area, will have an advantage.

In other areas, start-up 5B has a proven, novel solar-panel deployment system ready to expand globally, and SunDrive Solar has a breakthrough solar-cell manufacturing technology that could avoid the global dependence on silver for solar cells, enable lower costs and offer higher efficiency.

Decarbonised products

For years, commentators and politicians in Australia have criticised our role as a quarry to the world and argued that we should instead be adding value to our resources prior to export. It may have sounded like a worthy idea, but in reality there has been little economic imperative to do so. Our domestic market is small, our energy costs are not low because fossil-fuel exports expose us to international energy prices, and our salaries are high.[11] Now, for perhaps the first time, there is a strong economic imperative for Australia to add value to raw materials before export.

Most refining of ore into industry-grade chemicals is energy intensive. In Australia, we will be able to use our increasingly available renewable electricity at competitive prices to refine ores and to replace the use of fossil-fuel electricity at our aluminium smelters.

Beyond the use of zero-emissions electricity to refine our ores, there are enormous opportunities to add value by using locally available hydrogen to produce decarbonised products.

Many forecasts predict the cost of green hydrogen will eventually fall to US$1 per kilogram at the production facility. However, most models show that getting it to a port, liquefying it and shipping it is likely to add US$2 or more to the landed price in the importing country.[12] There is little optimism that the handling and shipping costs will fall rapidly or significantly. A simpler alternative is to completely avoid the handling and shipping costs by instead integrating hydrogen production into onshore facilities that will use the hydrogen to make decarbonised products.

Perhaps the biggest opportunity will be to use hydrogen produced onsite to chemically convert iron ore into elemental iron, to be shipped as hot-briquetted iron or equivalent. Shipping this green iron will make more economic sense than shipping the iron ore and the hydrogen separately to be processed into elemental iron overseas. In the latter scenario, the importing country would not only bear the hydrogen shipping costs but would also need its own zero-emissions electricity supply to operate the plant.

Australia is the world's largest exporter of iron ore, accounting for 54% of the world export market in 2021. For the electrostate down under, green iron is a major strategic opportunity to enhance our largest export commodity using our almost unlimited renewable energy resources.[13] Green iron is also a strategic threat, given Australia is also by far the world's largest exporter of metallurgical coal.

Green-iron production facilities will be dramatically different from the blast-furnace factories used for traditional iron production. Although blast-furnace factories are big, they take up less than a square kilometre. In contrast, green hydrogen facilities will use hundreds of square kilometres of land for gigawatt-scale solar and wind generation. The renewable electricity will supply the electrolysers and the hydrogen direct-reduction equipment. The last piece of the picture will be the rail line for the iron ore coming in and the hot-briquetted iron going out.

The main technical challenge is the iron ore itself. Most of Australia's iron-ore exports are hematite, with iron content of 50% to 63%, which is too low for immediate use in hydrogen direct reduced iron production. However, given the huge value of this resource, we can be confident solutions will be found through ongoing research and innovation.

More immediately, iron ore in magnetite form can be upgraded to a higher concentration that is suitable for green iron production. Fortescue Mining Group and its joint venture partners are on the verge of commissioning the Iron Bridge magnetite mine and processing facility in Western Australia. The processing facility will add value through an ore-processing plant that uses a dry crushing and grinding process to upgrade the low-grade ore into a concentrate containing 67% iron by weight.[14] This is not far short of the theoretical maximum of 72% iron in pure magnetite.

Once ore supply issues have been resolved, it is likely that international companies currently importing iron ore and coal will co-invest with Australian companies to develop fully integrated green iron facilities in Australia. This opportunity is within our grasp, with global players already making moves. In December 2022, the giant Korean steel maker POSCO declared its intention to invest US$40 billion in Australia alongside local partners for green hydrogen and green iron production.

Another potential local use of hydrogen will be in alumina refining. It is early days, but with part funding from the Australian government, Rio Tinto is studying whether hydrogen can replace natural gas at alumina refineries.[15]

There are also significant opportunities to use green hydrogen to make non-metallic products locally. Currently, Australia imports about 2% of the world's traded nitrogenous fertiliser, such as ammonium nitrate, nitric acid and urea.[16] These products are produced from ammonia, which in turn is produced from hydrogen derived from natural gas in a process powered by additional natural gas. In future, these nitrogenous fertilisers can be produced at low cost from green hydrogen in a process powered by renewable electricity.

Another product with huge potential, still in its embryonic stage, is synthetic jet fuel. Carbon dioxide from direct air capture facilities can be combined with hydrogen in synthesis plants to produce the aviation fuel. This would be a high-value product easily uploaded by aircraft and transported by sea. In the interim, and possibly making a long-term contribution, hydrogen can be used to increase the yield of sustainable aviation fuels from biomass.

Importantly, our future decarbonised commodities, and the products made by others using our commodities, will avoid punitive import taxes such as those that will be imposed under the European Carbon Border Adjustment Mechanism from January 2026. That commencement date is not very far away, and similar schemes are sure to follow. Our industries will need to move quickly.

To some extent, Australia's export industry for decarbonised products would benefit from uptake in the Australian domestic market. However, there are very few government programs at the state or federal level to increase demand for these products. In a report titled *The Next Industrial Revolution*, Tony Wood and colleagues from the Grattan Institute suggested that state governments could support demand for green steel, concrete, aluminium and glass by introducing an embedded energy standard for the construction industry.[17]

By getting on the front foot, Australia will be a supplier of choice in a world where purchasing power is increasingly looking for decarbonised products.

Credible carbon-offset exports

There is no doubt that international trade in carbon offsets will be required. No country can reduce its emissions to zero, and not all countries will have the nature-based or sequestration potential to balance the net-zero equation. The trick, as we have discussed, is to ensure the credibility of those traded offsets.

The highest-quality carbon offset is direct air capture and storage (DACS), because the act of removing one tonne of carbon dioxide from the air and burying it is easily monitored, quantified and guaranteed to be enduring. The problem, as we have seen, is the high cost, which is directly dependent on the price of the electricity to run the process. Because of our plentiful solar and wind resources and many potential geological locations for storage, Australia is well positioned to provide DACS services, with carbon offsets sold in domestic and international markets.[18]

Of course, it is a mug's game to predict the future, but modellers do it all the time. Most are confident that the market for carbon offsets will be large, with estimates for 2030 ranging from US$5 billion to US$190 billion.[19] The key reason for this huge disparity between estimates is the market's dependence on the strictness of the regulatory regime. If voluntary markets are regulated in future and obliged to offer only high-quality offsets, and if companies and countries are held to account on their emissions-reduction pledges, prices and volumes will rise, and the higher estimates look plausible. Global consultancy EY estimates that the price per offset could be in the range of US$80 to US$170 by 2030.[20] Bloomberg estimates that if carbon offsets are limited to carbon removal schemes, the carbon-offset price will be above US$220 by 2030.[21]

The question then becomes, can the DACS companies deliver? Most of the start-up companies are aiming for US$200 or less by the mid-2030s. A US Department of Energy program, Carbon Negative Shot, is ambitiously funding innovation to capture carbon dioxide from the atmosphere and store it for less than US$100 per tonne by the early 2030s.[22]

So, it is likely that the price companies are willing to pay will rise and the price for DACS carbon offsets will fall until they meet. When that happens, the market will be robust.

For Australia to be well positioned to be a key player, our industry must be able to compete with DACS projects in other countries. The United States is providing multi-billion-dollar government funding for direct air capture hubs and even more funding through its US$180 tax incentive per tonne of carbon dioxide sequestered. One way to provide additional funding for the Australian DACS industry would be to remove the prohibition on the Clean Energy Finance Corporation that prevents it from investing in carbon capture and storage projects (CCS). The prohibition could be selectively removed for non-fossil projects such as DACS and cement production. Another way to support the industry would be through production-linked incentives.

A possible concern is that if we start selling carbon offsets internationally, it will lead to much higher prices at home than if we only use our carbon offsets domestically. That may be the case, but arguably it would be the wisdom of the market in action. A way forward for future governments to consider would be to reserve a percentage of carbon offsets for the domestic market, not unlike the successful 15% domestic reserve for natural gas that the Western Australian government imposed many years ago.

Another potential service occasionally mentioned is sequestering carbon dioxide imported from our trading partners. The idea has not been costed and there are not yet any prominent project proposals, but the idea is inherently simple. Ships would carry green ammonia from Australia to countries that need it as a clean fuel. Instead of returning empty, the ships would pick up a load of carbon dioxide and return it to Australia for underground sequestration.

It is hard to see this one playing out successfully. Who pays and how carbon offsets are allocated would have to be determined. There would need to be an apportionment of responsibility for monitoring, measurement and verification. Political support would have to be gained, social-licence issues would have to be thrashed out, and the economic case for using sequestration sites for foreign waste carbon dioxide rather than carbon dioxide removed locally from the air would have to be evaluated.

In summary, with government encouragement for direct air capture and storage, we will have all we need to become an important global player in the international market for carbon offsets.

Risks

Every opportunity is accompanied by one or more risks. It is important to identify and manage the risks that might prevent or slow the development of new export and domestic industries.

Political uncertainty

For decades, Australia suffered from divisive 'climate wars'. No longer. The Albanese government, elected in May 2022, has a refreshing clarity of purpose.

As an advisor to two successive prime ministers and two successive energy ministers in previous governments, I could see that their aspirations were stymied by aggressive negativity from many of their colleagues. Cabinet and the back bench included too many reactionaries who objected to change. Even when Prime Minister Scott Morrison indicated to his colleagues the importance of tackling emissions so that Australia could be as successful in the future global economy as we had been in the economy of the past, he was met by stony silence.

In contrast, the Albanese government has ambitious targets, a strategic plan and strong coordinated support across its ministerial and backbench ranks, with much of the crossbench arguing for even more ambitious action. It is just the sort of approach that a nation needs to successfully tackle the enormous challenge of the clean energy transition.

Equally important, the Albanese government is working constructively with the state governments on new transmission lines, batteries, capacity mechanisms and earning community support. The states themselves have for years been systematically implementing policies to drive emissions down; now they can do so with increased cooperation from the federal government.

For three years at least, we can take political uncertainty off the list of risk factors.

Competition

Competition from other countries is a key risk. Many are well positioned and eager to gain an advantage in the global transition to net-zero emissions.

Take Chile. The German automobile manufacturer Porsche has proposed investing in a consortium that will build a facility in Punta Arenas for the industrial production of synthetic fuels, or what they call eFuels.[23] Porsche's sights are on the ground rather than in the air, with the prospect of using these synthetic fuels to eliminate emissions from internal combustion engines. The company has also stated its intention to invest in a similar facility in Tasmania.[24]

There is a national plan to use Chile's sundrenched, windswept countryside to produce electricity to power the facilities to make decarbonised products such as ammonia, methanol and synthetic fuels. The declared ambition of the Chilean government is to establish a hydrogen export corridor to Europe.[25]

Chile is already the top copper miner and second-largest lithium producer in the world. Its mining companies are not resting on their laurels. In addition to expanding production, they are investing in their sustainability credentials through the incorporation of desalination and renewable energy to reduce their mine-site carbon footprints.

Canada has huge hydropower capacity, ideal for powering electrolysers 24 hours per day. It also has a long-established fuel-cell manufacturer, Ballard Power, and many other hydrogen and fuel-cell technology companies. I visited the Ballard factory in Vancouver in 2019. Perusing their museum and speaking to their long-timers, it was evident how far fuel-cell technology has advanced in the last 40 years. The Canadian government is ambitious and aims to make the country one of the world's top-three clean hydrogen producers.[26]

Canada is already a major global producer of copper, nickel and cobalt. It has well advanced project proposals for rare earth elements, lithium and graphite. It has an excellent reputation for environmentally responsible mining, which it will leverage. Its mines and processing facilities produce relatively few emissions, and they are continuing to invest in electrification of equipment and vehicles.[27]

Aluminium from Canada is already the greenest in the world, especially in the province of Québec, where 94% of the electricity is hydropower and 5% is wind electricity. While little has been done in Canada to produce green iron, the potential is substantial, in particular because of the abundant hydropower for the cost-effective production of hydrogen.

Global supply chains will not sit idly by until Australia decides to help decarbonise them. If Australia wants to get ahead of the competition, we need to act swiftly with decisive, clear and attractive policies to encourage the industries of the future.

The Australian government is aware of this, and in late 2022 was actively consulting with industry and community stakeholders on the development of a national critical minerals strategy, inclusive of materials for batteries and other clean technologies.[28]

Australia cannot hope to match the level of subsidies that China, the United States and Europe are using to accelerate the growth of their clean energy industries, but we can focus support on commodities and products that have global potential, and we can utilise our renewable energy potential as a competitive advantage. Such support already exists but could be expanded. Mechanisms by which the government can reduce risks for investors and encourage private-sector finance include incentives to produce selected decarbonised products, capital support for the construction of facilities, and loan guarantees.

To have impact on a world scale given the enormous subsidies available in other countries, support from the Australian government will have to be sharply directed and considerable. For example, the capital costs for a green iron facility will be in the billions and any government support will need to be sufficient to make a difference. To be maximally effective, the government should consider prioritising a small number of projects rather than spreading its support widely.

We must also continue to invest in decarbonising the domestic electricity grid and expanding it to cover growing electricity demand in transport, heating and industry. As energy minister Chris Bowen has stated, that alone will require the installation of more than 22,000, 500-watt solar panels per day and at least one 7-megawatt wind turbine every day for the rest of this decade.[29]

In pursuing this domestic goal, we should not shy away from using gas-fired electricity to firm the solar and wind electricity. Gas for firming would help to accelerate the rate at which solar and wind electricity can expand to displace coal-fired electricity. An Australian electricity supply that reached 82% renewables and 18% gas for firming would be a world-class low-emissions supply, with a grid emissions intensity better than Denmark's today.[30] By using gas for firming, our electricity supply would also be reliable 24/7 and suitable for green aluminium smelting and critical mineral ore refining.

Workforce

There are widespread shortages of skilled workers in Australia, including mining engineers, geologists and electricians. You name it, there is a shortage; it is a problem across the economy. There is no easy solution in the short term other than skilled migration, but even there we will be competing with other countries, who are experiencing their own shortages. In the medium to long term, governments, universities and industries must make these skilled jobs attractive and train the workforce of the future. The solutions will include marketing programs and scholarships in areas of skills shortage, from apprenticeships to doctoral studies. Government support for a stepped-up national clean-energy apprenticeship scheme would be a logical commitment.

At the tertiary level, there are very few Australian PhD graduates whose doctorates are in rare earth element research, whereas in China there are 1,000 or more such graduates. Topic-specific PhD scholarships could help.

Several participants at the Sydney Energy Forum commented on the need to focus on skills rather than qualifications, perhaps by blending vocational and university education pathways. Jennifer Westacott, CEO of the Business Council of Australia, reflected on the need to rethink skills and training, as four-year degrees take too long, and we don't have the luxury of waiting. Another participant suggested implementing a Colombo Plan for the Pacific, with training for Pacific Islanders in Australia, after which they could choose to stay or return home.

If we get it right, rather than destroying jobs, the transition will create new jobs for all the coal miners, power-plant operators and others who are willing to reskill or relocate. Nevertheless, new jobs will not work for all existing workers, thus governments and companies must provide alternative pathways.

Ten years ago, futurists were routinely predicting that by now artificial intelligence would be causing a structural and permanent increase in unemployment. They were as wrong as could be. Instead, factors including technological innovation, rising socioeconomic expectations and climate change have contributed, and will continue to contribute, to new jobs and economic growth.

High costs

Another challenge at home is high costs. Everything seems to be expensive in Australia. Sometimes we manage, sometimes we struggle.

An excellent example of managing well despite high wages is the mining industry. The production cost for Western Australian iron-ore exports was US$32 per tonne in 2021, well below the world average of US$42 per tonne and below our main competitor, Brazil, at US$37 per tonne.[31] The reason why Western Australian mines are so price competitive is that the industry is highly innovative. Our mining companies make extensive use of automation, artificial intelligence and algorithmic process-control to optimise the efficiency of their end-to-end mining operations.

We manage in mining, but what about electricity prices? Most of the National Electricity Market was privatised in the late 1990s. While the virtues of privatisation are many, there are weaknesses, too. The virtues have included a reduction in excess reserve generation plants, increased efficiency and the construction of interconnectors between jurisdictions. One of the weaknesses is a side effect of how the market was designed. Retailers were introduced to ensure that generator companies would be able to sign contracts in advance to assist with their planning and financing. These retailers incur significant costs in hedging and arbitrage, and in marketing and managing customer churn. In 2014, David Richardson of the Australia Institute concluded that from 1995 to 2012, after allowing for the jump caused by the carbon tax introduced in 2012, the retail price of electricity increased 130%, while the consumer price index (CPI) rose just 60%.[32] Richardson's analysis attributed much of this price rise above inflation to a disproportionate increase in the indirect workforce in sales, management, clerical and administrative jobs.

Debates about the effectiveness of privatisation are not unique to Australia. In a 2022 study covering the period from 1994 to 2016, economists from the Massachusetts Institute of Technology and the Harvard Business School reported that electricity consumer prices in American states that deregulated rose faster than in states that remained tightly regulated.[33]

Another contributor to the faster than CPI rise in the retail price of electricity in Australia was the major investment in transmission lines in the first decade of the century.

The cost of building high-voltage transmission lines in Australia is high. For example, the planned 500-kilovolt, 2.5-gigawatt, 370-kilometre HumeLink overhead transmission line is expected to cost A$3.3 billion.[34] Comparable projects in the United States cost about half that much.[35]

These costs are compounded by delays in securing community support and landholder permissions. Encouragingly, things might be changing for the better, as there are signs that state governments are rising to their responsibility to work with industry, individuals and communities to tackle the problem.

For example, consider the opposition in Victoria to the Western Renewables Link, a 190-kilometre-long transmission line to carry new solar and wind electricity from a renewable energy zone in Western Victoria to the outskirts of Melbourne.[36] Local opponents say that the planning process did not consider matters beyond the efficient operation of the electricity grid. Instead, they argue, when choosing the optimal route for a transmission line, it is essential to first consider state-level economic development, and the environmental and societal impact.[37] The Victorian government is now moving to do exactly this, through its Victorian Transmission Investment Framework (VTIF).[38] The proposed framework seeks to integrate land-use considerations, environmental impacts and community views into the planning process for new transmission, generation and storage infrastructure. Communities will be engaged early in the planning process to make the most of regional development opportunities. This approach is constructive and considers all perspectives.

A second example is the NSW government's Strategic Benefit Payments Scheme, which recognises the urgent need to build a modern transmission network that maximises benefits for communities and households. Under the scheme, from 2022 the government will pay private landholders A$200,000 per kilometre for new transmission lines built on their land, in addition to the money landholders receive from the transmission-line company.[39] NSW treasurer Matt Kean stated that this payment will almost double the average payment landholders receive. In early 2023, to ensure an equitable approach for interconnections between Victoria and New South Wales, the Victorian government announced similar payments.[40]

The cost of transmission lines is further compounded by supply-chain constraints. Overseas steel manufacturers are quoting at least 12 months, and sometimes up to two years, for delivery. Transformers and voltage controllers are taking a similarly long time. This forces transmission-line companies to plan well in advance and order these components early. It also pushes many to diversify their sources of supply, with some now looking to India as an increasingly important provider.

Offshore wind-turbine deployments will be particularly squeezed by global shortages and international competition for materials. The UK is aiming to increase its installed offshore wind capacity from 11 gigawatts in 2021 to 50 gigawatts by 2030. Through the Esbjerg Declaration, Germany, Denmark, Belgium and the Netherlands aim to have 65 gigawatts of offshore wind power in operation by 2030.[41] The United States aims to increase from less than one gigawatt to 30 gigawatts of offshore wind power in operation by 2030.[42]

The first and only formally announced offshore wind commitment in Australia is two gigawatts in Victoria by 2032, rising to four gigawatts by 2035 and nine gigawatts by 2040. New South Wales is considering its first offshore wind opportunities. Internationally, the demand for offshore wind turbines and the ships to install them is exceeding supply. Because the *Inflation Reduction Act* tax credit of 30% is for offshore wind projects that begin construction before

January 2026, there is likely to be a peak in US demand in 2025.[43] Thus, Australian government and industry planners would benefit from making early, long-term commitments before the international growth spurt.

When it comes to natural gas, despite being one of the biggest exporters of liquefied natural gas, Australian consumers and industries in 2022 were paying nearly the same high prices as supply-constrained consumers in Europe. The Australian government had to act. Choosing against a windfall tax like in the UK, in December the federal and state governments jointly decided to impose price caps on domestic coal and gas. Some of the market interventions were temporary, such as a 12-month cap on the price of gas at A$12 per gigajoule, and a A$125 per tonne cap on the price of black coal. In addition, the Australian government announced it will make the existing voluntary code of conduct for the gas market mandatory and implement a provision to ensure reasonable pricing for domestic wholesale gas contracts.

It is unknown how these price interventions will play out. The gas and coal industries objected stridently, and some gas companies claimed that they would postpone their exploration and expansion plans, but it is not clear that any have actually done so. A month after the imposition of the price caps, finding that supply was not meeting demand, the NSW government imposed domestic reserve obligations on the state's coal miners to ensure that they supplied the domestic market as a priority over the more lucrative international market.[44] The gas industry argued that the best answer to high prices is to invest in increasing supply. In the short term, high international prices, driven by the Covid-19 pandemic and the war in Ukraine, are driving new gas exploration.

In the long term, the best way for Australia to decouple from international price volatility will be to transition quickly to a fully renewable electricity supply.

Regulatory uncertainty

As we have already noted, good regulations are essential. The protections they afford to the environment and communities cannot be bypassed. However, poorly designed regulations can cripple projects and lead to major cost blowouts. The Australian regulatory thicket is complex, with legislation at the Commonwealth, state and local levels.[45]

Companies have long advocated for the 'white space' – the time taken for application processing and decision making – to be tightened up, but approvals or rejections nevertheless take years. One way to address this would be for state government planning bodies to pre-apply for approvals for likely future projects, so that when the circumstances are right for commitment to a new generator or transmission project, as long as the project meets the pre-approval criteria it will get a head start. Such approaches are currently being developed in Queensland and New South Wales in collaboration with the Australian government. Reducing the legislated durations for reviews and appeals could also help to minimise white space.

In December 2022, the Australian government announced its intention to accelerate approvals for renewable energy projects. The federal environment minister, Tanya Plibersek, said, 'Nature is being destroyed. Businesses are waiting too long for decisions. That's bad for everyone. Things have to change.' With this, the minister indicated her clear grasp of the dual purpose of regulations. Let's hope this laudable intention is maintained during 2023, when new environmental legislation will be introduced to parliament.

Further uncertainty is created by activist decision making by the courts. For example, in November 2022, the Land Court in Queensland recommended that an application by Waratah Coal to build a new thermal coal mine in the Galilee Basin be rejected. The court upheld the plaintiff's claim that burning the coal overseas would worsen global climate change and thereby impinge on the human rights of Indigenous people and Queensland children. This ruling ignored the relatively diminutive impact of a single mine on a global scale, and the reality that international buyers will source their coal from other suppliers if not from this proposed mine. While I personally agree that that there are domestic political and local community reasons why the mine should not proceed, it is nevertheless extraordinary for the court to make its judgement based on such tenuous arguments. It would be much more appropriate for elected representatives in state and national parliaments to make such decisions, rather than leaving them to the judiciary.

Local objections

The problem of local objections to projects that would help the global environment is well known and has inspired several acronyms: NIMBYs – not in my backyard; NOTEs – not over there either; BANANAs – build absolutely nothing anywhere near anything.

The thing is, in most cases the locals have a legitimate complaint. But the planet needs large-scale projects if we are to replace high-emission fuels and technologies with zero-emission alternatives. Resolving this tension is not easy, but it is important. Governments and companies increasingly understand the importance of including local communities in early planning, sharing the project benefits, and investing in clear communication and forward planning so that communities can be confident in the long-term future of their area.

•　　•　　•

Without doubt, Australia is a lucky country to have world-class reserves of most of the energy transition materials, large-scale project experience, political ambition and an abundance of solar and wind energy.

But other countries have competitive advantages, too. This is not a winner takes all race; many if not all countries can benefit from the clean energy transition. Importantly, we can do better or worse economically, in our own emissions reduction and our contribution to global emissions reduction, depending on how we plan and engage. The Ancient Roman philosopher Seneca said 'Luck is what happens when preparation meets opportunity.' For Australia, now is the moment to prepare and deliver on the decades-old cry for us to add value.

Conclusion

It will not be easy getting to zero, but it is possible. This book has described a wide range of initiatives and policies to take us towards the global target; let's finish with a short recapitulation.

Best of times, worst of times

To be sure, there is a lot to worry about. Heat waves, fires, floods and cold snaps are becoming more extreme. Fossil fuel use is at record highs, and greenhouse gas emissions and global temperatures continue to rise. But there is also a lot to be optimistic about. Solar and wind electricity now provide more than 5% of global energy consumption. Starting from a low base, their combined output has quadrupled each decade. If this rate of growth can be kept up for two more decades their output will be nearly enough to replace fossil fuels entirely, putting us well on the way to eliminating three quarters of global emissions. Electric car uptake is booming, with new car sales taking 15% of the market and growing by more than 50% every year. In 2022, the global investment in zero-emission technologies surpassed US$1 trillion for the first time. More than 30 countries have now decoupled economic growth from emissions growth, laying bare the false dichotomy that we must choose between economic growth and decarbonising our economies. In response to the energy price shocks of 2022, governments have sharpened their focus on renewable electricity and nuclear power to improve their energy independence and reduce price volatility.

There is a lot to do. The clean energy transition is the biggest economic challenge in human history. Never before has a major source of energy been eliminated from the global economy, and now we are proposing to replace all three of the big ones.

The rise of subsidies

With a single legislative act, the Biden administration flipped the United States from being a net-zero hindrance to a colossus. The *Inflation Reduction Act* (IRA) was deftly steered through Congress by focussing on *carrots* (subsidies) rather than sticks (carbon pricing) and by appealing equally to Democratic and Republican state political interests. The enormity of the subsidies and sharp technological focus will provide enduring benefit for the planet. However, the IRA's *made-in-America* provisions are acting as a magnet, drawing talent, international finance and new factories to American shores, thereby reversing decades of free trade that has contributed to national wealth and low product prices. Other countries and jurisdictions are responding in kind, jostling to position themselves in the new economic zeitgeist. Again, good for the planet; not so good for free trade.

One of the biggest challenges for governments is to find the right balance between carrots and sticks – subsidies and carbon prices. The surge in the use of subsidies is highly effective because it accelerates investment in transformational technologies. Carbon pricing does not guarantee that kind of investment. It currently is running a distant second to subsidies, although the European carbon border adjustment mechanism (CBAM) is an important refinement that will improve the effectiveness of the European Emissions Trading Scheme in the medium and long term.

Electricity is magic

Electricity is the *magic* driving the clean energy transition. We must electrify everything we can, and where we cannot, we can use electricity to make hydrogen. That hydrogen can be used as a fuel for transport and long-duration electricity storage, or as a chemical to make ammonia, fertilisers, green iron and carbon-neutral jet fuel.

Electricity has two roles. It is the end product that will power households and our broader economy. It is also part of the supply chain; the factories that produce the electric vehicles, batteries, wind turbines and solar panels of the future all need zero-emissions electricity. For both roles, the electricity supply must be abundant, reliable, low-cost and zero emissions.

From petrostates to electrostates

We are in the early stages of a tectonic shift in the global energy superpowers. Yesterday's powerful petrostates will be replaced by emerging electrostates. They come in two flavours: those that supply the energy transition materials, and those that are shipping sunshine.

The energy transition materials – silicon, silver, lithium, manganese, nickel, cobalt, graphite, rare-earth elements, copper, aluminium, platinum and iridium – will be needed in massive quantities.

The expansion of mining is key to our green future. However, it must not be achieved at the expense of local communities and the local environment. Instead, responsible mining must become the norm. Consumers should exercise their purchasing power to demand that the products they buy are built from ethically mined, low-emissions materials. Advocates using the principle of *follow the money* can help hold miners and refiners to account, as can verifiable certification schemes and ethical stamps.

Another way to improve the ethical credentials of end products such as electric vehicle batteries is to develop new designs that do not require problematic materials. For example, there is a global effort, already delivering results, to produce cobalt-free batteries. But some ingredients, especially lithium, are irreplaceable, so in addition to expanding mining and reducing the emissions during refining, it will be important to invest in recycling and reuse.

'Shipping sunshine' is my turn of phrase for when the sun's energy, converted to solar, wind or hydropower electricity, is used to generate hydrogen that is then shipped from the producer country to the importing country. Equally important is indirect shipping of sunshine, by embedding hydrogen into decarbonised products. This is the *use it where you make it* philosophy. Renewable hydrogen can be used locally to produce green iron more economically than if the hydrogen and iron ore were separately shipped to a remote customer. Likewise, renewable hydrogen can be used locally to cost-effectively produce zero-emissions alumina, green fertiliser and modern biofuels.

Investment, not divestment

The best way to drive the clean energy transition is to improve the performance, lower the cost and increase the manufacturing capacity for zero-emissions technologies, so that their low price and convenience will make the high-emissions incumbents obsolete. To achieve this, the appropriate mantra is *investment, not divestment*. Instead of selling off their fossil-fuel assets or using their profits to expand into more coal, oil and gas projects, fossil-fuel companies should take the opportunity to reinvent themselves, to be part of the long-term future.

The existing practice of some publicly traded companies divesting their fossil-fuel assets is driven partly by the fact that most of the ESG funds that might invest in them have a singular mandate to invest in companies that are at low risk of being affected by climate change and low risk of being affected by activist investor pressure or restricted access to financing. Instead, ESG funds should adopt a *double materiality* mandate to invest in companies that are not only at low risk themselves but, importantly, acting to help the planet.

There is no room in the new economy for coal-fired electricity. As coal-fired plants approach closure, governments and regulators must work closely with the operators to provide support for displaced workforces and local communities. It is equally important for governments to ensure that zero-emissions electricity sources are deployed at a rate equal to or slightly faster than the rate of closure of coal-fired generators.

Dealing with the deficit

When governments, industry and individuals have done as much as possible, there will still be budget-busting annual emissions in the vicinity of 10 billion tonnes per year. Getting to net zero will require this quantity of carbon dioxide be removed annually from the atmosphere, either through nature-based or technology-based methods. Offsets from nature-based removal traded under government-regulated schemes are reliable, but those traded under the auspices of voluntary schemes have been described as worthless. In contrast, technology-based removal, such as direct air capture, is easily verified. Although technology-based removal projects are today only operating as pilot schemes, their potential to operate at scale is promising. The biggest challenge is the currently prohibitive cost, but as we have witnessed for solar, wind and batteries, costs will come down.

Release the parking brake

There is an urgent need to scale up the supply chain as rapidly as we can. International finance is eager, and government resolve is more clearly aligned than ever before. However, in most countries, the regulatory approvals system acts as a brake. We can all agree that robust regulation is absolutely essential to protect people and the environment. At the same time, regulation should facilitate commerce, especially when the commercial activities help with the global challenge of reducing emissions. Shortening the time taken to approve or disapprove projects will speed up the clean energy transition and reduce costs. Optimising the regulatory system is the responsibility of governments. A key plank in the European Green Deal Industrial Plan is to 'create a predictable and simplified regulatory environment for net-zero industries'.

Australia – the lucky country

Optimising the clean-energy supply chain is crucial for the global transition. Australia, the genuinely lucky country, is especially well placed to actively participate in the clean energy transition and become a responsible electrostate supplying the needs of other countries. Even luckier, we can excel in both interpretations of the term – supplying energy transmission materials and shipping sunshine.

Value-added products

The new era is truly full of opportunity for Australia. We already have an enviable position in resource exports including energy transition materials such as lithium, nickel, cobalt, aluminum, copper and rare earths. Until recently, exporting resources has been a 'dig and ship' activity, because it made no economic sense to do anything more. But now, there are financial drivers to export value-added products. Importing countries are looking to diversify the number of supplier countries for refined chemicals and metals, and materials refined using renewable energy will attract a premium. The shift to exporting refined products has already begun, with early investments in refining lithium rock to lithium hydroxide, refining nickel ores to nickel sulphate and refining rare-earth ores to their elemental form. Our free trade agreement (FTA) status with America helps us to be a preferred supplier of both raw and refined energy transition materials. If we are successful in our current negotiations with the European Union to establish an FTA, that may help us to become a preferred supplier there, too.

We are well placed to produce decarbonised products, such as green iron that has been processed using hydrogen instead of carbon. This, too, is a transformational value-adding opportunity. The challenge will be the upfront investment costs. Green iron will require large integrated facilities for solar and wind electricity, hydrogen production and the hydrogen direct reduction plant. The capital expense at full scale will be billions of dollars per facility. Private enterprise and finance will bear the brunt of the effort, but to prevent key opportunities being ceded to other countries, new financial support from government will be required, as will simplified access to existing funding mechanisms.

To capture these opportunities for the use of hydrogen as an energy carrier and as a critically important input to decarbonised export products, it is timely that the federal government has announced a refresh to the national hydrogen strategy. Direct export of hydrogen and the use of hydrogen to replace distributed natural gas in our metropolitan areas are less of a priority now than first thought. The *use it where you make it* philosophy should be given a starring role so that we can add value to our exports and develop smart integrated facilities that will compete internationally despite the financial support given to competitor producers in the United States, the European Union and other countries. Government incentives to help Australian producers get over the starting line should favour specific solutions such as green iron rather than generic capabilities such as hydrogen hubs. Such carefully targeted financial support will need to be substantial to be effective.

Certification schemes to verify the emissions intensity of hydrogen and decarbonised products are required for markets to operate efficiently. Australia has already taken a leading role developing a hydrogen certification scheme that can ultimately be expanded to cover ammonia and decarbonised iron and aluminium. Continued engagement with industry and other national governments is essential.

To help deal with the global emissions deficit, Australia can build on its available land and abundant solar power to develop a new industry, exporting highly credible carbon offsets based on direct air capture and removal.

Finally, we have unrealised start-up opportunities to invest in manufacturing complex products that will be needed at large scale on shore, such as electrolysers to produce hydrogen for decarbonised products, and devices to capture carbon dioxide from the atmosphere to support our future carbon offsets export industry and to synthesise carbon-neutral jet fuel.

Enablers

Like nearly every developed country, Australia has a complex regulatory system that adds years of delay to major projects. Simplifying and speeding up the process without sacrificing the important provisions that protect communities and the environment is a daunting challenge that will require political commitment at the highest level.

Besides our material resources, Australia has the competitive advantage of a reputation for responsible mining, modern labour-force practices and consideration for Indigenous and other landholders and communities. We have large-scale project management experience and low sovereign risk. In a sense, we have an excellent national ESG profile that we must defend by continuing to invest in best practices.

We will need an increasingly skilled workforce across all the relevant clean energy technologies for deployment, customisation and improvement. A vibrant research system stretching from universities to companies will be essential. At the time of writing, the Chief Scientist of Australia is leading a review of the national science and research priorities. Australia would be well served by including the clean energy transformation as one of the priorities.

Underpinning all these opportunities is the decarbonisation of our existing electricity system. It is not feasible to do so only in pockets where the mining and refining takes place. Thus, it is essential that the government continues to vigorously pursue its legislated commitment to 82% renewable electricity by 2030. Achieving that target will depend on long-duration energy storage, most likely from pumped hydro and hydrogen. In the meantime, gas-fired electricity generation can provide the firming services that will unlock the potential of solar and wind electricity. Speedy upgrading and construction of transmission lines will be important so that investors and developers can be confident they will be able to connect the generators they intend to build.

Further expanding our electricity system to electrify transport, heating, hot water and industrial processes will lower our national emissions and bring benefits of scale and flexible loads. Vehicle procurement policies and support for the widespread deployment of charging stations will help with electrification of transport, and subsidies for heat pumps will help with electrification of heating and industrial processes.

•　　•　　•

If we move quickly and effectively, we will continue to be a lucky country. Even those Australians who think the threat of climate change is overstated should be able to see the economic opportunity. Ross Garnaut popularised the use of the term *superpower* to describe Australia's potential in a post-carbon world. If we get it right, we could go further. As the world shifts from the Industrial Age to the Electric Age, Australia will build on its three superpowers – renewable energy, decarbonised products and energy transition materials – to become the world's electrostate superhero.

Acknowledgements

My engagement in energy policy began with a series of seminal reviews providing evidence-based advice in the energy sector. I thank the ministers who trusted me to chair the Independent Review of the Future Security of the National Electricity Market (Malcolm Turnbull, Josh Frydenberg), the National Hydrogen Strategy (Josh Frydenberg), the Low Emissions Technology Roadmap (Angus Taylor), the Sydney Energy Forum (Anthony Albanese, Scott Morrison) and the advice on the US *Inflation Reduction Act* (Chris Bowen). In particular, the Sydney Energy Forum was the catalyst for this book. Without possibly being able to list them, I deeply thank the expert members of the panels I chaired, the superbly capable public servants who managed the research and report preparation, and the participants in public and private consultations who gave so freely of their wisdom.

Commentators on the drafts have been crucial to honing my arguments. I thank Bruce Mountain for intense debates on the role of gas in the generation mix, international and national economic levers to drive decarbonisation and the moral responsibility of individuals and nations; Tim Buckley and Tony Wood for their detailed and strong economic insights and broad advice; Natalie Bugalski and David Pred for introducing me to the issues surrounding land rights and ethical development and the concept of follow the money; Kate Temby for insights into what lies beyond conventional ESG reporting; Greg Bourne on ethical investing; David Lloyd for comprehensive advice and specialised insights into sustainable fuels; Noe van Hulst for insights on hydrogen logistics in the Netherlands; Daniel Westerman for discussions on reliable operation of the electricity network and the role of storage;

Raghunath Mashelkar for constant inspiration; Sanjiva de Silva on international policies; Karen and Tarun Weeramanthri for early discussions. For extensive and detailed commentary, I thank Michael Belchamber, Herbert Huppert, Jana Howden, John Dixon, Peter Tidswell, Andrew Dyer, Sam Lowe, Tom Biegler, Jens Goennemann, Matt Stocks and Rohan Gillespie. My wife Elizabeth gets a special thank you for her patience, her intellectual probing and her high expectations. My son Victor's ever-growing expertise in the energy sector kept me on my mettle, and my son Alex's sharp intellect and curiosity helped me with formulating my ideas. May the Force be with you and your generation. To my centenarian friend, Bella Hirshorn, thank you for your incisive questions. Denise O'Dea, I thank you for your skilful editing, suggestions and insights; and Chris Feik, thank you for your confidence and deft steering during our early brainstorming.

I acknowledge my colleagues across the private sector from whom I have learned so much. I declare that I am an adviser and investor in Australian direct air capture company Southern Green Gas and Australian electrolyser company Hysata, and that I am an adviser to Indian conglomerate company Reliance Industries and Australian mining company Rio Tinto.

Endnotes

1. Setting the Scene

1   Matthew Agius, 'As Europe Burns, Australia Needs to "Prepare for 50C,"
    Say Experts', *Cosmos Magazine*, 23 July 2022.

2   OECD emissions tables including LULUCF, worldbank.org/indicator/
    EN.ATM.GHGT.KT.CE.

3   Electricity production in 2021 was 28,500 TWh. Total energy demand
    from the graph in the text was 176,400 TWh. So, electricity is only 16% of
    the total, globally. Hannah Ritchie and Max Roser, 'Energy Production
    and Consumption', ourworldindata.org, 2002.

4   Data on energy consumption from 'Energy Consumption by Source:
    World', ourworldindata.org.

5   Alan Finkel, *Getting to Zero*, Quarterly Essay 81. Melbourne: Black Inc.,
    2021.

6   More than 10% solar and wind, https://ember-climate.org/insights/
    research/global-electricity-review-2022/

7   6.6 million of new car sales were electric, https://www.iea.org/news/
    global-electric-car-sales-have-continued-their-strong-growth-in-2022-
    after-breaking-records-last-year

8   New car sales of electric vehicles in China, https://www.bloomberg.
    com/news/articles/2023-01-12/electric-vehicles-look-poised-for-
    slower-sales-growth-this-year

9   New car sales in Norway, https://www.cbsnews.com/news/electric-
    vehicle-europe-norway-tesla-sales/

10 Economic growth no long means higher emissions, https://www.
    economist.com/finance-and-economics/2022/11/08/economic-growth-
    no-longer-means-higher-carbon-emissions

11 Comparative efficiency of BEV versus ICE, https://www.fueleconomy.
    gov/feg/evtech.shtml

12 Number of human cells, https://www.ncbi.nlm.nih.gov/pmc/articles/
    PMC4991899/

13 IEA net zero roadmap, https://www.iea.org/reports/net-zero-by-2050

14 Oil and gas profits, Exxon, https://corporate.exxonmobil.com

2. Energy Transition Materials: Mining and Refining

1   No net zero without mining, https://ministers.treasury.gov.au/ministers/jim-chalmers-2022/speeches/address-australian-critical-minerals-summit-sydney

2   World Bank estimates, https://www.worldbank.org/en/topic/extractiveindustries/brief/climate-smart-mining-minerals-for-climate-action

3   94 gigawatts of wind deployed, https://gwec.net/global-wind-report-2022/

4   An electric car uses four times as much copper, https://investorintel.com/market-analysis/market-analysis-intel/follow-the-copper/ Although the IEA says 2.5 times as much, https://www.iea.org/data-and-statistics/charts/minerals-used-in-electric-cars-compared-to-conventional-cars

5   Conductivity, https://www.thoughtco.com/electrical-conductivity-in-metals-2340117

6   Joanne Freeze, https://www.economist.com/news/2022/03/30/whos-set-to-win-and-lose-from-the-green-energy-revolution

7   Aluminium smelting, https://www.aluminalimited.com/bauxite-process/

8   Tomago uses about 10% of NSW electricity, https://www.tomago.com.au/capral-and-tomago-aluminium-agreement-to-local-aluminium-remelting/

9   Aluminium carbon dioxide emissions, https://international-aluminium.org/statistics/greenhouse-gas-emissions-aluminium-sector/ and https://www.statista.com/statistics/276629/global-co2-emissions/

10   Steel-making emissions are approximately 3 billion tonnes, https://cen.acs.org/environment/green-chemistry/steel-hydrogen-low-co2-startups/99/i22

11   Cement CO2 emissions in 2021 were 2.6 billion tonnes, https://apnews.com/article/climate-science-china-pollution-3d97642acbb07fca7540edca38448266

12   Aluminium production, USGS, https://www.usgs.gov/centers/national-minerals-information-center/aluminum-statistics-and-information

13   HRW report, https://www.hrw.org/report/2021/07/22/aluminum-car-industrys-blind-spot/why-car-companies-should-address-human-rights

14   Vision 2050 Report, https://www.european-aluminium.eu/vision-2050/

15   'Total final consumption by sector: oil' for road transport, aviation and navigation, https://www.iea.org/reports/key-world-energy-statistics-2020/final-consumption#abstract

16   Electric starter motor, https://www.wired.com/2010/11/1124automatic-automobile-starter/

17   Whittingham quote, https://www.barrons.com/articles/meet-the-creator-of-lithium-ion-batteries-exxon-mobil-51607605202

18   Akira Yoshino, https://ethw.org/Akira_Yoshino

19   McKinsey, https://www.mckinsey.com/capabilities/operations/our-insights/unlocking-growth-in-battery-cell-manufacturing-for-electric-vehicles

20   Range is a rough estimate based on the cars on this site, https://www.drive.com.au/caradvice/electric-cars-australia-2022-longest-range/

21   Gigafactory construction pipeline, https://www.benchmarkminerals.com/membership/global-gigafactory-pipeline-hits-300-china-maintains-lead-but-west-gathers-pace/

22   China's large share of battery manufacturing, https://www.economist.com/business/2022/08/14/could-the-ev-boom-run-out-of-juice-before-it-really-gets-going

23   Battery prices up slightly, https://www.statista.com/statistics/1042486/india-lithium-ion-battery-packs-average-price/

24   Graphite mine production, USGS, https://www.usgs.gov/centers/national-minerals-information-center/graphite-statistics-and-information

25   Synthetic graphite 1.8 million tonnes in 2021, https://www.researchandmarkets.com/reports/4763878/synthetic-graphite-market-growth-trends-covid. Other sites say as little as 300,000 tonnes.

26   Top producers of artificial (synonym for synthetic) graphite, https://oec.world/en/profile/hs/artificial-graphite

27   Graphite production and reserves by country in 2020, https://www.nrcan.gc.ca/our-natural-resources/minerals-mining/minerals-metals-facts/graphite-facts/24027

28   Battery-grade graphite demand growing at 30% per year, https://electrek.co/2021/12/20/graphite-will-be-in-deficit-from-2022-heres-what-ev-battery-makers-need-to-do-to-secure-the-critical-mineral/

29   Graphite demand growth, https://investingnews.com/daily/resource-investing/battery-metals-investing/graphite-investing/graphite-outlook/

30   Silicon is king, lithium is queen, https://cosmosmagazine.com/science/physics/long-live-the-power-of-lithium/

31   Lithium reserves in millions of tonnes, https://www.statista.com/statistics/268790/countries-with-the-largest-lithium-reserves-worldwide/

32   Lithium production, USGS, https://www.usgs.gov/centers/national-minerals-information-center/lithium-statistics-and-information

33   Lithium demand growth, https://panasiametals.com/conversion-tables

34 Lithium in the United States, https://www.cnbc.com/2022/01/15/how-the-us-fell-way-behind-in-lithium-white-gold-for-evs.html

35 Why manganese is important, https://investingnews.com/innspired/manganes-critical-steel-battery-ev-metal/

36 Manganese mine production, USGS, https://www.usgs.gov/centers/national-minerals-information-center/manganese-statistics-and-information

37 Manganese consumption dominated by steel, https://www.fastmarkets.com/insights/overlooked-battery-material-manganese-sulfate-could-experience-supply-deficit-in-next-ten-years

38 China imports of manganese ore, https://www.wsj.com/articles/china-hones-control-over-manganese-a-rising-star-in-battery-metals-11621597490

39 https://www.reportlinker.com/p092570/World-Manganese-Market.html

40 Nickel use increasing, https://www.statista.com/statistics/1257902/share-of-nickel-consumption-for-batteries-worldwide/

41 Nickel demand for batteries is accelerating, https://aheadoftheherd.com/worlds-running-short-on-nickel-supply-for-battery-use/

42 Nickel production, https://www.usgs.gov/centers/national-minerals-information-center/nickel-statistics-and-information

43 Nickel demand to 2030, https://www.minerals.org.au/sites/default/files/Commodity-Outlook-2030.pdf

44 Fitch Solutions nickel forecasts, https://www.fitchsolutions.com/metals/battery-grade-nickel-assessing-global-supply-bottlenecks-and-opportunities-30-12-2021

45 BHP acquisition of OZ Minerals, https://www.afr.com/companies/mining/bhp-oz-minerals-agree-scheme-deed-in-9-6b-deal-20221222-p5c87r

46 See NREL CEMAC report, 2019.

47 Many forms of cobalt, https://www.tandfonline.com/doi/abs/10.1179/aes.2001.110.2.75?journalCode=yaes20

48 200 thousand artisanal miners, https://www.pactworld.org/blog/combating-modern-slavery-artisanal-cobalt-mining-vital-achieving-paris-agreement-targets

49 Artisanal mining conditions in Congo, https://www.economist.com/middle-east-and-africa/2022/07/05/how-the-world-depends-on-small-cobalt-miners. Of which, 35,000 are children, https://www.theguardian.com/global-development/2018/oct/12/phone-misery-children-congo-cobalt-mines-drc

50 Cobalt resource review, https://ceder.berkeley.edu/publications/2020_cobalt_resource_review.pdf

51 Cobalt reserves, https://www.nsenergybusiness.com/features/largest-cobalt-reserves-country/

52 Mass of cathode metals, https://www.nature.com/articles/d41586-021-02222-1. NMC532 with 35 kWh energy capacity, the cathode material content would be approximately 8 kilograms of lithium, 35 kilograms of nickel, 20 kilograms of manganese and 14 kilograms of cobalt.

53 Car sales in 2021, https://www.statista.com/statistics/200002/international-car-sales-since-1990/

54 Rare earth elements in smartphones, https://www.visualcapitalist.com/visualizing-the-critical-metals-in-a-smartphone/

55 Purifying the rare earth elements is complex, personal communication from Amanda Lacaze, and evident in the description here: https://www.britannica.com/science/rare-earth-element/Preparation-of-the-metals

56 China refining far higher than its production, at 90%, https://www.ft.com/content/5a974ea5-c863-406f-bab1-3cc6fe8d6ad2

57 Lynas and Sojitz rare earths import deal, https://www.ussc.edu.au/analysis/rare-earths-is-there-a-case-for-government-intervention

58 Rare earth elements production, USGS, https://www.usgs.gov/centers/national-minerals-information-center/rare-earths-statistics-and-information

59 Shifting location of rare earth elements refining, https://www.marketplace.org/2021/04/30/the-u-s-is-trying-to-reclaim-its-rare-earth-mantle/

60 Lynas Rare Earths changed focus in 2001, https://en.wikipedia.org/wiki/Lynas#History

61 Oxides produced at Lynas Malaysia, https://lynasrareearths.com/about-us/locations/kuantan-malaysia/

62 Lynas production broght forward from '25 to '23, https://www.afr.com/companies/mining/lynas-looks-for-relief-in-countdown-to-rare-earths-deadline-20221113-p5bxr1

63 Rare earth element mining projects outside of China, https://www.mining-technology.com/analysis/mapping-rare-earths-projects-outside-china/

64 Polysilicon production in 2011, https://en.wikipedia.org/wiki/Polycrystalline_silicon

65 Polysilicon production estimate to 2030, https://rethinkresearch.biz/wp-content/uploads/2022/02/Executive-Summary-of-Polysilicon-manufacturing-forecast-to-2030-b3175.pdf

66 Global polysilicon production per IEA, https://iea-pvps.org/trends_reports/trends-2022/

67 IEA special report on solar, https://iea.blob.core.windows.net/assets/4eedd256-b3db-4bc6-b5aa-2711ddfc1f90/SpecialReportonSolarPVGlobalSupplyChains.pdf

68   Achieving American leadership in solar, https://www.energy.gov/sites/default/files/2022-02/Solar-Energy-Supply-Chain-Fact-Sheet.pdf

69   Risk of disrupted supply if China-Taiwan tensions increase, https://www.canarymedia.com/articles/solar/china-owns-the-solar-supply-chain-jeopardizing-the-energy-transition

70   United States Forced Labor Prevention Act, https://www.state.gov/implementation-of-the-uyghur-forced-labor-prevention-act/

71   Silver mine production, USGS, https://www.usgs.gov/centers/national-minerals-information-center/silver-statistics-and-information

72   Silver in PV cells expected to exceed 30% according to IEA, https://www.iea.org/reports/solar-pv-global-supply-chains/executive-summary

73   Platinum uses, https://www.rsc.org/periodic-table/element/78/platinum

74   Finding platinum, https://www.thenaturalsapphirecompany.com/education/precious-metal-mining-refining-techniques/platinum-mining-refining/

75   Platinum and gold mining in tonnes, https://www.statista.com/statistics/238414/global-gold-production-since-2005/ and https://www.statista.com/statistics/1170691/mine-production-of-platinum-worldwide/

76   Platinum mine production USGS, https://www.usgs.gov/centers/national-minerals-information-center/platinum-group-metals-statistics-and-information

77   600 thousand troy ounces is 19 tonnes. Demand for platinum in 2030, https://www.h2bulletin.com/platinum-hydrogen-economy-wpic/

78   Platinum mining perhaps in Australia, https://www.australianresource-sandinvestment.com.au/2022/05/10/australias-platinum-future/

79   Platinum and iridium prices on 10 October 2022 from https://www.metalsdaily.com/live-prices/pgms/. Gold and silver prices on 10 October 2022 from https://www.kitco.com/market/

80   Iridium production, https://www.woodmac.com/news/opinion/why-iridium-could-put-a-damper-on-the-green-hydrogen-boom/

81   Iridium production, https://en.wikipedia.org/wiki/Iridium

82   Irena prediction of iridium requirements, https://www.irena.org/-/media/Files/IRENA/Agency/Publication/2020/Dec/IRENA_Green_hydrogen_cost_2020.pdf

83   Iridium in PEM electrolysers, https://www.h2-view.com/story/iridium-availability-why-it-should-not-stall-electrolyser-growth/

84   Artisanal gold mine in Guinea, https://www.inclusivedevelopment.net/cases/guinea-anglogold-ashanti-gold-mine/

85   Gold mine in Liberia, https://www.inclusivedevelopment.net/cases/liberia-holding-avesoro-resources-to-its-community-development-promises/

86   Eliminating artisanal cobalt, https://www.economist.com/middle-east-and-africa/2022/07/05/how-the-world-depends-on-small-cobalt-miners

87   BMW cobalt sourcing, https://www.bmwgroup.com/en/sustainability/our-focus/co2-reduction.html

88   United Nations guiding principles on business and human rights, https://www.ohchr.org/documents/publications/guidingprinciples-businesshr_en.pdf

89   ReSource blockchain cobalt tracing, https://re-source.tech/#vision

90   Glencore fined US$1 billion, https://www.theguardian.com/business/2022/may/24/glencore-to-pay-1bn-settlement-amid-us-bribery-and-market-abuse-allegations. Fined US$180 billion, https://www.aljazeera.com/news/2022/12/6/glencore-to-pay-180m-over-drc-corruption-claims

91   Glencore worst record in human rights, https://www.bloomberg.com/news/articles/2022-05-04/glencore-human-rights-record-worst-in-green-metals-group-says?sref=wpjMCURG

92   IBM blockchain, https://www.ibm.com/blogs/blockchain/2020/12/blockchain-and-sustainability-through-responsible-sourcing/

93   Fair Cobalt Alliance members, https://www.faircobaltalliance.org/supply-chain-wide-collaboration/our-members/

94   Announcement of Climate Smart Mining, https://www.worldbank.org/en/news/press-release/2019/05/01/new-world-bank-fund-to-support-climate-smart-mining-for-energy-transition

95   Nike in 2018, https://cleanclothes.org/news/2018/06/11/adidas-and-nike-pay-record-breaking-amounts-to-footballers-but-deny-decent-wages-to-women-stitching-their-shirts

96   Nike in 2020 Uyghur scandal, ASPI, https://www.aspi.org.au/report/uyghurs-sale

97   Criticism of lithium mining in Chile and Argentina, https://www.volkswagenag.com/en/news/stories/2020/03/lithium-mining-what-you-should-know-about-the-contentious-issue.html

98   European battery passport, https://www.euractiv.com/section/circular-economy/news/digital-product-passports-become-the-norm-in-eus-green-economy-plan/

99   Tesla to take 42,000 tonnes of nickel per year from Prony Resources, https://www.mining-journal.com/energy-minerals-news/news/1419535/prony-tesla-strike-nickel-supply-deal

100 Bloomberg Green on Mattel toys, https://www.bloomberg.com/news/features/2022-10-21/mattel-remakes-barbie-with-recycled-plastic

101 Follow the Money, https://www.inclusivedevelopment.net/following-the-money/

3. Energy Transition Materials: Minimising Future Demand

1   Recycled silver, https://www.statista.com/statistics/1231248/recycled-silver-volume-worldwide/

2   Recycled copper, https://www.statista.com/statistics/1236581/worldwide-annual-copper-scrap-use-by-manufacturers/

3   Word Economic Forum on recycling aluminium, https://www.weforum.org/agenda/2021/12/aluminium-emissions-recycling-circular-economy/

4   Global EV sales, https://www.visualcapitalist.com/visualizing-10-years-of-global-ev-sales-by-country/

5   Average battery size, https://www.statista.com/statistics/309584/battery-capacity-estimates-for-electric-vehicles-worldwide/

6   Some examples in *The Economist* of gigafactories anticipating recycling, https://www.economist.com/science-and-technology/2022/10/26/gigafactories-are-recycling-old-ev-batteries-into-new-ones

7   Northvolt claim to source 50% of metals for battery cell production from recycling by 2030, https://northvolt.com/articles/revolt/

8   Northvolt, https://www.economist.com/podcasts/2022/08/31/will-the-electric-vehicle-boom-go-bust

9   US$248 million for recycling of US$9 billion rare earth market, https://energyindustryreview.com/metals-mining/rare-earth-recycling/

10   Recycling rare earths, https://ensia.com/features/rare-earth-recycling/

11   Re-use of batteries, https://batteryline.com/sustainable-manufacturing/second-life-batteries-and-their-applications-and-challenges/

12   Relectrify and Vector battery re-use trial, https://www.relectrify.com/newsblog/vector-and-relectrify-use-second-life-batteries-for-distribution-grid-storage

13   I-Pace battery re-use, https://www.autodaily.com.au/jaguar-recycling-i-pace-batteries-for-portable-power-packs/

14   Hummer battery, https://spectrum.ieee.org/manganese-ev-batteries

15   Tesla reducing cobalt dependence, https://about.bnef.com/blog/tesla-targets-cobalt-free-batteries-in-all-models/

16   Mass compounding effect, https://www.greencarcongress.com/2018/01/20180114-doe.html

17   Time to charge a car, https://www.nationalgeographic.com/environment/article/will-charging-electric-cars-ever-be-as-fast-as-pumping-gas

18   Toyota says 3–5 minutes to fill a hydrogen car, https://www.toyota.co.uk/hydrogen/how-do-i-charge-a-hydrogen-car

19   Platinum in a fuel cell, https://www.cell.com/one-earth/pdf/S2590-3322(19)30018-1.pdf

20 Iron catalyst for fuel cell, https://www.pv-magazine.com/2022/04/26/the-hydrogen-stream-fuel-cell-that-uses-iron-instead-of-expensive-platinum/

21 Hysata efficiency, https://www.rechargenews.com/energy-transition/worlds-cheapest-green-hydrogen-start-up-with-ultra-efficient-electrolyser-to-develop-pilot-factory-after-securing-29m/2-1-1270403

22 Hysata design is iridium free, https://www.nature.com/articles/s41467-022-28953-x

23 PGM-free catalysts for PEM electrolysers, https://www.sciencedirect.com/science/article/abs/pii/S2211339821000757

24 Reduced use of silver in solar cells, https://www.silverinstitute.org/wp-content/uploads/2020/06/SilverSolarPower_CRU2020.pdf

25 SunDrive Solar, https://www.pv-magazine-australia.com/2022/09/05/sundrive-hits-efficiency-high-with-copper-based-solar-cell-technology/

26 First solar thin film cells, https://www.firstsolar.com/en/Technology/CadTel

27 United States defense stockpile, https://www.defensenews.com/congress/2022/05/23/congress-and-pentagon-seek-to-shore-up-strategic-mineral-stockpile-dominated-by-china/

28 Innovation Metrics Review, https://www.industry.gov.au/sites/default/files/2022-09/improving-innovation-indicators.pdf

29 Fortescue trains, https://www.fmgl.com.au/in-the-news/media-releases/2022/03/01/fortescue-williams-(wae)-settlement-powers-development-of-world-first-infinity-train

30 BHP hyperspectral imaging, https://www.afr.com/technology/bhp-turns-vc-to-back-mining-ai-star-s-25m-round-20220320-p5a692

31 Silver mining automation, https://www.ey.com/en_us/mining-metals/how-silver-miners-can-build-long-term-competitiveness

32 BHP copper mine desalination in Chile, https://www.mining-technology.com/analysis/copper-mining-tech/

33 Machine learning in copper mining, https://www.datacenterknowledge.com/companies/codelco-turns-ai-squeeze-out-more-copper-aging-mines

34 Direct lithium extraction, https://www.innovationnewsnetwork.com/ibats-direct-lithium-extraction-technology/20994/

35 Lithium from brine, https://samcotech.com/what-is-lithium-extraction-and-how-does-it-work/

36 Direct lithium extraction, https://www.ibatterymetals.com/insights/all-you-need-to-know-about-the-direct-lithium-extraction-process. In much greater details, see here: https://www.innovationnewsnetwork.com/ibats-direct-lithium-extraction-technology/20994/

37 Direct lithium to product, https://ibcmrt.com/markets-and-applications/direct-lithium-to-producttm-dlptm/

38   Sustainability of bauxite mining, https://rmis.jrc.ec.europa.eu/uploads/
      library/jrc125390_sustainability_profile_bauxite__aluminium_online.pdf

39   Bauxite mine rehabilitation, https://bauxite.world-aluminium.org/min-
      ing/responsible-sourcing/

40   Relative emissions of bauxite mining, alumina refining and alumini-
      um smelting, see Figure 14 on page 19, https://rmis.jrc.ec.europa.eu/
      uploads/library/jrc125390_sustainability_profile_bauxite__aluminium_
      online.pdf

41   Rio Tinto and ARENA looking at hydrogen instead of natural gas,
      https://aluminium.org.au/news/could-hydrogen-help-reduce-
      emissions-in-the-aluminium-industry/

42   Alumina mechanical vapour recompression, https://icsoba.org/assets/
      files/publications/2019/AA08S.pdf

43   Apple supporting ELYSIS project, https://www.elysis.com/en/what-is-elysis

44   Mining accounts for 11% of global energy use, https://www.worldbank.
      org/en/topic/extractiveindustries/brief/climate-smart-mining-
      minerals-for-climate-action

45   McKinsey report in 2020, 'The mining industry has only just begun
      to set emission-reduction goals. Current targets published by min-
      ing companies range from 0 to 30 percent by 2030, far below the
      Paris Agreement goals', https://www.mckinsey.com/capabilities/
      sustainability/our-insights/climate-risk-and-decarbonization-what-
      every-mining-ceo-needs-to-know

46   Fast charging of haul trucks, https://www.bhp.com/news/media-centre/
      releases/2022/05/mining-giants-back-eight-winning-ideas-in-global-
      charge-on-innovation-challenge

47   Peak oil, https://www.forbes.com/sites/rrapier/2016/09/08/what-
      hubbert-got-really-wrong-about-oil/

48   IEA oil production per day, https://www.iea.org/reports/oil-2021

49   Deep see mining, https://news.mongabay.com/2022/09/regulator-
      approves-first-deep-sea-mining-test-surprising-observers/

50   Processing copper tailings, https://link.springer.com/article/10.1007/
      s40831-020-00325-z

4. Renewable Electricity

1   Geothermal running for 100 years without problem, https://www.un-
      .org/en/climatechange/what-is-renewable-energy

2   All figures other than nuclear taken from IRENA dashboard. Bioener-
      gy taken as the sum of solid biofuels, municipal waste, liquid biofuels
      and biogas. Wind as the sum of onshore and offshore, https://www.
      irena.org/Statistics/View-Data-by-Topic/Capacity-and-Generation/

Technologies. Nuclear figures taken from https://ourworldindata.org/nuclear-energy

3   Theoretical and practical solar cell efficiency, https://www.nature.com/articles/s41598-019-48981-w

4   Blakers and Green, https://aip.scitation.org/doi/10.1063/1.96799

5   Solar cell learning curve, https://ourworldindata.org/cheap-renewables-growth

6   Solar rooftop subsidies in Japan, https://www.japanfs.org/en/news/archives/news_id027851.html

7   Solar installed in 2021, https://www.solarpowereurope.org/press-releases/world-installs-a-record-168-gw-of-solar-power-in-2021-enters-solar-terawatt-age

8   Historical IEA solar forecasts, https://www.carbonbrief.org/exceptional-new-normal-iea-raises-growth-forecast-for-wind-and-solar-by-another-25/

9   2022 solar installations about 270 GW, https://www.renewable-energy-industry.com/countries/article-6246-solar-expansion-accelerates-global-pv-market-on-course-for-record-growth-in-2022

10   Rapid growth in polysilicon manufacturing, https://www.bloomberg.com/opinion/articles/2022-09-06/solar-industry-supply-chain-that-will-beat-climate-change-is-already-being-built?sref=wpjMCURG

11   5B Solar speed record, https://reneweconomy.com.au/5b-claims-world-speed-record-for-solar-build-but-global-rollout-still-too-slow/

12   India solar manufacturing to reach 43 GW by 2025, https://www.pv-magazine.com/2022/01/24/indias-solar-module-manufacturing-capacity-on-track-to-soar-400-in-four-years/

13   Advantages of offshore wind, https://www.energy.gov/eere/wind/articles/top-10-things-you-didnt-know-about-offshore-wind-energy

14   Capital cost of wind, https://www.statista.com/statistics/499491/us-wind-turbine-price-index/

15   Wind installed capacity , https://ourworldindata.org/grapher/cumulative-installed-wind-energy-capacity-gigawatts

16   Wind turbine manufacturers, https://gwec.net/gwec-releases-global-wind-turbine-supplier-ranking-for-2020/

17   Transporting an 88- metre blade, https://www.youtube.com/watch?v=v1r7CFaresM

18   Transporting blades in one piece, https://www.utilitydive.com/spons/wind-turbine-blade-sizes-and-transport-a-guide/623444/

19   Offshore visibility, https://blmwyomingvisual.anl.gov/docs/

20   Depth for offshore wind, https://www.americangeosciences.org/critical-issues/faq/what-are-advantages-and-disadvantages-offshore-wind-farms

21 Deep coastal waters in Japan, https://www.cnbc.com/2021/08/24/japan-targets-floating-wind-farms-for-its-deep-coastal-waters.html

22 Equinor information about their world- first floating rigs, https://www.equinor.com/energy/floating-wind

23 Floating offshore wind projects, https://en.wikipedia.org/wiki/Floating_wind_turbine#Operational

24 US Department of Energy, https://www.energy.gov/eere/wind/floating-offshore-wind-shot

25 Load-following capabilities, 54 minutes into this presentation, https://www.youtube.com/watch?v=JhrxFCtCPUo

26 Poland going nuclear, https://www.politico.eu/article/poland-20-billion-nuclear-power-us-westinghouse/

27 Land use in Japan, https://www.statista.com/statistics/1276355/japan-land-use-distribution-by-category/

28 Japan's offshore wind potential, https://www.powermag.com/rapid-progress-for-japans-offshore-wind-ambitions/

29 Nuclear power plants in Japan, https://www.nippon.com/en/japan-data/h00967/

30 Japan restarting reactors, https://world-nuclear.org/information-library/country-profiles/countries-g-n/japan-nuclear-power.aspx

31 Hinkley price is adjusted for inflation, https://www.bbc.com/news/uk-england-somerset-58724732

32 One of many articles indicating consumers will wear the cost of Hinkley C, https://www.iisd.org/story/the-united-kingdom-is-to-subsidize-nuclear-power-but-at-what-cost/

33 Resources for a nuclear station, https://www.nextbigfuture.com/2007/07/constructing-lot-of-nuclear-power.html

34 Nuclear generation, https://ourworldindata.org/nuclear-energy

35 Number of operable reactors, https://pris.iaea.org/PRIS/WorldStatistics/WorldTrendNuclearPowerCapacity.aspx

36 Solar and wind combined in 2021 was 2,894 TWh, https://ourworldindata.org/renewable-energy

37 NuScale dimensions, https://www.nuscalepower.com/technology/technology-overview

38 NuScale final ruling is pending, https://www.nrc.gov/reading-rm/doc-collections/rulemaking-ruleforum/active/ruledetails

39 GE Hitachi BWRX-300 details, https://nuclear.gepower.com/build-a-plant/products/nuclear-power-plants-overview/bwrx-300

40 Price of SMR nuclear, https://ieefa.org/resources/eye-popping-new-cost-estimates-released-nuscale-small-modular-reactor

41 Hydrogen fusion efficiency, https://physicstoday.scitation.org/do/10.1063/PT.6.2.20221213a/full/

42 Thorium complexities and fifty years of development, https://www. forbes.com/sites/energysource/2012/02/16/the-thing-about-thorium-why-the-better-nuclear-fuel-may-not-get-a-chance/

43 Nuclear poll by the Lowy Institute, https://poll.lowyinstitute.org/charts/nuclear-power-in-australia/

44 Deep repository nuclear waste disposal, https://www.government.se/articles/2022/01/final-disposal-of-spent-nuclear-fuel/

45 Forsmark, https://www.government.se/press-releases/2022/01/government-to-permit-final-disposal-of-spent-nuclear-fuel-at-forsmark/

46 November 2020 decision to build big battery, https://www.theage.com.au/national/victoria/victoria-to-build-one-of-the-world-s-biggest-batteries-near-geelong-20201105-p56brg.html

47 Northern Territory, Scientific Inquiry into Hydraulic Fracturing, https://frackinginquiry.nt.gov.au/inquiry-reports/final-report.

48 BloombergNEF Power Transition Trends, https://assets.bbhub.io/professional/sites/24/BNEF-Power-Transition-Trends-2022_FINAL.pdf

5. Firming: Unlocking the Full Potential of Renewables

1 Daniel Westerman, https://www.energymagazine.com.au/aemo-ceo-shares-lessons-from-most-difficult-period-on-record/

2 Go for net zero, https://grattan.edu.au/report/go-for-net-zero/

3 Worldwide installed battery storage, https://about.bnef.com/blog/global-energy-storage-market-to-grow-15-fold-by-2030/

4 *AFR* article based on SunWiz report, https://www.afr.com/companies/energy/record-battery-installations-in-2021-20220323-p5a72v

5 Round- trip efficiency for lithium battery storage and other storage types, https://www.pnnl.gov/ESGC-cost-performance

6 Vanadium redox battery in China, https://www.energy-storage.news/first-phase-of-800mwh-world-biggest-flow-battery-commissioned-in-china/

7 Redflow in California, https://www.bestmag.co.uk/redflow-completes-installation-its-biggest-zinc-bromine-flow-battery-date/

8 Pumped hydro worldwide, https://www.iea.org/reports/grid-scale-storage

9 Queensland Burdekin pumped hydro, https://statements.qld.gov.au/statements/96237. Queensland Borumba Dam pumped hydro, https://www.epw.qld.gov.au/about/initiatives/borumba-dam-pumped-hydro. 24 hours at full power, https://reneweconomy.com.au/has-queensland-overpumped-its-pumped-hydro-plans/

10 Snowy 2.0 delays and costs are increasing, https://www.theaustralian.com.au/commentary/six-years-of-bungled-billions-time-to-cut-losses-on-snowy-20/news-story/d486f6656e8978e7b2a2110c90f88325

11   Ardent Underground, https://ardentunderground.com//

12   Natural gas generator ramp times, https://www.wartsila.com/energy/
learn-more/technical-comparisons/combustion-engine-vs-gas-tur-
bine-ramp-rate

13   Natural gas peaking generation for firming in Germany, https://www.
energycouncil.com.au/analysis/a-view-from-the-spree-australian-ener-
gy-delegation-to-berlin/

14   Natural gas storage at Iona, https://www.lochardenergy.com.au/iona/

15   Bioelectricity in Denmark, https://www.irena.org/IRENADocuments/
Statistical_Profiles/Europe/Denmark_Europe_RE_SP.pdf. In Australia,
biogas and biomass provided 0.13% (0.05+0.08) of our 2020 electricity,
https://opennem.org.au/energy/au/?range=all&interval=1y

16   Geothermal in New Zealand, https://www.mbie.govt.nz/building-and-
energy/energy-and-natural-resources/energy-statistics-and-modelling/
energy-statistics/electricity-statistics/

17   Nuclear in France, https://www.statista.com/statistics/270367/share-
of-nuclear-power-in-the-power-supply-of-selected-countries/

18   Renewable Electricity Storage Target by Brue Mountain et al., https://
www.vepc.org.au/_files/ugd/92a2aa_3abddb7f37994760b86e-
0c921a692b5b.pdf

19   Capacity reserve by Nelson et al., https://onlinelibrary.wiley.com/doi/
abs/10.1111/1759-3441.12374

20   Paper from University of Delaware, https://www.sciencedirect.com/sci-
ence/article/pii/S0378775312014759

21   In Germany, underground transmission lines are being built because of community resistance to overhead lines, https://www.
energygridalliance.com.au/underground-dc-to-transmit-wind-
generated-power-across-germany/

22   Underground transmission lines are four to ten or more times
more expensive than overhead, https://www.power-grid.com/td/
underground-vs-overhead-power-line-installation-cost-comparison/
and https://www.tdworld.com/intelligent-undergrounding/
article/21215620/overhead-or-underground-transmission-that-is-still-
the-question

23   Repairs to underground lines can be up to five or ten times higher,
https://www.power-grid.com/td/underground-vs-overhead-power-
line-installation-cost-comparison/

24   SuedLink is US$11 billion, https://www.jacobs.com/projects/Germany-
SuedLink.

25   California wildfire sparked when transmission lines came in
contact with tree, https://edition.cnn.com/2022/01/05/us/dixie-
fire-power-lines-cause-pge/index.html, not so in Australia, https://

www.energynetworks.com.au/resources/fact-sheets/bushfire-factsheet-2020/

26 Solar installations rates in Australia in 2021, https://apvi.org.au/australia-leads-the-world-in-pv-installation-rate/

27 15 GW cumulative installed rooftop solar by end of 2021 rising to 69 GW by 2050, or rising to about 33 GW from Figure 11 in the AEMO ISP 2022, https://aemo.com.au/en/energy-systems/major-publications/integrated-system-plan-isp/2022-integrated-system-plan-isp

28 AEMO planning for 100%, https://aemo.com.au/newsroom/news-updates/orchestrating-the-pace-of-change

29 Digitalisation per the IEA, https://www.iea.org/reports/digitalisation-and-energy

30 Germany's efficiency strategy, https://www.energypartnership.cn/fileadmin/user_upload/china/media_elements/Documents/200407_BMWi_Dossier_Energy_Efficiency_Strategy_2050.pdf

6. Shipping Sunshine: Green Hydrogen

1   List of hydrogen strategies by country, https://research.csiro.au/hyresource/policy/international/

2   Hyundai Tucson ix35, https://en.wikipedia.org/wiki/Hyundai_ix35_FCEV. Toyota Mirai, https://en.wikipedia.org/wiki/Toyota_Mirai.

3   US Henry Hub prices, https://www.eia.gov/dnav/ng/hist/rngwhhdm.htm

4   SEQ price of natural gas from AER, https://www.aer.gov.au/wholesale-markets/wholesale-statistics/gas-market-prices

5   Germany natural gas price, https://ycharts.com/indicators/germany_natural_gas_border_price/chart/

6   Natural gas price in Japan, https://ycharts.com/indicators/japan_liquefied_natural_gas_import_price/chart/

7   In Germany, for July, August and September 2022 the average price was about US$55 per million BTU being US$52 per GJ, https://ycharts.com/indicators/germany_natural_gas_border_price

8   Incredibly cheap electricity in the Middle East, https://onlinelibrary.wiley.com/doi/full/10.1002/pip.3414

9   Lazard estimates of solar and wind electricity prices, https://www.lazard.com/perspective/levelized-cost-of-energy-levelized-cost-of-storage-and-levelized-cost-of-hydrogen/

10 US DOE estimates of hydrogen price, https://www.hydrogen.energy.gov/pdfs/20004-cost-electrolytic-hydrogen-production.pdf. Uses combined solar and wind. The difference between $1.5 million and $1 million of electrolyser capex is 77 cents, so the contribution of the electrolyser capes is is three times that, or $2.21.

11   Cumulative installed electrolysis capacity and forecast, https://www.iea.org/reports/electrolysers

12   EU delegated act to tighten the rules on green hydrogen, https://www.euractiv.com/section/energy-environment/news/germany-welcomes-eus-new-green-hydrogen-rules-activists-divided/

13   Strangling the hydrogen economy, https://www.rwe.com/en/press/interviews/eu-regulation-strangles-hydrogen-economy

14   IRENA Outlook 2022, https://www.irena.org/publications/2022/Mar/World-Energy-Transitions-Outlook-2022

15   Underground hydrogen storage at Chevron Phillips Clemens Terminal in Texas, https://www.aissoftware.com/storing-hydrogen-underground/

16   Energy to liquefy hydrogen, https://www.idealhy.eu/index.php?page=lh2_outline

17   Next generation LH2 ship, https://www.argusmedia.com/en/news/2324383-japans-khi-develops-liquefied-hydrogen-carrier.

18   Calculations based on figures in Table 1 at https://www.iea-amf.org/content/fuel_information/ammonia

19   30% co-firing in Japan, https://power.mhi.com/news/20221207.html

20   Repurposing gas pipelines in the Netherlands, https://www.gasunie.nl/en/projects/hydrogen-network-netherlands

21   Underground hydrogen storage in Groningen, https://www.chemengonline.com/bilfinger-supporting-gasunie-collaborate-on-green-hydrogen-storage-project-in-the-netherlands/?printmode=1

22   Hydropower emissions, https://www.un.org/esa/sustdev/sdissues/energy/op/hydro_tremblaypaper.pdf

23   Emissions from hydroelectric reservoirs, see curve b) 100 year potential in Figure 1, https://www.nature.com/articles/s41467-019-12179-5

24   Atmospheric implications of increased hydrogen use, https://www.gov.uk/government/publications/atmospheric-implications-of-increased-hydrogen-use

25   Fugitive Hydrogen Emissions in a Future Hydrogen Economy, https://www.gov.uk/government/publications/fugitive-hydrogen-emissions-in-a-future-hydrogen-economy

26   HySupply State of Play report, September 2021, https://www.globh2e.org.au/_files/ugd/8d2898_153f1369fe4742be9a95d34cb6866394.pdf

27   Steel growth to 2050, https://rethinkresearch.biz/articles/global-steel-demand-to-grow-60-through-2050/

28   Shaft temperature is 800C, https://www.sciencedirect.com/science/article/pii/S0959652618326301

29 Stochiometric hydrogen requirement per tonne of iron, https://www.mdpi.com/2075-4701/10/7/922/htm

30 Actual hydrogen requirement per tonne of iron, https://www.teriin.org/sites/default/files/2021-08/policybrief-green-steel.pdf

31 Coal used in steel production, per tonne, https://www.bhp.com/what-we-do/products/metallurgical-coal

32 Forecast price of metallurgical coal, https://www.statista.com/statistics/779868/forecasted-price-of-coking-coal-by-type/

33 Magnetite vs hematite, https://ieefa.org/resources/iron-ore-quality-potential-headwind-green-steelmaking-technology-and-mining-options-are

34 H2 Green Steel €260 million equity plus €3.5 billion debt raised, https://sifted.eu/articles/h2-green-steel-e3-5bn-debt/

35 H2 Green Steel advanced contracts, https://greensteelworld.com/h2-green-steel-signs-contracts-for-over-1-5-million-tonnes-of-green-steel

36 Boston metal, https://www.bostonmetal.com/transforming-metal-production/

37 Ammonia production, https://en.wikipedia.org/wiki/Ammonia#Applications

38 Uses of ammonia, https://iea.blob.core.windows.net/assets/6ee41bb9-8e81-4b64-8701-2acc064ff6e4/AmmoniaTechnologyRoadmap.pdf

39 Type of ships for which ammonia fuel would be suitable, https://www.emsa.europa.eu/newsroom/latest-news/item/4833-potential-of-ammonia-as-fuel-in-shipping.html

40 Types of ships, https://www.statista.com/statistics/264024/number-of-merchant-ships-worldwide-by-type/

41 Ammonia SOFC and PCFC fuel cells, https://www.ammoniaenergy.org/wp-content/uploads/2021/01/ganley_fuelcell.pdf

42 Viking Energy to run on ammonia SOFC, https://almacleanpower.com/news/clara-previously-prototech-awarded-contract-to-supply-2mw-zero-emission-ammonia-fuel-cell-module

43 SOFC efficiency with ammonia is greater than 60%, https://iopscience.iop.org/article/10.1149/10301.0185ecst

44 Breeding and fertiliser in the green revolution, https://mlpp.pressbooks.pub/americanenvironmentalhistory/chapter/chapter-8-green-revolution/.

45 Borlaug said we would need 1.8 billion hectares of additional agricultural land instead of the 600 million that is used if it were not for the green revolution, https://en.wikipedia.org/wiki/Norman_Borlaug. That is a factor of four. Elsewhere, Vaclav Smil has estimated closer to a factor of three.

46 Transesterification, https://afdc.energy.gov/fuels/biodiesel_production.html

47   Neste release on production, https://www.neste.com/
      releases-and-news/renewable-solutions/liebherr-expands-its-use-
      neste-my-renewable-diesel

48   Amount of renewable diesel in US, https://afdc.energy.gov/fuels/emerg-
      ing_hydrocarbon.html, converted at 3.8 litres to a US gallon.

49   Total diesel consumption in the United States, https://www.eia.gov/en-
      ergyexplained/diesel-fuel/use-of-diesel.php

50   Acreage analysis, https://www.dtnpf.com/agriculture/web/ag/news/
      business-inputs/article/2021/12/16/renewable-diesel-plans-outstrip-
      soy

51   IRRI on rice stalks, https://www.irri.org/rice-straw-management;
      particulate pollution in India, https://www.fao.org/energy/news/news-
      details/en/c/1461055/

52   Nordic prefeasibility study to convert biogas to SAF, https://
      findresearcher.sdu.dk/ws/portalfiles/portal/155625931/Nordic_avia-
      tion_fuel_production_28_10_2019_final.pdf

53   Department of Energy article on SAF, https://www.energy.gov/eere/bio-
      energy/sustainable-aviation-fuels

54   HEFA process for sustainable aviation fuel, https://skynrg.com/
      sustainable-aviation-fuel/technology-basics/

55   Neste presentation to European parliament claimed 1.5 million tonnes
      in 2023, https://www.europarl.europa.eu/cmsdata/232175/Presen-
      tation_Thorsten-Lange_2021-04-14_Neste-SAF.pdf. Global jet fuel
      consumption in 2019 was 95 billion gallons, https://www.statista.com/
      statistics/655057/fuel-consumption-of-airlines-worldwide/

56   Air transport action group, https://aviationbenefits.org/downloads/
      waypoint-2050-summary/

57   Solar kerosene, https://www.sciencedaily.com/releas-
      es/2021/11/211104115245.htm

58   Shell makes synthetic kerosene, https://www.shell.com/business-
      customers/aviation/the-future-of-energy/sustainable-aviation-fuel/
      synthetic-kerosene.html

59   10 gigatonnes to be removed by 2050 per year, https://www.wri.org/ini-
      tiatives/carbon-removal

60   DACS price by end of decade, https://www.spglobal.com/
      commodityinsights/en/market-insights/latest-news/
      energy-transition/042222-cost-of-capturing-co2-from-air-to-drop-to-
      250-300mtco2e-end-decade-climeworks

61   Stripe paying top dollar, more than US$2000 per tonne, https://www.
      datacenterdynamics.com/en/news/microsoft-buys-carbon-removal-
      credits-from-direct-air-capture-heirloom/

62   Climeworks, https://climeworks.com/roadmap/

63   Carbon Engineering, https://carbonengineering.com/news-updates/construction-direct-air-capture-texas/

64   Cement emissions, https://phys.org/news/2022-06-cement-carbon-dioxide-emissions-quietly.html. Global emissions of carbon dioxide in 2021 were 36 billion tonnes, https://www.iea.org/news/global-co2-emissions-rebounded-to-their-highest-level-in-history-in-2021

65   Half of emissions in cement production are heat and the other half chemistry, https://news.climate.columbia.edu/2012/05/09/emissions-from-the-cement-industry/

66   Concrete use, https://www.nature.com/articles/d41586-021-02612-5

67   Cement flue gas mix, https://www.sciencedirect.com/science/article/pii/S1876610209000216/pdf

68   Electrical safety, https://www.cullanlaw.com/blog/2015/may/may-is-national-electrical-safety-month-do-you-k/

69   Alstom sale to Lower Saxony, https://www.alstom.com/press-releases-news/2022/8/world-premiere-14-coradia-ilint-start-passenger-service-first-100

70   Alstom other contracts, https://www.railexpress.com.au/coradia-ilint-on-first-hydrogen-powered-passenger-train-route/

71   Amazon using Plug Power hydrogen, https://www.businesswire.com/news/home/20220824005803/en/Amazon-Adopts-Green-Hydrogen-to-Help-Decarbonize-its-Operations

7. Getting the Policy Settings Right

1   Danish response to oil crisis, https://thesolutionsjournal.com/2016/06/16/denmarks-energy-revolution-past-present-future/

2   Germany spending on subsidies over eight years to 2020, https://www.bloomberg.com/news/articles/2021-01-12/germany-paid-record-38-billion-for-green-power-growth-in-2020 and over all years to 2025, https://www.forbes.com/sites/michaelshellenberger/2019/05/06/the-reason-renewables-cant-power-modern-civilization-is-because-they-were-never-meant-to

3   China green power revolution, https://www.theguardian.com/world/2009/jun/09/china-green-energy-solar-wind

4   Stimulus in China for solar, in 2010, https://www.climatescorecard.org/2021/04/the-chinese-government-as-solar-power-entrepreneur-and-the-examples-of-suntech-and-longi-green-energy-technology-company/

5   Subsidies for renewables in China reported in 2016 at US$8.8 billion per year, https://www.efdinitiative.org/story/review-finds-chinas-renewable-energy-subsidies-are-unsustainable

6   World Bank report on carbon pricing in 2021 issued in 2022, https://

www.worldbank.org/en/news/press-release/2022/05/24/global-carbon-pricing-generates-record-84-billion-in-revenue.

7   Global carbon pricing, https://carbon-price.com/history/

8   EU trading scheme price history, https://tradingeconomics.com/commodity/carbon

9   EU ETS covers carbon dioxide but not methane, https://climate.ec.europa.eu/eu-action/eu-emissions-trading-system-eu-ets_en

10   Family climate action incentive payments in Canada, https://www.canada.ca/en/environment-climate-change/services/climate-change/pricing-pollution-how-it-will-work/putting-price-on-carbon-pollution.html

11   Carbon pricing returns in Australia, from *The Superpower Transformation* by Ross Garnaut (Melbourne: Black Inc., 2002).

12   CBAM, https://www.h2-view.com/story/eu-agreement-on-carbon-pricing-of-imported-goods-including-hydrogen/.

13   Phasing out of free allowances under the EU-ETS, https://www.europarl.europa.eu/news/en/press-room/20221212IPR64509/deal-reached-on-new-carbon-leakage-instrument-to-raise-global-climate-ambition

14   Asset divestments, https://www.nytimes.com/2022/05/10/climate/oilfield-sales-pollution.html

15   Engie mission statement, https://www.engie.com/en/group/purpose

16   Engie investments in Australia, https://engie.com.au/home/assets

17   Credit Suisse estimate of IRA spending, https://www.theatlantic.com/science/archive/2022/10/inflation-reduction-act-climate-economy/671659/

18   Cutting emissions by 42%, https://repeatproject.org/docs/REPEAT_IRA_Prelminary_Report_2022-08-04.pdf

19   Production tax credit for renewables other than solar, https://www.mossadams.com/articles/2022/08/inflation-reduction-act-clean-energy-credits. This article also covers CCS.

20   Department of Energy estimate for new generation, https://www.eia.gov/outlooks/aeo/pdf/electricity_generation.pdf

21   CCS costs, https://www.iea.org/commentaries/is-carbon-capture-too-expensive

22   CCS rates under IRA, https://www.globalccsinstitute.com/news-media/latest-news/ira2022/

23   Hydrogen production tax credit, https://www.utilitydive.com/news/the-ira-will-accelerate-electrolyzed-hydrogens-future-heres-what-that-me/632925/

24   *Inflation Reduction Act* summary from the CBO, https://www.crfb.org/blogs/cbo-scores-ira-238-billion-deficit-reduction

25   Whitehouse fact sheet, https://www.whitehouse.gov/briefing-room/
     statements-releases/2022/08/19/fact-sheet-the-inflation-reduction-
     act-supports-workers-and-families/

26   Article in *The Atlantic* about the Act, https://www.theatlantic.com/
     science/archive/2022/08/inflation-reduction-act-america-world-
     diplomacy/671293/

27   Formal discussion on EV subsidies, https://www.reuters.com/
     technology/us-eu-launch-formal-group-discuss-conflict-over-ev-
     subsidies-2022-10-26/

28   Macron annoyed by IR Act, https://www.cnbc.com/2022/11/09/
     europe-shows-a-united-front-against-bidens-inflation-reduction-
     act.html

29   Europe to copy US subsidy models, https://www.politico.eu/article/
     germany-france-biden-green-subsidy-inflation-reduction-act-robert-
     habeck-bruno-le-maire/

30   Chinese comments to the WTO, https://www.globaltimes.cn/
     page/202212/1280903.shtml

31   Panasonic battery plant plans, https://www.reuters.com/business/
     autos-transportation/panasonic-plans-additional-4-bln-ev-battery-
     plant-us-wsj-2022-08-26/

32   Honda and LG Energy, https://electrek.co/2022/10/11/honda-major-ev-
     battery-production-investment-us/

33   FT reports enormous investment in first six months after IRA legislated,
     https://www.ft.com/content/0f8bf631-f24c-48da-905f-e37f8dc5d5f8

34   US$250 billion loan program, https://www.energy.gov/lpo/inflation-
     reduction-act-2022

35   CHIPS and Science Act, https://www.nga.org/updates/the-chips-and-
     science-act-of-2022/

36   EY analysis on IIJ Act, https://www.ey.com/en_us/infrastructure-
     investment-and-jobs-act

37   US$3.5 billion for DAC hubs, https://www.energy.gov/articles/
     biden-administration-launches-35-billion-program-capture-carbon-
     pollution-air-0 and US$4.9 billion for CCS, https://www.energy.gov/
     articles/biden-harris-administration-announces-49-billion-deploy-
     infrastructure-necessary-manage

38   High wind -producing states, https://www.politico.com/newsletters/
     the-long-game/2022/08/18/red-states-reap-inflation-bills-green-
     benefits-00052463

39   Grants to republican states, https://www.nytimes.com/2022/10/19/
     business/electric-vehicles-republicans-investment-south.html

40   Enel expansion plans, https://electrek.co/2022/11/16/largest-american-
     solar-panel-maker/

41 EU response to IRA, https://www.euractiv.com/section/energy-environment/news/eu-loosens-subsidy-rules-for-green-tech/

42 EU Critical Raw Materials Act, https://www.reuters.com/world/europe/eu-set-up-central-buying-agency-critical-minerals-draft-law-2023-03-07/

43 California legislation, https://www.nytimes.com/2022/09/01/climate/california-lawmakers-climate-legislation.html

44 California to phase out gasoline vehicles by 2035, https://www.gov.ca.gov/2020/09/23/governor-newsom-announces-california-will-phase-out-gasoline-powered-cars-drastically-reduce-demand-for-fossil-fuel-in-californias-fight-against-climate-change/

45 California incentives for zero-emissions trucks, https://www.greencarcongress.com/2023/01/20230119-nikola.html

46 German investment in hydrogen, https://www.gtai.de/en/invest/industries/energy/green-hydrogen

47 Heat pumps in Germany, https://www.euractiv.com/section/energy-environment/news/boost-for-germanys-heat-pump-makers-as-industrial-policy-meets-climate-action/

48 Germany funding the clean transition in 2022, https://www.dw.com/en/german-parliament-approves-200-billion-energy-relief-plan/a-63517489

49 GX Roadmap, https://eneken.ieej.or.jp/en/chairmans-message/index.html

50 Open NEM, https://opennem.org.au/energy/au/?range=all&interval=1y

51 Per capita solar, https://apvi.org.au/wp-content/uploads/2022/05/APVI-Media-Release-T1-Snapshot-2022-Google-Docs.pdf

52 Offshore electricity framework, https://www.claytonutz.com/knowledge/2022/september/australian-offshore-wind-guide-2-0

53 Australian budget November 2022, Table 3.7, A$3.478 billion for supporting the transformation to net zero, https://budget.gov.au/2022-23-october/content/bp1/download/bp1_bs-3.pdf

54 National reconstruction fund, https://www.industry.gov.au/news/national-reconstruction-fund-diversifying-and-transforming-australias-industry-and-economy

55 Safeguard mechanism, https://www.cleanenergyregulator.gov.au/NGER/The-safeguard-mechanism

56 OECD explanation of baseline and credit schemes, https://www.oecd.org/env/tools-evaluation/emissiontradingsystems.htm

57 Safeguard treatment of trade exposed industries, https://www.cleanenergyregulator.gov.au/NGER/The-safeguard-mechanism

58 Tailored treatment under the Safeguard Mechanism, https://www.gtlaw.com.au/knowledge/safeguard-mechanism-reform-consultation-paper-released-feedback

59 Australian CBAM, https://www.aigroup.com.au/news/
media-centre/2022/revamped-safeguard-needs-to-support-
competitiveness-and-reduce-net-emissions/

60 NSW roadmap, https://www.nsw.gov.au/media-releases/electricity-
infrastructure-roadmap-tenders-open

61 NSW targeting 70% cut by 2035, https://www.theguardian.com/
australia-news/2022/dec/23/matt-kean-announces-nsw-target-to-cut-
carbon-emissions-by-70-by-2035

62 Queensland plan, https://www.afr.com/companies/energy/qld-to-cut-
off-coal-power-by-2035-20220928-p5bljs

63 Victorian emissions reduction targets, https://www.energy.vic.gov.au/
renewable-energy/victorian-renewable-energy-and-storage-targets

64 India's population will overtake China's in 2023, https://www.
economist.com/graphic-detail/2023/01/05/india-will-soon-overtake-
china-as-the-worlds-most-populous-country

65 Indian economy overtook UK, https://www.statista.com/chart/28258/
gdp-of-india-and-united-kingdom/

66 India energy use doubled in two decades from 2000, https://www.iea.
org/reports/india-energy-outlook-2021

67 Central Electricity Authority, https://cea.nic.in/annual-report/?lang=en

68 India targets, https://www.reuters.com/business/energy/
india-annually-invite-bids-8-gw-wind-power-projects-2030-govt-
order-2023-01-12/

69 Indian customs duties on solar, https://www.reuters.com/business/
energy/india-may-exempt-30-gw-solar-plants-equipment-duty-
sources-2023-01-11/

70 National Green Hydrogen Mission, https://mnre.gov.in/img/docu-
ments/uploads/file_f-1673581748609.pdf

71 Reliance US$10 billion for manufacturing, https://www.ril.com/Our-
Businesses/New-Energy.aspx#

72 Reliance commitment to Gujarat, https://www.pv-magazine.
com/2022/01/14/reliance-industries-commits-over-us75-billion-for-
green-energy-projects-in-india/

73 IRENA data, https://www.irena.org/publications/2022/Jul/Renewable-
Energy-Statistics-2022

74 Number of nuclear power plants under construction, https://world-
nuclear.org/information-library/current-and-future-generation/
plans-for-new-reactors-worldwide.aspx

75 BYD passes Tesla in 2022, https://observer.com/2023/01/china-byd-
beat-tesla-world-top-ev-seller/

76 Battery manufacturers, top, https://www.scmp.
com/business/china-business/article/3205675/

who-powers-worlds-evs-china-has-6-top-10-ev-battery-makers-60-cent-market-share-led-catl-and-warren

77 Buses in Shenzhen, https://iea.blob.core.windows.net/assets/db408b53-276c-47d6-8b05-52e53b1208e1/e-bus-case-study-Shenzhen.pdf

78 London has 8,600 buses, https://londonist.com/2016/09/london-bus-facts, NYC has nearly 14,00 cabs, https://www.nyc.gov/site/tlc/businesses/yellow-cab.page

79 Mandates and assistance help BYD outsell Tesla, https://www.ev-volumes.com/

80 Tim Buckley, https://www.smh.com.au/environment/climate-change/what-if-china-saved-the-world-and-nobody-noticed-20220818-p5bavz.html

81 China dominance in technology, https://www.smh.com.au/politics/federal/wake-up-call-china-takes-stunning-lead-in-race-for-tech-domination-20230301-p5conv.html

82 Worldwide investment in 2022 reached US$1.1 trillion, https://about.bnef.com/blog/global-low-carbon-energy-technology-investment-surges-past-1-trillion-for-the-first-time/

83 Deglobalisation defined by Chatham house writers, https://www.cha-thamhouse.org/2021/10/what-deglobalization

84 Polycrisis, per Ngozi Okonjo-Iweala, https://www.reuters.com/world/wto-chief-seeks-one-or-two-deals-warns-road-will-be-rocky-2022-06-12/

85 Deglobalisation, https://link.springer.com/article/10.1057/s41267-019-00219-7

86 Pakistan debt crisis, https://www.bloomberg.com/news/articles/2022-11-14/climate-debt-trap-risks-pushing-emerging-markets-to-the-brink?sref=wpjMCURG

87 54 countries on the default watch list of the UN, https://www.theguardian.com/environment/2022/nov/10/54-poor-countries-in-danger-of-bankruptcy-amid-economic-climate-cop27

88 COP27 basics in the FT, https://www.ft.com/content/e2020621-fbde-44ab-9497-a540bfc7425f

89 Netherlands halving its dairy industry, https://www.nytimes.com/2022/08/20/world/europe/netherlands-farmers-protests.html

90 *The Economist*, https://www.economist.com/special-report/2022/07/21/a-broken-system-needs-urgent-repairs

91 Goldman Sachs under ESG investigation, https://www.bloomberg.com/news/articles/2022-06-10/goldman-sachs-facing-sec-probe-of-esg-funds-in-asset-management

92 Tesla dumped from ESG index, https://www.reuters.com/business/
sustainable-business/tesla-removed-sp-500-esg-index-autopilot-
discrimination-concerns-2022-05-18/

93 BHP in the Australian S&P ESG index, https://www.spglobal.com/
spdji/en/documents/education/education-the-sp-asx-200-esg-index-
defining-the-sustainable-core-in-australia.pdf

94 ESG failures in Myanmar investigated by IDI and ALTSEAN-Burma,
https://www.inclusivedevelopment.net/myanmaresgfiles/

95 ESG failures in Myanmar per United Nations, https://www.bloomberg.
com/news/articles/2022-12-21/myanmar-energy-ties-are-flying-under-
the-esg-radar

96 SEC clean- up of ESG reporting, https://www.sec.gov/news/press-
release/2022-46

97 EU Commission plans to update ESG reporting, https://www.
consilium.europa.eu/en/press/press-releases/2022/06/21/
new-rules-on-sustainability-disclosure-provisional-agreement-
between-council-and-european-parliament/

98 Australia ESG reporting requirements are coming, https://www.afr.
com/companies/financial-services/esg-reporting-standards-and-rules-
need-to-speed-up-20220928-p5blt9

99 ISSB and GSSB joining forces, https://www.globalreporting.org/news/
news-center/ifrs-foundation-and-gri-to-align-capital-market-and-
multi-stakeholder-standards/

100 ISSB intentions, https://www.ifrs.org/groups/international-
sustainability-standards-board/

101 Financing the Transition, https://www.weforum.org/projects/
sustainable-banking

102 EU sustainable finance disclosure regulation described by KPMG,
https://assets.kpmg/content/dam/kpmg/ie/pdf/2021/03/ie-
sustainable-finance-disclosure-reg-sfdr.pdf

103 Double materiality from the European Commission, https://www.wlrk.
com/docs/Double_Materiality.pdf

104 Difference between carbon credits and carbon offsets, https://carbon-
credits.com/carbon-credits-vs-carbon-offsets-whats-the-difference/

105 Estimating carbon in forests, https://www.terraformation.com/blog/
how-to-measure-carbon-capture-potential-forests

106 Chubb review of ACCUs, https://www.dcceew.gov.au/climate-change/
emissions-reduction/independent-review-accus

107 CDM fraud, https://www.theguardian.com/environment/2008/may/21/
environment.carbontrading

108 Carbon credit numbers in 2021, https://www.sylvera.com/blog/carbon-
projects-rated-by-sylvera

109   Voluntary offsets based on weak additionality, https://www.bloomberg.com/graphics/2022-carbon-offsets-renewable-energy/

110   FIFA World Cup offsets, https://www.bloomberg.com/news/articles/2022-11-17/how-the-2022-world-cup-rebuilt-a-market-for-renewable-energy-carbon-offsets

111   Live carbon prices from Carbon Credits, accessed 6 March 2023, https://carboncredits.com/carbon-prices-today/

112   Verra offsets, https://www.theguardian.com/environment/2023/jan/18/revealed-forest-carbon-offsets-biggest-provider-worthless-verra-aoe

113   Verra response, https://verra.org/verra-response-guardian-rainforest-carbon-offsets/

114   Verra nature- based offsets, https://carboncredits.com/carbon-prices-today/

115   Premature deaths from indoor fires, https://www.who.int/news-room/fact-sheets/detail/household-air-pollution-and-health.

116   India state bank and KfW agreement, https://economictimes.indiatimes.com/markets/stocks/news/sbi-gets-rs-1240-crore-from-german-kfw-for-solar-projects/articleshow/95562902.cms

1   Resources and Energy Quarterly, https://www.industry.gov.au/sites/default/files/minisite/static/ba3c15bd-3747-4346-a328-6b5a43672abf/resources-and-energy-quarterly-september-2022/documents/Resources-and-Energy-Quarterly-September-2022.pdf

8. Opportunities for Australia

2   Likely preferential treatment of FTA countries under Critical Raw Materials Act, https://www.acea.auto/publication/position-paper-critical-raw-materials-act/

3   Refining rare earth ores, https://iluka.com/products-markets/rare-earth-products

4   BHP refining of nickel ores into battery grade nickel sulphate, https://www.bhp.com/what-we-do/products/nickel

5   FY 2021 electricity generation in Australia, https://www.energy.gov.au/data/electricity-generation

6   Australia's LNG exports in 2021, https://www.upstreamonline.com/lng/australia-remains-worlds-top-lng-exporter-but-it-could-lose-its-crown-this-year/2-1-1147625

7   AMGC Manufacturing Competitiveness Plan, https://www.amgc.org.au/wp-content/uploads/2022/04/AMGC-Manufacturing-Competitiveness-Plan_2022.pdf

8   Assuming 50% capacity factorand 66 kWh/kg for production, handling, pipelining and shipping. Capacity factor is here, https://researchdata.edu.au/renewable-energy-capacity-maps-2021/1680981

9   Cumulative installed electrolysis capacity, https://www.iea.org/reports/
     electrolysers

10   Map of CCS sites, https://www.globalccsinstitute.com/resources/
     publications-reports-research/national-carbon-mapping-and-infra-
     structure-plan-australia-full-report/

11   LNG prices in Australia, https://www.accc.gov.au/
     regulated-infrastructure/energy/gas-inquiry-2017-25/lng-netback-
     price-series

12   Hydrogen intermediate transport, storage, conversion, carrier to port,
     fixed and variable shipping and reconversion costs are A$3.50 for am-
     monia, A$4.13 for ammonia, into the future, per HySupply, https://
     www.globh2e.org.au/hysupply-publication

13   Australia exported 54% of exported iron ore in 2021, https://www.
     statista.com/statistics/300328/top-exporting-countries-of-iron-ore/.
     Australia produced 35% of global iron ore in 2021, https://www.nrcan.
     gc.ca/our-natural-resources/minerals-mining/minerals-metals-facts/
     iron-ore-facts/20517

14   Iron Bridge ore processing, https://www.fmgl.com.au/about-fortescue/
     our-operations

15   Rio working on hydrogen to replace natural gas at alumina re-
     fineries, https://www.riotinto.com/en/news/releases/2021/
     Rio-Tinto-and-ARENA-to-study-using-hydrogen-to-reduce-carbon-
     emissions-in-alumina-refining

16   Fertiliser trade, https://fertilizer.org.au/Fertilizer-Industry/
     Australian-Fertilizer-Market

17   Tony Wood, https://grattan.edu.au/news/careful-compromise-or-
     huge-headache/

18   Numerous CCS sites in Australia, https://www.ga.gov.au/scientific-
     topics/energy/resources/carbon-capture-and-storage-ccs/
     geological-storage-studies

19   Carbon credit markets in 2030 estimated by the World Bank at US$167
     billion, https://www.ieta.org/resources/International_WG/Arti-
     cle6/CLPC_A6-report_no-crops.pdf, estimated by McKinsey as being
     from US$5 billion to more than US$50 billion, https://www.mckinsey.
     com/capabilities/sustainability/our-insights/a-blueprint-for-scaling-
     voluntary-carbon-markets-to-meet-the-climate-challenge, and by
     Bloomberg as being as much as US$190 billion, https://www.bloomberg.
     com/professional/blog/carbon-offsets-price-may-rise-3000-by-2029-
     under-tighter-rules/

20   EY carbon credits 2030 price estimate, https://assets.ey.com/content/
     dam/ey-sites/ey-com/en_au/topics/sustainability/ey-net-zero-centre-
     carbon-offset-publication-20220530.pdf

21   Bloomberg carbon credit estimates, https://www.bloomberg.com/
     professional/blog/carbon-offsets-price-may-rise-3000-by-2029-under-
     tighter-rules/

22   DACS shot program, https://www.energy.gov/fecm/carbon-negative-shot

23   Porsche investing in synthetic fuels in Chile, https://newsroom.porsche.
     com/en_AU/2022/sustainability/porsche-invests-development-
     industrial-efuel-production-chile-usa-australia-27945.html

24   Porsche to invest in Tasmania, too, https://themarketherald.com.au/
     fancy/porsche-backed-e-fuel-group-to-build-sustainable-plant-in-
     tasmania/

25   Chile's ambitions, https://energydigital.com/renewable-energy/chile-
     plans-green-hydrogen-export-corridor-europe

26   Canada's hydrogen ambitions, https://canada-next-best-place-to-home.
     ft.com/canadas-clean-hydrogen-gets-set-to-power-the-world?twclid=2
     2io596q3h1rb41kgc62l94y2a

27   Minerals production in Canada, https://www.nrcan.gc.ca/our-
     natural-resources/minerals-mining/minerals-metals-facts/
     minerals-and-the-economy/20529#critical

28   Critical minerals strategy in Australia, https://www.pm.gov.au/media/
     support-critical-minerals-breakthroughs

29   22,000 panels per day and 40 wind turbines per month, https://
     reneweconomy.com.au/the-staggering-numbers-behind-australias-82-
     per-cent-renewables-target/

30   Open Cycle Gas Turbines (OCGT) lifecycle emissions with upstream
     emissions included are 776 kg CO2e/MWh. Combined Cycle Gas Tur-
     bine (CCGT) lifecycle emissions with upstream emissions included are
     490 kg CO2e/MWh. From the Scientific Inquiry into Hydraulic Fractur-
     ing in the Northern Territory Final Report table 9.6:
     •   If OCGT were to contribute 18% of grid electricity, the grid emis-
          sions intensity with upstream included would be 0.18 * 776 = 140 kg
          CO2e/MWh.
     •   CCGT is much better, yielding a grid intensity of 0.18 * 490 = 88 kg
          CO2e/MWh with upstream emission included.
     •   Denmark's grid intensity in 2021 was 207 kg CO2e/MWh, per the
          Danish Energy Agency.
     •   Australia's electricity emissions intensity in 2021 was 605 kg/MWh,
          from the Quarterly Update March 2022 and Australia Energy Up-
          date 2021.

31   Production cost for iron ore in Australia, https://www.wa.gov.au/

32   Australia Institute 2013 report by David Richardson, https://
     australiainstitute.org.au/wp-content/uploads/2020/12/TB-22-
     Electricity-and-privatisation.pdf

33   Deregulations not so great for prices, https://climate.mit.edu/posts/
     deregulation-market-power-and-prices-evidence-electricity-sector
34   Cost of HumeLink, https://www.afr.com/companies/energy/transgrid-
     facing-hurdles-on-vital-3-3b-humelink-20220901-p5belw
35   AEMO Transmission Cost Database Report 2021, https://aemo.com.au/
36   Western Renewables Link, https://www.westernrenewableslink.com.au/
37   Energy Grid Alliance Community First Framework, https://www.
     energygridalliance.com.au/community-first-framework-for-electricity-
     transmission-development/
38   VTIF, https://engage.vic.gov.au/victorian-transmission-investment-
     framework
39   NSW Strategic Benefits Payments Scheme, https://www.nsw.gov.
     au/media-releases/australias-first-benefit-sharing-scheme-for-
     landowners-hosting-new-transmission-lines
40   Victorian government to pay $200,000 over 25 years, https://www.
     premier.vic.gov.au/sites/default/files/2023-02/230224-Landholder-
     Payments-For-A-Farier-Renwables-Transition.pdf
41   Esbjerg Declaration, https://www.bechbruun.com/en/news/2022/the-
     esbjerg-declaration-the-north-sea-to-be-europes-green-power-house#
42   Whitehouse commitment to 30 GW offshore wind by 2030, https://
     www.whitehouse.gov/briefing-room/statements-releases/2022/09/15/
     fact-sheet-biden-harris-administration-announces-new-actions-to-
     expand-u-s-offshore-wind-energy/
43   IRA 30% for offshore wind before January 2026, https://crsreports.con-
     gress.gov/product/pdf/IN/IN11980
44   NSW to even the playing field among coal producers, https://www.
     theguardian.com/australia-news/2023/jan/19/nsw-to-intervene-in-
     coal-market-to-even-playing-field-among-producers
45   Regulatory thicket, https://uk.practicallaw.thomsonreuters.com/
     1-502-8908